"SINCE RIKYU'S TIME, THE WAY OF TEA H
ENTIRE HISTORY OF TEA CULTURE, BUT THRC
COMPLEXITY OF JAPANESE CULTURE IN GENE
INFLUENCE ON THE FORMATION OF SOME OF THE MOST
ACTERISTICS OF THE ETHICAL-ESTHETIC SENSITIVITY OF THE JAPANESE AND
THEIR BEHAVIORAL NORMS, UP TO THE LEVEL OF EVERYDAY LIFE."

HORIGUCHI

Quoted from Masao Yanagi, *Proportion in der Architektur – dargestellt in der Gegenüberstellung
der Villa Barbaro (Palladio) und des Chashitsu Taian (Rikyû)*

"SINCE RIKYU'S TIME, THE WAY OF TEA H
ENTIRE HISTORY OF TEA CULTURE, BUT THRC
COMPLEXITY OF JAPANESE CULTURE IN GENE
INFLUENCE ON THE FORMATION OF SOME OF THE MOST
ACTERISTICS OF THE ETHICAL-ESTHETIC SENSITIVITY OF THE JAPANESE AND
THEIR BEHAVIORAL NORMS, UP TO THE LEVEL OF EVERYDAY LIFE."

HORIGUCHI

Quoted from Masao Yanagi, *Proportion in der Architektur – dargestellt in der Gegenüberstellung
der Villa Barbaro (Palladio) und des Chashitsu Taian (Rikyû)*

"For Kerstin who showed me Japan."

Text and concept: Wolfgang Fehrer, Aarau
Design: Urs Stuber, Frauenfeld
Editing: Cosima Talhouni
Typesetting: Johannes Rinkenburger

niggli

THE
JAPANESE TEAHOUSE

Wolfgang Fehrer

CONTENTS

7   **INTRODUCTION**

9   The procedure of a tea ceremony

15   **SPATIAL PRINCIPLES**

15   Emptiness, dynamism and the concept of ma
19   The concept of oku
23   Japanese space and sequence
25   Inhomogeneity and symbolic meaning
27   Building with nature
29   Spatial references

33   **PHILOSOPHICAL AND RELIGIOUS BACKGROUND**

33   The influence of Zen Buddhism
35   The seven characteristics of Zen design
37   Transience and renewal
38   The temporary hut
41   The wabi esthetics
43   I-Ching and the teaching of the "five elements"

47   **ESTHETIC PRINCIPLES**

47   Fundamentals
47   Asymmetry
51   The significance of the surface
53   Permeable borders
55   Light
57   Rikyū gray

61   **TEA ROOM STRUCTURE**

61   Division of space
63   Flexibility
65   Functions in the teahouse
69   The tea room
72   Two essential elements – tatami and tokonoma

81   **CONSTRUCTION**

81   Timber construction
89   Basic structure

105   **THE TEA GARDEN**

107   Historical development of tea gardens
111   Elements of the tea garden

123   **THE DEVELOPMENT OF THE SŌAN TEAHOUSE**

123   The beginning of Japanese tea culture
129   The kaisho
131   The shoin style and the first tea room
135   Murata Shukō and the beginning of the wabi tea
137   Sōju and the shimogyo-chanoyu
140   Takeno Jōō and the sōan teahouse prototype

SEN NO RIKYÛ AND HIS TIME   **143**
Tea ceremony and power structure   143
Sen no Rikyû   145
The sôan teahouse   149

THE DAIMYÔ TEA AFTER RIKYÛ   **155**
The beginning of the daimyô-cha   155
The En-an teahouse   157
The Joan teahouse   161
Teahouses of Hosokawa Sansai   165
Kobori Enshu and the peak of daimyô-cha   167

**SUKIYA ARCHITECTURE
AND THE RETURN OF THE WABI**   **173**
The sukiya style   173
The tea of courtly society   173
Villa Katsura   175
Kanamori Sôwa and the Teigyokuken teahouse   183
The restoration of the Sen family   183
Sen no Sôtan   185
Teahouses of Sen no Sôtan   187

**THE INFLUENCE OF THE BOURGEOISIE
AND THE MEIJI RESTORATION**   **193**
Katagiri Sekishu and Hon'ami Koetsu   193
New teahouse concepts   197
Changes in the Meiji restoration   199
Okakura and "The Book of Tea"   203

TEAHOUSE TODAY   **207**
Kisho Kurokawa   209
Hiroshi Hara   209
Arata Isozaki   211
Shigeru Uchida   211
Kan Izue   211
Tadao Ando   213
Sabie-Zen   215

APPENDIX   **219**
Important terms of the tea ceremony   220
Important terms of teahouse architecture   222
Chronological table   224
Bibliography   227
Picture credits   231
Acknowledgements   232

"The tea room *sukiya* wants to be nothing more than a simple cottage – a straw hut, as we call it. The original characters for *sukiya* mean place of fantasy. Later, the various tea masters used various other signs that corresponded to their concept of the tea room, and *sukiya* can mean place of emptiness or place of asymmetry. It is a place of fantasy insofar as it is built to be a temporary home of poetic emotion. It is a place of emptiness inasmuch as it is without adornment, except for the few things needed to satisfy an instantaneous esthetic need. It is a place of the asymmetrical in that it is dedicated to the worship of the imperfect, leaving with intent something imperfect in order to be completed in the play of imagination."

FROM DAS BUCH VOM TEE

Unlike the teahouses of China or the Middle East, which are public places, comparable to Western coffee houses, the Japanese teahouse is of a private nature. Only those who have been invited to a tea gathering are allowed to enter this building, which is usually located away from the main house, at the back of the property. The teahouse is the place where the Japanese tea ceremony is held, a kind of meditation in which a host communicates with the guests through the medium of tea. This tea ceremony or *chanoyu*_A, as it is called in Japan, is a unique art form that combines a highly refined version of the Chinese custom of drinking tea with certain aspects of Zen philosophy. It goes far beyond the art of preparing and enjoying a bowl of tea according to certain rules and encompasses all the activities and actions associated with it, all the equipment and utensils and, last but not least, the surroundings of the tea room and garden. Different artistic genres such as architecture, garden design, ikebana, calligraphy and pottery are merged into a new whole.

The ceremonial way of drinking tea has been carried out throughout history in various rooms: The variety of architectural variations ranges from the magnificent, large *shoin* reception rooms in the palaces of the ruling shoguns and samurai to the simple grass-roofed *sôan* hut modeled on the hermit's mountain hermitage. After many changes, the *sôan* teahouse finally emerged as the most suitable architectural form for the tea ceremony. The classic tea room, first built by tea master Jôô in the 16th century_B and brought to perfection by his student Sen no Rikyû, is a room the size of 4½ *tatami* mats with a floor area of around eight square meters: Usually it does not offer space for more than five people. The extreme simplicity of the hut at first glance reveals nothing of its architectural complexity, and yet the teahouse stands at the intersection of various currents of Japanese philosophy, art, and esthetics. Despite the small size of the rooms and the simplicity of the materials used, every detail is the result of centuries of development and the highest artistic care.

The tea room itself is absolutely empty most of the time. The tea preparation utensils and individual decorative objects are only in the room during the tea ceremony. The light is also dimmed during the day: A wide roof overhang and a few windows covered with paper and bamboo roller blinds (*shoji*) allow little light into the interior and create a mystical atmosphere. The variable lighting that can be selected by opening and closing the *shoji* and bamboo roller blinds in combination with the choice of flowers and the hanging scroll as decoration provides almost unlimited possibilities to adapt the atmosphere of the tea room to the respective conditions of the time of day or year, the com-

1 Before the guests arrive, the tea master sprinkles the tea garden with water.

A The literal translation of this expression means "hot water for tea".

B If in the following it is mentioned that this or that tea master has erected a building, it is to be assumed as a rule that he did not participate in the building himself. Rather, craftsmen were employed who, over the course of time, were able to acquire increasingly specialized knowledge of the peculiarities of teahouse construction.

2

position of the guests or the mood of the host. Everything in the tea room has a certain patina. The asymmetry and an apparent imperfection in the design of the buildings and tea utensils evoke an association of transience and impermanence. However, you will never find even a single grain of dust in the tea room; everything is cleaned with the utmost care by the host before the guests arrive. The preparation of the tea room is an integral part of every tea ceremony.

While the rooms of Japanese residential buildings are open to a wide variety of uses and thus flexible, the teahouse is tied to a specific purpose. The overall mood and position of the individual elements – the crawl-in entrance, the position of the *tatami*, the arrangement of the sunken stove and the niche (*tokonoma*) – define the use of the space and dictate to each visitor the rhythm of movement of the tea ceremony, from which he/she can hardly escape. For the dense atmosphere of the small teahouses with a floor area of less than 4½ *tatami* mats in particular, hardly any other use than that of the tea ceremony is conceivable. There are tea rooms with a floor area of no more than 1½ *tatami* mats, less than three square meters. This limitation of space to a minimum is intended to create an atmosphere as dense as possible, which is conducive to concentration and spirituality.

The tea ceremony is still a living art form today and is practiced by countless followers around the world. Despite the high costs, teahouses are still being built today, and the design of a teahouse is still a great challenge for Japanese architects and designers.

THE PROCEDURE OF A TEA CEREMONY

"Chanoyu to wa
tada yu wo wakashi
cha wo tatete
nomu bakari naru
koto wo shiru-beshi."
SEN NO RIKYU c

"Chanoyu: that means,
you have to be aware of that,
to just boil water,
to prepare tea
and drink it."

A tea ceremony begins long before tea is served; in fact, the tea is prepared at the very end of the ceremony. It is the culmination of a long process that unfolds gradually. A full ceremony lasts up to four hours: It begins as soon as the first guest enters the tea garden.

If guests are invited to a tea ceremony, they will find the area in front of the house sprinkled with water and the gate to the tea garden open. The last guest closes the gate and the participants gather in a waiting room where they get rid of their outer wear and slip into the *tabi*, the white socks with the separated big toe. Straw sandals (*zori*) or wooden sandals (*geta*), in case of rain or snow, are available for guests. These are asked not to wear jewelry or perfume. Also, no eye-catching garment should disturb the concentration of the tea ceremony. Since the time in the tea room is removed from the everyday world, no clocks are allowed. The tea ceremony is outside of time.

Once all the guests have gathered, they go into the garden to a covered waiting bench (*koshikake-machiai*). After a brief moment of contemplation, they hear a rippling sound as the host fills fresh water into a sink near the teahouse. Then the host appears and greets the guests with a deep, formal bow, and they in turn stand up and return the bow. Not a word is spoken, everything happens in complete silence. The host goes to the teahouse, and shortly afterwards the guests also make their way in a row through the outer tea garden. The main guest (*shôkyaku*) leads the procession. He or she is either

2   Preparation of the "thick" tea (*koicha*), 13th scene of a series of woodcuts of the tea ceremony by Toshikata Mizuno (1866–1903)

c   *Rikyû hyakushu* ("The hundred doctrinal poems of Rikyû"), quoted from Horst Hennemann, *Chasho – Geist und Geschichte der Theorien japanischer Teekunst*, p. 235

3

4

10

determined by the host at the time of the invitation, or the guests agree on their roles in the waiting room. In any case, the main guest must be a connoisseur of the tea ceremony, as he or she will be given the right of way everywhere and will conduct the highly ritualized communication with the host. The *shôkyaku* arrives at a gate and opens it to enter the inner garden. From here you may be able to take a first look at a corner of the teahouse. The path leads over stepping stones past a low stone washbasin filled with water on which lies a bamboo ladle (*hishaku*). The guests sit one after the other in front of this basin and scoop water with which they clean their hands and rinse their mouths. It is the same ritual that is performed before entering a Shinto shrine. Then they proceed to the teahouse. The first guest enters the high stone in front of the entrance, bends down and opens the "crawl-in entrance" (*nijiriguchi*) which is so small that the teahouse can only be entered on hands and knees in a bent posture. Before entering, he or she removes his or her sandals and leans them against the wall of the teahouse.

The guests crawl one by one into the tea room. In the *tokonoma* hangs a scroll, either an ink painting or calligraphy of a famous Zen master, which is silently admired by every guest after a bow. In another corner stands the *furo*, a fire basin made of metal or ceramic in which the host has already artfully arranged the charcoal with the kettle on top. This arrangement is also considered by each guest before they all take their place. The *shôkyaku* sits closest to the *tokonoma* and determines the seating order of the other guests. The last guest closes the *nijiriguchi* behind him or her. The audible click is the sign for the host that all guests are gathered together. Shortly afterwards the host enters the tea room from the adjoining preparation room and bows to the guests. In the first part of the ceremony the host serves a light meal – *kaiseki*~D~. The dishes, which are served in several courses, are of selected quality, served with sake. At the end of the first part of the tea ceremony sweets are served. To allow the guests to rest their legs a little after eating the meal – they have been sitting in the kneeling position (*seiza*) for some time now – they return from the teahouse to *koshikake-machiai*. There a short conversation usually unfolds before the sound of five gong beats announces the end of the break (*nakadachi*~E~) and the further course of the ceremony – the preparation of the "thick tea" (*koicha*).

Following the same order as at the beginning, the guests enter the tea room, which has been rearranged by the host in the meantime: For the final second part of the ceremony, the scroll is removed; a simple flower arrangement adorns the *tokonoma* instead. The water in the kettle begins to boil. In the silence one can clearly hear the soft hissing that carries the poetic name *matsu-kaze* ("wind in the pines"). Next to the *furo* there is a vessel with fresh water and in front of it a ceramic vessel with powder tea, which is packed in a silk bag. The host appears and brings the tea utensils into the room: a tea bowl (*chawan*) containing the bamboo broom for beating the tea (*chasen*) and a white linen cloth, the bamboo teaspoon (*chashaku*), a container for used water, and a ladle (*hishaku*) similar to the one in the tea garden. The host sits in front of the *furo*, arranges the utensils and is now ready to prepare the tea. Each of his or her movements is calm and concentrated. The individual steps of the tea ceremony are carried out in a precisely defined sequence of movements. He or she unpacks the tea container, takes a silk cloth (*fukusa*) from the belt of his or her kimono and performs a ritual cleaning of the tea container and the *chashaku*. The host then moistens the *chasen* with warm water and checks whether all the bamboo fibers are intact. The tea bowl is heated with hot water and ritually cleaned. Of course, all tea utensils are already immaculately clean when they are brought into the tea room. The purification before the guests symbolizes the purification

5

3   On the way to the teahouse: middle gate of the Omotesenke tea school
4   The sweets (*o-kashi*) served with the "thin" tea (*usucha*) vary depending on the season.
5   Before entering the teahouse, the guests remove their sandals.

D   *Kaiseki* was the name for a warm stone that monks in Buddhist monasteries laid on their stomachs to alleviate the feeling of hunger during meditation.
E   Literally translated *nakadachi* means "getting up in the meantime".

11

6

of the mind and the heart – all thoughts about the outside world are discarded. The tea powder is filled into the bowl with the *chashaku*, infused with hot water and stirred with the tea broom to a thick tea. Folding the *fukusa*, holding the ladle, opening the tea container, tapping the teaspoon – each movement follows a traditionally fixed form, whereby the different tea schools differ in individual details.

Only one bowl is prepared from the *koicha*. Each guest takes only a few sips after having eaten a piece of the served sweets and bowed to the host, but also to the guests sitting next to him or her. After drinking, each person wipes the part of the tea bowl from which they have drunk with a piece of paper and passes it on to the next guest. The quality of the tea and the beauty of the bowl are praised. When everyone has drunk, the *chawan* is returned to the host, who in turn cleans all the equipment. Afterwards the first guest asks to be allowed to inspect the tea utensils. Each object is examined in detail and a dialog unfolds between guests and host about the origin, name and age of the tea utensils.

7

Now the fire is rekindled. Another sweet is served, but different from the one served with the *koicha*. The host now prepares the "thin tea" (*usucha*). He or she uses another tea container made of lacquer and a different type of tea. The tea is whipped to a foamy liquid; each guest receives an own bowl. This part of the ceremony takes place in a slightly more relaxed atmosphere than the *koicha* procedure, as *usucha* serves as refreshment before one separates. After the tea has been drunk and the utensils have been inspected, the host and guests exchange their last greetings. The guests then leave the tea room and walk through the tea garden to the waiting room, where they say goodbye to each other with a final bow.

The type of tea ceremony described here corresponds to the noon ceremony according to the style of Urasenke tea school. There are many variations, because the course of a ceremony changes depending on the occasion, the time of day, and the season.

6   At the tea ceremony every hand movement is performed with the highest concentration.

7   Each time a threshold is crossed, the guest is brought closer to the peace and concentration of the tea room.

8

Enjoying a wonderful apartment and delicious food are ordinary, worldly pleasures. A house through whose roof it doesn't rain is enough for us.
SEN NO RIKYŪ[A]

EMPTINESS, DYNAMISM AND THE CONCEPT OF THE MA

In Japan, although strongly influenced by China and Korea, a completely independent cultural tradition has developed. Music, literature, painting, the performing arts, cuisine, and not least the tea ceremony were able to develop undisturbed by external influences during the almost complete isolation of the country that lasted several centuries. This uniqueness of Japanese culture manifests itself not least in architecture and in the way space is perceived and designed. The teahouse as an expression of this special Japanese sense of space occupies a central position in this respect: Just as there is no ritual in the West that resembles the tea ceremony, there is no Western room that resembles the interior of a teahouse. Just as a Japanese ink drawing only begins to live through the empty spaces between the black brush strokes, the architectural space in Japan is also formed by the in-between, limited by the constructive elements of the building. Space in Japan is first and foremost thought of as "empty space", as a potential in which human activities can develop. Just as holistic thinking in Japan differs from the rationalistic-scientific concept of the West, the concept of "space" is also defined differently. While in the West "space" is defined as an objectively measurable static entity defined by form and size, Japanese space is connected to experience: No abstract concept, it is perceived with all five senses in movement. The whole body, but also feelings, intuition and memory play a decisive role in this process. Accordingly, Japanese space always remains related to the viewer; it is relative, kinetic and situational.

In the word *kukan*, which in Japanese describes space, decisive concepts of Japanese spatial thinking are laid out: If *ku* denotes the area between heaven and earth – the emptiness – then *kan* means – the character can also be read as *ma* – interval. The concept of *ku* is a very old philosophical system deeply rooted in the Asian way of thinking. Already in the 6th century BC, emptiness was one of the most important prerequisites and characteristics of everyday life for Lao Tse, the Chinese philosopher and founder of Taoism. In his book *Tao Te-King* he says: "Thirty spokes unite to form a hub: The adequacy of their nothing is the carriage's usefulness; one kneads the clay with regard to the pot: The adequacy of its nothing is the pot's usefulness; one lifts out door and window with regard to the house: The adequacy of their nothing is the house's usefulness. So: The purpose of being is advantage, the purpose of nothing is usefulness."[B]

The empty space is more important than the solid, because the reality of a space is not to be found in its enclosing surfaces, not in the floor, roof or walls, but only in its emptiness itself. And yet none of these aspects exist by themselves, independently of the others: Building structure and empty space are mutually dependent. This concept of emptiness had a great influence on the view of Buddhism, in whose philosophy these ideas were adopted as *ma*, as the idea of "nothing".[C] With the spread of Buddhism in Japan since the 6th century, the concept found its way into domestic thinking, and to this day it is a central component of spiritual life. From an esthetic point of view, it corresponds to the sensibility for the beauty of empty spaces and surfaces (*yohaku-no-bi*), which is of great importance in various Japanese art genres. Zen masters refer to it as "painting by not painting", meaning the balance of

8 A straw rope separates a space of special quality from its surroundings. Shimogamo shrine, Kyoto

A Quoted from Horst Hennemann, p. 222
B Lao Tze, *Tao Te King – Das Buch vom rechten Weg und rechten Gesinnung*, p. 65
C *Ku* is an ancient Buddhist principle that was formulated under the Sanskrit name *sunyata* by the Indian philosopher Nagarjuna in the 2nd or 3rd century AD in the *Mula-madhyamaka-sutra*.

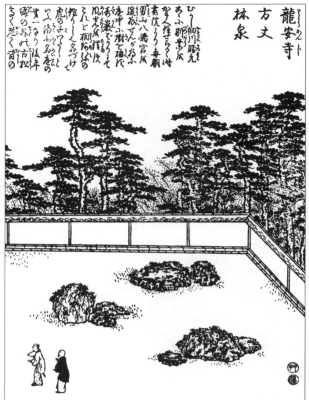

9

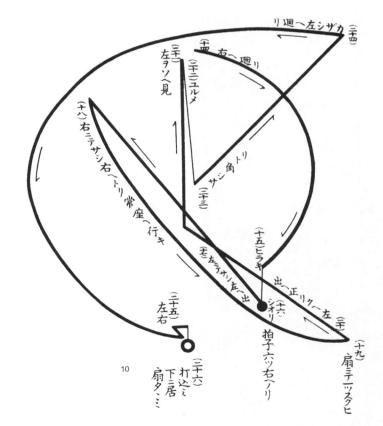

10

9   The empty space dominates the famous
    kare-sansui garden of Ryoan-ji in Kyoto.
    Woodcut from the *Miyako Rinsen Meisho
    Zue* (an illustrated handbook on famous
    gardens in Kyoto)

10 Information on the actor's movements and
    gestures in a program booklet for a Nô drama

form and emptiness that characterizes many masterpieces of Japanese art. It can be found in the white areas of the ink paintings and calligraphies as well as in the barren gravel areas of the dry gardens (*kare-sansui*) of the Zen monasteries. In architecture, this view finds its culmination in the teahouse, a "mode of symbolic building wherein nothing was symbolized, or, more precisely, where void, emptiness or no-thingness (mu) was symbolized"[D]; here an architectural expression is given to a line from the Buddhist heart sutra "emptiness is form, form is emptiness".[E]

In the Buddhist worldview, things are not only empty in their essence, they are also transient. Buddha teaches that people suffer because they persist in ignorance and strive for things that are not permanent. Nothing is, in his view, free from transience, because all being is embedded in a flowing, uninterruptedly changing reality. These thoughts are the basis for another essential characteristic of the Japanese spatial concept: Space is not a fixed entity, but a continuum subject to dynamic changes and permanent modifications. This aspect is also contained in the word *kukan*: The character *kan* or *ma*[F] means interval, both spatially and temporally.[G] In Japan, space and time have never been understood as independent facts, but have always flowed together in a concept that seeks to overcome this duality. Without exception, every spatial experience is bound to time, just as every experience in time is a spatially structured process.[H]

Already in early Shintoism, when sacred buildings were as yet unknown, sacred places (*yorishiro*) were marked by four corner pillars and the inner area was marked by a simple straw rope. It was believed that gods would descend into these empty areas and fill them with their spiritual energy. Here, too, space was synonymous with the phenomena and processes that take place within it and was therefore always perceived in relation to temporary phenomena.[I] The concept is particularly vivid in the Nô theater, where *ma* uses the term *senuhi-ma* to describe the time between the individual actions of the actor. It is an interval that is more than just a "pause" in which one does not act, but the moment of greatest concentration. "It is the moment when nothing is portrayed and yet everything happens."[J]

In the arts of calligraphy, painting, or tea ceremonies as well, *ma* forms a space of imagination that is not filled with objective content, but must first be brought to life by one's own mind. The term that used to refer to the architectural design still contained the *ma* concept: *madori* literally means "to grasp the space". Not only the spatial connections were structured, but all temporary processes such as the replacing of furniture according to specific use or the removal of individual sliding doors to expand the space were also made possible. Today, however, the term *madori* is increasingly replaced by imported *dizain*, derived from English *design*.

D   Botond Bognar, quoted from Robin Noel Walker, *Shoko-ken, A Late Medieval daime sukiya Style Japanese Tea-house*, p. 68

E   The literal translation of the core sentence of the heart sutra is: "The appearing is just the emptiness, the emptiness is just the appearing, appearance is (as) emptiness, emptiness (as) appearance." See the article "Japan und einige Aspekte der Weltgeschichte des Nichts", in: Peter Pörtner (ed.), Japan – Ein Lesebuch, p. 65ff.

F   In Japan, the Chinese script has been adopted since about the 5th century due to the lack of a native writing system. However, since the language structures of Japanese and Chinese differ greatly, there is a purely Japanese reading for each character in addition to the Sino-Japanese.

G   The literal translation covers both areas, in the *Iwanami Wörterbuch alter Begriffe* (from Botond Bognar, *Contemporary Japanese Architecture*, 1985) ma is described as the "natural distance between two or more things existing in continuity" or "the natural pause or interval between two or more phenomena occuring continuously".

H   See Günter Nitschke, "*Ma* – Place, Space, Void", in: Günter Nitschke, *From Shinto to Ando*, p. 48ff.

I   Arata Isozaki, "*Ma*: Japanese Time-Space", in: *Japan Architect*, p. 71

J   Masao Yanagi, p. 74

11

The beginning of rice cultivation in the Yayoi period meant a turning point for the inhabitants of Japan, as the adoption of this cultivation technique meant a shift in the most important areas of life from the mountain regions to settlements on the plains. In this context, the world was divided into a human realm and a sphere reserved for the gods: Dense forests, small islands off the mainland and mountainous regions covered in mist became realms far removed from every-day human activities; forbidden and sacred zones worshipped as *go-shintai*, the seat of a deity.[K] The organization of the settlements took this into account: Villages were often arranged along a reference line in the direction of a mountain overlooking the surrounding rice fields. This is how a religious axis was created that led from the village to the shrine at the foot of the mountain and on to hidden mountain regions, a pattern that can still be found throughout the country today.

With this arrangement of sanctuaries, which were so far away that they could not usually be visited by people (they were obviously forbidden zones), the spatial concept of the *oku* developed according to the theory of the archi-tect Fumihiko Maki.[L] This describes a hidden center, a core or the innermost part of a spatial formation that seeks its symbolism in depth and concealment and unfolds primarily in a horizontal direction. *Oku* is a concept that is difficult to define because it can hardly be attached to concrete phenomena. However, a comparison with Western principles of spatial organization is helpful for the clarification: While in Japan the remote depths of the mountain world became the object of worship, in the West the idea of the center itself – the mountain top – was reproduced in the cities. In Western settlements, the church formed the center of a city, with the church tower being the center around which the city was arranged and separated from the surrounding chaos of nature. In Japan people were looking for something invisible instead of a visible center. This imperceptible center seems to have been realized in the concept of the *oku* as the innermost, hidden zone of a spatial constellation surrounded by several lay-ers of outer spatial areas. This "wrapping" is a fundamentally different process than the delimitation of a field or object practiced in Western culture. A more passive than active principle, it adapts to the wrapped object and shows a wide range of variations depending on the nature of the wrapped object.

Within this context, there is probably also the fact that no culture has pro-duced such a range of beautiful, functional and versatile packaging materials as the Japanese. In the relationship between teahouse and tea garden, this spatial configuration is realized in an exemplary way: The teahouse, hidden deep in the garden and only perceptible to the guest at the last moment, represents the invisible core of a spatial structure that is enveloped in several layers by the inner and outer tea garden and, so to speak, "wrapped".

In the context of the teahouse, another aspect of the *oku* becomes appar-ent, since it serves not only to describe spatial configurations, but also to express psychological depth as an abstract and esoteric concept. The view into the inte-rior of the teahouse thus represents not only the direct sensual experience but also a view into the interior of the human self.

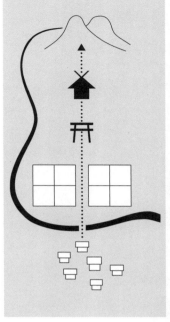

12

11 Sanctuary in the mountains in the south of Kyoto

12 The religious axis runs from the village through the rice fields to a shrine and on to remote mountain regions.

K   Günter Nitschke, *Japanische Gärten – Rechter Winkel und natürliche Form*, p. 10
L   Fumihiko Maki, "Japanese City Spaces and the Concept of *oku*", in: *Japan Architect*, p. 51ff.

13

13 A fence separates the everyday world from
the teahouse. Koetsu-ji, Kyoto
14 View from the teahouse into the tea garden

As a consequence of the idea of the *oku*, another spatial concept characterizing Japanese architecture follows: The aspects of passage and rapprochement have always characterized local architecture and reach far back into the traditions of the country. Even in the shrine buildings of Shintoism, which served as storage places for sacred objects, the interiors are not decisive, because they are taboo for ordinary people and, with the exception of a few chosen ones, may not be entered by anyone. Rather, these buildings are symbolic objects, remote places that can be approached but never reached, never entered. Within this context, Maki and Bognar[M] interpret the theory of *oku* as a convergence towards zero. Japanese buildings are rarely designed to be viewed as a whole from a distance. In most cases, they stand at the end of a spatial-temporal sequence that makes it possible to perceive the buildings only step by step. Shrines and temples are often built deep in the woods, and the paths that lead there are correspondingly remote and entwined. Just as enlightenment can only be attained by a laborious stony path, so the approach to a sanctuary is also a slow and gradual process. More than just the way to a certain goal, the conscious experience of space under a time parameter is one of the most essential components of the Japanese spatial concept. Japan's insularity and the high density of Japanese settlements may also have contributed to this development. Confronted with the feeling of limited personal space, people from time immemorial were forced to subjectively expand narrow boundaries and develop concepts that counteracted this scarcity of space and allowed depth to be experienced even in spatially cramped conditions. A tradition of paradoxical esthetics was the result, in which infinite expansion is represented by an extremely compressed space, suggesting eternity for a moment.[N]

As a tried and tested means of "stretching" the limited space, design measures were taken to slow down the speed at which the user traversed given distances in order to extend the experienced time span. In his essay "Time is money, space is money"[O] Günter Nitschke meticulously describes the factors used in this process using two entrances to buildings from different eras: The entrance areas of the Shisen-do temple in Kyoto from the 17th century and the Rokko church of Tadao Ando in Kobe use very similar means to influence the time experienced – and thus the subjective perception of space: "Both are passages leading to places of silence, places which are sacred in that they invite true rest and induce insight."[P]

The conscious setting of abstract and physical thresholds, the ritual cleansing in several stages, the play with light and shadow, the only step-by-step approach and the repeated turning of the path are concepts that are also directly implemented in the tea garden. In garden design, a special technique – *miegakure*[Q] – is used that does not allow any visual axes and has unsymmetrical paths, thus creating a sequence of divided spaces that obscures the view of the whole and can only be perceived through movement. Perhaps there are parallels to the Chinese idea that ghosts could only move along straight lines, which in China led to construction measures such as ghost walls or zigzag bridges.

Another principle plays an important role in the tea garden, as the path through the garden symbolizes a process of cleaning. As one approaches the teahouse, one passes through a series of stations and thresholds at which both physical and mental purification is carried out in several stages. Not only the visual perception is involved in this complex process, but the whole person is included.

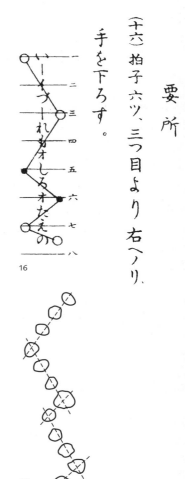

16

17

15 The teahouse is hidden in the tea garden and only becomes visible to visitors at the last moment.

16 Movement pattern of a Nô actor

17 The arrangement of the stepping stones is reminiscent of the movement patterns of the Nô actors (see caption 16)

M See Fumihiko Maki and Botond Bognar

N Tadao Ando, quoted from Robin Noel Walker, p. 3

O Günter Nitschke, "Time is money, space is money", in: Günter Nitschke, *From Shinto to Ando*, p. 32ff

P Günter Nitschke, p. 33

Q Literally: "hide and reveal"

18

If one follows Mircea Eliade's[R] theories, for a religious person space is not homogeneously structured. The sacred appears in different places and thus forms points of reference and orientation in the person's chaotic and disordered life. As a result, for the believer, places of special quality and density are created, which do not differ from their surroundings in purely external terms. In early Japan there were certain mountains, rivers and forests, but also stones and trees, which were regarded as residences of gods and thus elevated from the usual profane world of mankind. The least accessible areas were those to which the strongest spirituality was attributed. This special spatial quality – that space disintegrates into units of different meaning and that certain places in space occupy an outstanding position – was able to assert itself over centuries in connection with the *oku* concept in Japan. According to Buddhist cosmology, in which the universe is perceived without beginning, middle and end, Japanese buildings with their additive spatial development have no highlights in themselves: Unlike the West, the rooms of a Japanese house are not arranged axially, and there is hardly any furniture that could define directions or set focal points within the room. Also, the formation of spatial sequence from spaces of minor importance to higher ranking is almost entirely unknown to Japanese architecture. Roland Barthes speaks of it in his book *Das Reich der Zeichen* when he describes a Japanese room: "There is no room here for a piece of furniture [...]. In this corridor – just like in the Japanese ideal house – which is free of furniture (or contains very little furniture), there is no place that describes even the slightest property: neither armchair nor bed nor table, from which the body could constitute itself as the subject (or master) of a space: There should not be a center (what burning frustration for Westerners who are the owners of a domestic place everywhere, provided with their armchairs and their beds)."[S]

Yet in order to meet the need for a – spiritual – center of the house or individual rooms, the picture niche (*tokonoma*) was developed.[T] Usually serving as a decorative niche, in which a picture scroll hangs or a flower arrangement is placed, it turns into a sacred place on special occasions.[U] At the same time a functional, spiritual and esthetic concept, both spatial organization and constructive details assign it a special position in the structure of the house. Special attention is paid to the design of the *tokonoma* post (*toko-bashira*). In Japanese architecture, the column has always had a special significance that goes beyond the symbolism common in other cultures – as a sign of power or the will to build: Already in Shintoism, trees were thought of as a means for gods to descend and columns as seats of deities (*kami*), which led to the fact that in many shrines the columns were particularly accentuated at the gable ends. Visible from afar, they carried the ridge beam and thus the main load of the building. In the highest Shinto sanctuary, the Ise shrine, it is even a pillar that serves as the central object of worship. The "sublime pillar of the heart" (*shin no mihashira*) measures about one and a half meters and is completely buried under the inner shrine. Above this place there is a small hut, which indicates its location.

This tradition was taken up and continued in the farmhouses (*minka*) of rural Japan. There the cult column (*daikoku-bashira*) marks the spiritual center of the house next to the god board and the place of the hearth deity. This column, dedicated to the lucky gods Ebisu and Daikoku, is primarily symbolic and marks the place of ceremonial actions. In many cases, despite its considerable thickness, it is not assigned any constructive task at all. In the tea room there are two pillars that represent symbolism and around which the room seems to be condensed: Next to the *toko-bashira*, which is part of the decorative niche and has the task of closing it off laterally and anchoring it in the

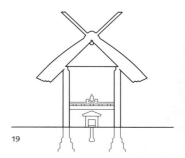

19

18 A straw rope marks places with a special symbolic meaning.

19 Section of the inner shrine (*naiku*) of the Ise sanctuary with the buried pillar (*shin-no-mihashira*) (according to Nitschke, 1993)

R   Mircea Eliade, *Das Heilige und das Profane*
S   Roland Barthes, *Das Reich der Zeichen*, p. 148f.
T   See chapter "Tea room structure", p. 77
U   During New Year, for example, traditional balls made of mashed rice (*mochi*) are placed in the *tokonoma* to serve as food for the gods when they visit the houses.

25

room, there is the center post (*naka-bashira*), which separates the host's area from that of the guests and at the same time indicates the position of the sunken stove. The symbolic relevance of both objects is immediately apparent, as they mark the functional and spiritual centers of the tea room with the place of tea preparation and the *tokonoma*.

Both columns already differ in their nature from the rest of the construction: They are made of special wood or bamboo, the trunks are mostly used with their natural curvature, and this natural form of the supports disrupts the tension structure of the space that is otherwise characterized by rectangular patterns. In many cases the bark was left on the trunk to emphasize its natural state. If the pillars were rectangular in shape, they stood out from other supports in terms of surface treatment, were differently hewn, chamfered, dyed or polished.

BUILDING WITH NATURE

The particularly intimate relationship of the Japanese to nature[v] had a decisive impact on the built environment. Space in Japan was always seen as something universal and, in accordance with Shintoism, was based on unity with surrounding nature. Thus, spatial phenomena were more likely to belong to the sphere of topography than to the buildings themselves, since they could only be thought of along with spiritual qualities of natural phenomena. Even today, it is still a tradition in many places to hold a so-called earth calming festival (*jichin-sai*) before the construction of a building begins. During the celebration a simple Shinto shrine will be built. In this context, Kisho Kurokawa describes Japanese spatial thinking as a continuity, which he opposes to the dominant attitude of architecture in the West as spatial confrontation.[w] Buildings are designed to blend into their surroundings so as to appear not as the focus of an architectural composition, but as part of an overall picture. Again and again, unity with nature is sought; the two poles of nature and culture are understood as equal, complementary systems. The emphasis on horizontality is an expression of this philosophy: The buildings were mostly one- to two-story buildings; stairs were never an important element of Japanese houses. Heavy roofs with wide overhangs bind the buildings to the ground and determine the direction. Vertical structures were never able to establish themselves in Japan, and even in the pagodas, the only type of building in Japan's architectural history with a clear vertical orientation, the idea of the horizontal is realized through the expansive roofs staggered one above the other. This form obviously corresponds most closely to the Japanese worldview.

The teahouse fulfils this requirement in a perfect way, as its outer appearance blends in perfectly with the surroundings of the tea garden. Only a small hut, which can hardly be seen between the bushes and trees, the teahouse mostly recedes behind its surroundings. Nature is also permanently present inside: The exclusive use of materials that are as natural as possible – any surface treatment seems to have the sole aim of emphasizing the natural beauty of the materials – creates a perfect harmony of colors, shapes and textures. Zen master Takuan describes the plan to build a teahouse in harmony with nature: "Let us then construct a small room in a bamboo grove or under trees, arrange streams and rocks and plant trees and bushes, while [inside the room] let us pile up charcoal, set a kettle, arrange flowers, and arrange in order the necessary tea utensils. And let all this be carried out in accordance with the idea that in this room we can enjoy the streams and rocks as we do the rivers and mountains in Nature, and appreciate the various moods and sentiments suggested by the snow, the moon, and the trees and flowers, as they go through the transformation of seasons, appearing and disappearing, blooming and withering. As visitors

20 Flower decoration on a *tokonoma* post; the wooden surface of these columns is often of special texture.

v   See the contributions by Pamela J. Asquith/Arne Kalland, Peter Ackermann, Joy Hendry and Joseph A. Kyburz, in: Pamela J. Asquith/Arne Kalland (eds.), *Japanese Images of Nature – Cultural Perspectives*
w   Kisho Kurokawa, *Rediscovering Japanese Space*

21

22

are greeted here with due reverence, we listen quietly to the boiling water in the kettle, which sounds like a breeze passing through the pine needles, and become oblivious of all worldly woes and worries; we then pour out a dipperful of water from the kettle, reminding us of the mountain stream, and thereby our mental dust is wiped off. This is truly a world of recluses, saints on earth."[x]

The fact that sometimes only a single flower is present in the tea room can suggest a stronger connection with nature during the tea ceremony than a clear view of the garden would be able to create. This oneness with the surrounding nature is so intense that a view outside is no longer necessary; such a view would even disturb this intensity. As Sen no Rikyû says:

"People keep looking outside, not knowing whether the cherry blossom is appearing on that hill or in that wood, unaware that both the cherry blossom and the red maple are in their own hearts."[y]

SPATIAL REFERENCES

In their analysis of the structure of Japanese space[z], Willi Flindt and Manfred Speidel place the tea room in a level with the residential building, the pilgrim temple and the stage of the Nô theater. According to the authors, all these buildings are based on a common concept that can be divided into five sub-areas. Area 1 refers to the access corresponding to the tea garden in the teahouse and area A to the middle gate. Area 2 is a transition area, where B is equivalent to the crawl-in entrance (nijiriguchi). The innermost area – the tea room itself – is represented by 3, while 4 and 5 designate the non-accessible area and the outside area. If you take a closer look at this spatial structure, you will notice two different interior-exterior references with the tea garden as the pivotal point: As a garden, it is of course an exterior space, but its position changes with regard to the structure of the entire property: Isolated from the outside world by walls and fences, hidden from the public eye and not visible from the street, it has become an interior space due to several layers of wraps and can therefore be regarded more as an area of the interior, the oku.

The analysis of the direct relationship between the teahouse and the tea garden provides the second aspect, whereby the difference to the Japanese residential houses is obvious at first: In these houses, the absence of fixed exterior walls allows the building to open completely to the garden by removing the sliding elements. The reason for this construction method is certainly mostly to be found in the Japanese climate with its hot, humid summers. Already in the 14th century the hermit Yoshida Kenko writo: "When you build a house, you should remember summer. In winter you can live anywhere, but there is nothing worse than a house that proves unsuitable for the hot season."[Ä] Only a few supports, the surface of the raised floor, and the protruding roof mark the interior of the house, which together with the transitory space of the veranda forms a continuum with the exterior space.

The early teahouses still conveyed an idea of the openness of the living spaces (1): They were entered via a veranda by light-transmitting shoji arranged in pairs, which could be opened as required and provided a view of the garden. However, in front of the veranda there was a walled courtyard, which made it impossible to see the entire garden. Above the walls only the trees behind were visible, the courtyard itself remained as empty as possible to avoid any distractions from the tea ceremony (2).[Ö] The centripetal development of Sen no Rikyû was promoted in the further development of tea rooms: He eliminated the veranda at his teahouses and connects the tea garden directly to the teahouse. The nijiriguchi is the only connection to the garden and marks a clear boundary between interior and exterior space. The introversion of the tea room

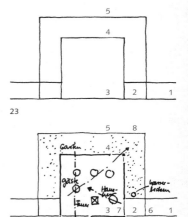

23

24

21 The dominance of the horizontal in a view of Tokyo from the 19th century; drawing by Edward S. Morse

22 A design as close to nature as possible integrates the teahouse into its surroundings. The Shoka-do teahouse in an illustration from the *Miyako Rinsen Meisho Zue*

23 General structure of the Japanese room (according to Flindt/Speidel, 1978):
  1 Access
  2 Transition area
  3 Innermost space
  4 Non-accessible area
  5 Outdoor area

24 Teahouse structure:
  1 Waiting area
  2 Transition area – inner tea garden
  3 Tea room
  4 Non-accessible area of tea garden
  5 Outdoor area
  6 Middle gate
  7 Nijiriguchi
  8 Fence

x   Daisez T. Suzuki, *Zen and Japanese Culture*, p. 276f.
Y   Quoted from Shuichi Kato, *Form. Style. Tradition. Reflections of Japanese Art and Society*, p. 159 (own translation)
Z   Willi Flindt/Manfred Speidel, "Zur Struktur des japanischen Raumes", in: Manfred Speidel (ed.), *Japanische Architektur – Geschichte und Gegenwart*, p. 18
Ä   Quoted from Karin Kirsch, *Die neue Wohnung und das alte Japan*, p. 65
Ö   See chapter "The tea garden", p. 105

25

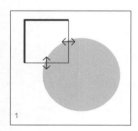

1

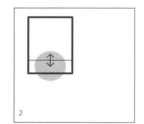

2

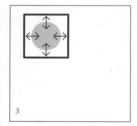

3

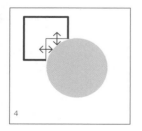

4

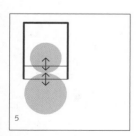

5

26

thus reached a climax (3). A paradoxical relationship manifests itself here: On the one hand, following the example of the temporary grass hut, all boundaries between man and nature are abolished as far as possible, while at the same time isolation from the outside space is perfected. The tea masters after Rikyû gradually deviated from the complete focus on the inside; they allowed more windows and provided views from the tea room again. Although this was the beginning of a development that lead away from the hermetic isolation of the interior, even in later buildings a complete opening of the rooms to the garden as in residential houses was never realized. In the subsequent development elements of the tea garden were increasingly incorporated inside the teahouse.[Ü] The stepping stones of the garden path led into the interior of the building, creating an area where the interior and exterior overlap (4). The highlight of this development was marked by the teahouse designs of Hosokawa Sansai and the Teigyokuken teahouse of Kanamori Sowa: In these buildings, a buffer zone is placed between the tea garden and the actual tea room, in which elements of the tea garden are located (5). Neither exterior nor interior, this transition area is used to create a new, complex room quality for the teahouse.

25 Only the roof and the veranda separate the house from the garden. Shisen-do, Kyoto
26 The changes in the relation of interior and exterior space

Ü   Example: En-an teahouse by Furuta Oribe, Joan teahouse by Oda Uraku, see p. 157ff.

"It was statesmen, commanders, warriors, merchants, monks who followed the Way of Tea or even became masters of it. But no matter what social class a person following this path belonged to, we hardly find one among them who would not have gone through the school of a master in Zen in one of the great temples or monasteries." [A]

THE INFLUENCE OF ZEN BUDDHISM

The history of the Japanese tea ceremony shows the close connection between the Way of Tea (*chanoyu*) and Zen Buddhism, since it was Japanese monks who got to know both on their travels to China and brought them to Japan at the end of the 12th century. All great tea masters were themselves Zen priests or closely connected to Zen, a fact which in Japan became proverbial as *Cha Zen ichimi* ("Tea and Zen are one"). *Chanoyu* can be seen as an esthetic form of Zen Buddhism, a way of practicing Zen. Many rules of the tea ceremony are derived from the simple and practical habits of the daily life of monks in a Zen monastery, and therefore it is not surprising that the ceremonial form of tea drinking was strongly influenced by the teaching to which it has always been strongly attached. As in other Buddhist schools, the goal in Zen is the enlightenment of the individual, but the paths that lead to this goal are different. The term "Zen" is derived from the Sanskrit word "Dhyana", which was used to describe meditation. While certain regionally practicing schools hope for salvation through belief in a higher being – for example in the Buddha of western paradise in Amida Buddhism – Zen encourages the individual to attain salvation through discipline and meditation.

Enlightenment can take place everywhere and in every place. Therefore, Zen teachers reject all written records because they believe that enlightenment can only be experienced directly through intuition. This teaching takes on an artistic form in the *chanoyu* when a sacred place of enlightenment is created in the middle of everyday life in a teahouse away from the world. Removed from the world of everyday life, the moments of the tea ceremony are nevertheless experiences of daily life: a fire is kindled, water is boiled, tea is drunk, nothing else. Profane and sacred meet at this moment. What Ôhashi says in the description of the Ryoan-ji-Zen garden also applies to the tea room: Here the "shapeless sacred and the esthetically shaped" [B] meet, interpenetrate, and both can retain their independence. The conventional separation between art as a field of esthetics and religion as inherently unformed is dissolved and brought together into a new unity.

The frequent naming of the tea rooms according to the number of their windows – always six or eight – also points to the special significance of Zen Buddhism to the architecture of the teahouse. The Hasso-no-seki, today in the National Museum in Nara, the Hassoken in the Manjuin temple in Kyoto, the Yatsumado Kakoi of the Shôkintei in the Villa Katsura, the Hasso-no-seki in the Konchiin sub-temple of the Nanzen-ji in Kyoto, and the Roku-soân in the National Museum in Tokyo can serve as examples. In this context, the "six" symbolizes the old Buddhist concept of the six eyes or sense organs: eye, ear, nose, tongue, body and mind. The "eight" refers to a similar idea that lists eight senses. The eyes and ears are counted twice. With the designation of a tea room according to the number of its windows it is equated with the human body. It serves the tea master as a sense organ, human being and space thus become an indissoluble unity.

28

27 Asymmetry and closeness to nature as formative design features; garden in the Daitoku-ji, Kyoto
28 Harmony-Respect-Purity-Tranquility (*wa-kei-sei-jaku*) – the four key principles of the tea ceremony; calligraphy by Sen Sôshitsu, the 15th grandmaster (*iemoto*) of the Urasenke tea school

A Horst Hammitzsch, *Zen in der Kunst des Teeweges*, p. 79
B Ryôsuke Ôhashi, *Kire – Das Schöne in Japan. Philosophisch-ästhetische Reflexionen zu Geschichte und Moderne*, p. 79

29

30

The idea of equality and brotherhood that manifested itself in the democratic organization of Zen monasteries was maintained during the period of strict social hierarchy of the feudal era: Everyone could gather in the tea room regardless of their social background, because entering the tea room through the crawl-in entrance (*nijiriguchi*) made all guests equal. From the 16th century onwards, the military rulers saw the tea ceremony not least as a ritual of peace and consensus. De facto, the tea room was the only place in public where members of the ruling samurai class entered without a sword. Tea huts and rooms thus became antipodes of war and violence.

THE SEVEN CHARACTERISTICS OF ZEN DESIGN

Hisamatsu Shinchi, one of the most important Zen philosophers of modern times, describes in his book *Zen and the Fine Arts* seven characteristics that are indispensable for the esthetic development of a Zen work of art. All these principles are effective as esthetic concepts within the tea ceremony and were directly implemented in the design of the teahouse, tea garden, and utensils. They support the efforts of the tea masters to create a framework for *chanoyu* that corresponds to its spiritual severity – Sen no Rikyû's *wabi* tea style can be regarded as the culmination of this development.

The first principle Hisamtsu referred to is asymmetry and irregularity in form (*fukinsei*). It refers to the closeness to nature of the Japanese, whose origins can be traced back to Shintoism. This principle permeates the entire Japanese culture and is also realized in artistic creation beyond Zen Buddhism. The second characteristic refers to simplicity (*kanso*), achieved through restraint in the choice of means of expression and derived from the Buddhist principle of "nothing" (*mu*). In painting and calligraphy, for example, this means the restriction to the color black; in the architecture of teahouses this corresponds to the principle of reduction to only a few, discreet color shades. *Kokô* speaks of a "sober sublimity" or a "sublime dryness". If in nature the drying out, of a plant for example, is usually associated with destruction, Zen Buddhism regards this very moment of transformation, in which the actual mode of being of a form of existence becomes visible and all essential aspects of life manifest themselves, as central. The same applies to works of art and architecture, which can only reveal their deepest truth in the absence of any sensual or superfluous element. Botond Bognar sees Japanese architecture permeated by a spatial logic that carries within it a hidden system of esthetically expressing what does not exist. It is precisely in this way that it "reminds us of the poignancy of things on the verge of disappearing or, conversely, at the moment of emerging."c For the artists, this means completely turning away from any emotional emphasis or immaturity and no longer allowing themselves to be guided by it.D The fourth principle is the spontaneous naturalness of a work of art (*shizen*). However, this has nothing to do with naturalism, but is rather the result of a pure, unmediated intention of the artist. Hisamatsu quotes a poem from the *Nampôroku*:

29 "Ocean of Happiness", "Mountain of Long Life"; calligraphy of Sokuhi (1616–1671)
30 Subtlety and restraint characterize the buildings inspired by Zen.

c Botond Bognar, quoted from Robin Noel Walker, p. 68
D Horst Hennemann
E Quoted from Horst Hennemann, p. 65

"Omowaji to	"To intend yourself,
omou mo mono wo	not wanting to intend,
omou nari	is intentional. That's what it's all about,
omowaji to dani	my dear, not intentional
omowaji ya kimi."	intention not to intend."E

31

There is no distance between the creator and the work in the act of creation; as a consequence, nothing seems intentional about it. Bruno Taut speaks of this in his reflections when he gives his impression of the teahouse architecture: "If you look around here [inside the teahouse], there is something quite different from architecture. Even the architect has to forget his profession, because sticking plaster to round bamboo poles this way and to work so completely subjectively with an apparently naïve and yet extremely refined technique – this disarms critical architects. It is as it were improvised like a sketch, as much the expression of momentary intuition as some of the great masterpieces of Japanese and Chinese scroll paintings in ink painting seem to be."[F]

32

The fifth characteristic of a Zen work of art stands for unfathomable, deep subtlety and restraint (*yûgen*). It is created by a "non-exhibition" of the content and results in a calm darkness, a darkness that can be found in the meditative atmosphere inside a teahouse. *Datsuzoku* describes the detachment from the connectedness of habits, conventions and formulas. This overcoming of the world and the absence of any authority, which only enable real freedom of thinking and acting, have always been inherent in Zen thinking. The tea masters tried to realize this in their work and countless stories about Sen no Rikyû and other masters tell of their ability to seek solutions off the beaten track, to break with conventions and to disregard authorities. *Seijaku*, as the seventh and last characteristic, describes an even inner peace, which is radiated by all inwardly turned works of Zen Buddhism – an atmosphere which is also sought to be achieved during a tea ceremony in the tea room.

TRANSIENCE AND RENEWAL

The decline of the Heian period and the rise of the samurai class in the Kamakura period brought about a radical change in social and philosophical values. A search for new ideals also began within Buddhist teaching. As is often the case in times of great instability, this led to the emergence of apocalyptic doctrines accompanied by an ethetics of inconsistency. It was believed that Buddhism would pass through three stages of development in the two thousand years following the death of the historical Buddha: the age of true law (*shôbô*), the age of imitative law (*zôbô*,) and the end of law (*mappô*). The latter was regarded as a time of decay of religion and morality, and people were convinced that this was the era they were living in. This mood led to the development of the philosophical and esthetic view of life and nature that influenced Japanese art and literature since the Heian period. Subtle shades, ephemeras were preferred, monochromes prized above colorfulness, autumn and winter above spring and summer, evening and night above morning and day. The beginning of the *Heike Monogatari*[G] illustrates the basic feeling of those days:

"The Jetavana hermitage bells dying away,
He is singing the song of all the events of the changeable
The Sâla twin tree's shimmering pallid yellow blossoms
Proves, as well as the strong downfall certain.
The ones that go up there won't last long,
They are like a dream on a spring night.
Even controversial heroes have finally fallen,
Not unlike the dust that the wind drives before it."[H]

The concept of the philosophy of the impermanence and transience of all things (*shogyô mujô*) derives from the first of the "Three laws of Buddhism" – "All being is fleeting". This principle, which has its origins in a time of political and military turmoil, also has positive connotations: Inconsistency is seen as an

31 "Improvised like a sketch" (Bruno Taut) and yet of the highest perfection.
32 Transient materials testify to the impermanence of all being. Window in the Karakasatei, Kodai-ji, Kyoto

F   Bruno Taut, *Das japanische Haus und sein Leben – Houses and People of Japan*, p. 162
G   "The Tale of the Heike" is about the decline of the ruling Taira clan
H   Franziska Ehmcke/Heinz Dieter Reese (eds.), *Von Helden, Mönchen und schönen Frauen – Die Welt des japanischen Heike-Epos*, p. 33f.

ideal in the sense that eternity on earth can only be represented by its opposite – the shortest possible moment. As opposed to the schools of Hinayana Buddhism that promise its followers the prospect of gradual enlightenment, Zen Buddhism postulates this precisely – sudden enlightenment that can arise from a single moment. The consciousness of impermanence could thus become a tool of liberation, a key to understanding human existence.

Japan has always been a culture of timber, and since time immemorial people have been accustomed to having to replace built structures on a regular basis. At the same time, the imponderables of natural phenomena – the inhabitants of Japan were struck at regular intervals by earthquakes, volcanic eruptions, typhoons, tidal waves and firestorms – may have shaped the awareness of the transience, imperfection and incompleteness of all being. Therefore, the house is only a temporary refuge for the body, just as the body can only be the seat of the soul for a limited period of time. In the design of the teahouse, this idea finds its direct counterpart in the use of natural and transient materials. The name *sôan* already refers to the temporary character of the building: The term derives from the terms for grass – *sô* – and hermitage – *an* – and refers in its original meaning to a temporary refuge of a traveler in ancient times: High rush grasses were bundled as they stood on the field and knotted at the upper end – a simple grass tent was created as a shelter for the night. In the morning the knot was loosened and the tent disappeared in a moment., The teahouses with their small size, built of light materials, perfectly corresponded to the idea of temporary dwelling. They could easily be disassembled and reassembled. The Japanese construction system with its prefabricated elements and the renunciation of fixed metal connections made such projects much easier. It was quite common not to leave teahouses in a certain place but to move them, and many of the teahouses that still exist today from past centuries no longer stand in their original place. Some tea rooms were even designed from the outset as temporary structures: The "Golden Tea Room" of the shogun Toyotomi Hideyoshi was only built on certain occasions, during the rest of the time it was stored in disassembled condition in the cellar of Hideyoshi's castle.,

Irrespective of the need to rebuild destroyed buildings, Japan has a long tradition of periodically renewing architectural structures. This originates from Shintoism, in which renewal plays a central role as an act of symbolic purification. The Ise shrines, the most important sanctuary of Shintoism, for example, have been rebuilt every twenty years since the 7th century, with the process of rebuilding taking eight years. Through the renewal, the shrine always shines in new splendor, even though it goes back to ancient Japanese history. Ritual renewals also took place on a larger scale in early Japan, for example when the entire capital had to be relocated after the death of an emperor. This custom was only abandoned with the foundation of Heian-kyo, today's Kyoto.

THE TEMPORARY HUT

The ideal of a building that was limited in size and equipment as much as possible as the site of the tea ceremony was certainly strongly influenced by the remote mountain hermitages in which Japanese philosophers and hermits traditionally sought refuge from the world. Even well-known personalities like the nobleman Kamo no Chômei, who retired to a hut in the mountains to lead a secluded life there around the year 1150, followed the ideal of the Taoist hermit, who lives in and with nature in order to strive for the Tao – the source of all being. In his *Hôjôki* notes, Kamo no Chômei describes the basic feeling of those days in the style of Heian court literature: "The river never ceases to flow, but its water is never the same. Foam bubbles dance in shallow places, disappear and form again – they are certainly not of great duration. The same applies to people and their dwellings [...] Now I have reached my sixtieth year, and my life seems to dwindle like a drop of dew. So I once again built myself a dwelling for the last years of my existence – like a wanderer who prepares a shelter for a night ..."ₖ

His hut was "ten feet square", about three by three meters, which is exactly the size of the 4½-mat teahouses. Yoshida Kenkô (1283–1350), another celebrated poet of the court nobility who also retired to a mountain hut as a hermit, describes in his work *Tsurezuregusa* the transience of the luxury he had left behind in the capital: "But if rare and splendid utensils are lined up next to each other, which were manufactured preciously by many artists from China and Japan, and if the grasses and trees are artfully trimmed in the garden, then this is a very sad sight. Who can live forever between these things? When I see such things, I always have to think: In a moment everything can pass like smoke."ₗ

The ideal of retreating into a mountain hermitage lost nothing of its attraction over the centuries, although very few people actually left the city for the mountains. Instead, the urban population tried to implement their everyday escape and longing for nature in rural, thatched huts built in the backyards in the middle of the city. These buildings were an important impulse for the development of the teahouse, which was to culminate in the *sôan*-style buildings.ₘ In this context, the Buddhist myth of Vimalakirtin, a layman Buddhist in ancient India, also plays an important role: He is said to have received and hosted 84,000 Bodhisattvasₙ in his three by three meter hut. The *Vimalakirti-nirdesa-sutra*, in which this event is told, was very popular among followers of Zen philosophy. One can assume that the early tea masters had known the story when they sought to convey the impression of an infinite space within a tea hut of similar dimensions. The 4½-mat room, the standard size of the teahouse, may seem small, but Zen thinking gives it the spaciousness of hundreds of mats and turns it into a place of endless expanse.

33

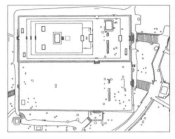
34

33 Every morning the flowers in the water basin of the Honen-in in Kyoto are renewed.
34 The inner shrine area (*naiku*) of the Ise shrine: On the two adjoining properties, the buildings are rebuilt alternately every twenty years.

I   According to Tetsuo Izutsu, *Die Theorie des Schönen in Japan – Beiträge zur klassischen japanischen Ästhetik*
J   See chapter "Sen no Rikyû and his time", p. 143
K   Kamo no Chômei, *Aufzeichnungen aus meiner Hütte*, p. 7 f.
L   Yoshida Kenkô, *Betrachtungen aus der Stille – Tsurezuregusa*, p. 12
M   See chapter "Sen no Rikyû and his time", p. 149
N   Bodhisattvas are buddha-like existences

35

"miwataseba	"You look around you:
hana mo momiji mo	neither cherry blossoms nor red colored leaves
nakarikeri	are there
ura no tomaya no."	at the reed hut near the bay." _O

"hana wo nomi	"If you can only show the ones
matsuran hito ni	who merely await the flowers impatiently,
yamazato no	the spring
yukima no kusa mo	of the grasses in the thawing snow
haru o miseba ya."	of the mountain village." _P

More than in other cultures, beauty is present in almost all aspects of Japanese life. Since the Heian period, works such as *The Tale of Genji* or *The Pillow Book* of Lady Sei Shonagon have testified to a high esthetic consciousness. Since the Middle Ages, certain aspects of esthetic sensitivity have stood in contrast to the admiration for materialized beauty. The four principles – the respect of subtle and ephemeral beauty (*mono-no-aware*), the view of the true nature of things (*yûgen*), cold (*hie*), and drought (*kare*) – were the precursors of an esthetics that was to find its perfection in the concept of *wabi*. In classical literature, the latter was already familiar long before it was established in tea ceremonies and the fine arts, but it only received its current form in connection with the Way of Tea.

Wabi describes an esthetic principle that is often translated as a style of restraint and temperance, imperfection and irregularity. The term derives from the Japanese expression "wabishî", which in the literal translation means "unhappy", "lonely" or "disappointed". "*Wabi* means lacking things, having things run entirely contrary to our desires, being frustrated in our wishes." _Q The term describes the esthetic equivalent of a mood in which one prefers to solitude to company, nature to culture, the unregulated to the regular, the imperfect to the perfect, the asymmetry to symmetry. From an esthetic point of view, *wabi* is an extremely economical and austere design style that prefers rough and unpolished materials and objects. Here, too, the Zen idea of simplicity and lack of ornament is an expression of the deepest human humility in the face of the endless variations in nature. *Wabi* does not simply mean simplicity, but it is a transformation of material insufficiency into spiritual freedom. Leonard Koren describes this mechanism as follows: "The materials used to make objects with *wabi-sabi* characteristics attract these special feelings. The way paper lets light shine through diffusely, how clay cracks when it dries; the change in color and structure of metal when it tarnishes and rusts. All this embodies the physical forces and deep structures that underlie our daily lives." _R

The objects in *wabi* tea style used in the tea room are simple and essential. The contrast to the perfection of the *shoin* tea ceremony and the Chinese utensils used becomes particularly clear. The preference for imperfection and asymmetry is also evident in the *Nampôroku*:

35   *Wabi*: Beauty comes from the simple, the unfinished.

O   Poem by Fujiwara no Teika (1162–1241), used by Takeno Jôô to illustrate the *wabi* feeling; quoted from Horst Hennemann, p. 257f.
P   Poem by Fujiwara no Ietake (1158–1237), used by Sen no Rikyû to illustrate the *wabi* feeling; quoted from Horst Hennemann, p. 258
Q   Zen-Cha-roku, quoted from Kôshirô Haga, "The Wabi Aesthetic through the Ages", in: Paul Varley/ Isao Kumakura (eds.), *Tea in Japan – Essays on the History of Chanoyu*, p. 195
R   Leonard Koren, *Wabi-sabi, für Künstler, Architekten und Designer*, p. 87

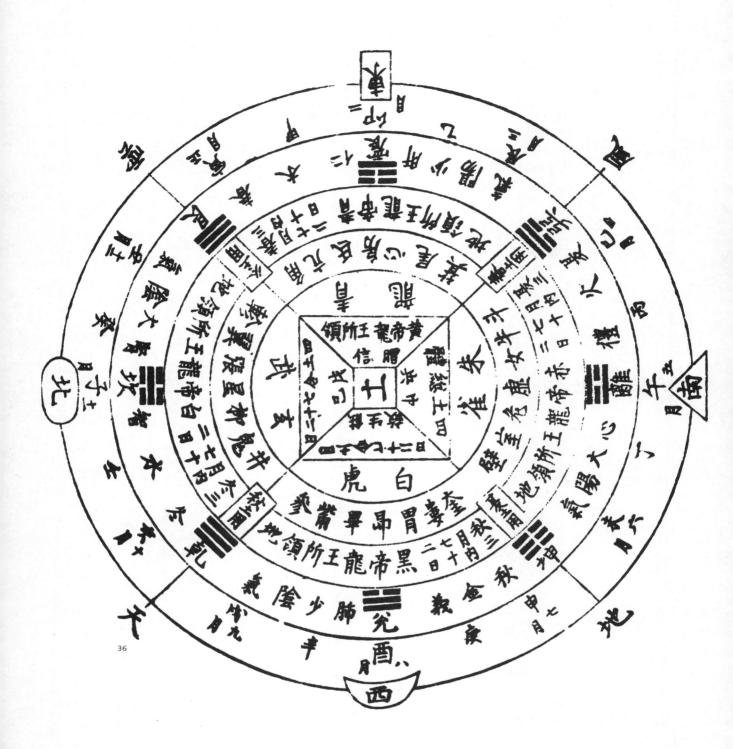

"Utensils used in the small tea room need not to be entirely perfect. There are people who dislike even slightly damaged objects. This, however, is merely indicative of thinking that has not attained true understanding."[s] Developed in the context of Zen, *wabi* always contains an aura of spiritual discipline: Beauty comes from the simple, from the unfinished, by enabling the viewers to complete the work of art in their minds. Beauty is not inherent in the object, but requires the active participation of the viewer. Perfection cannot be achieved in form, but only in the spiritual depth of mind or heart. Kakuzo Okakura describes this effect when he writes: "Only the one could discover true beauty who could complete the unfinished in mind. The power of life and art lay in its ability to grow. In the tea room, it is up to each guest to complete the fantasy of the entire effect in its relationship to his or her ego."[T]

Wabi is therefore a subjective quantity. With their works, the *wabi* artists disturb the expectations of the viewer, who believes to find a perfected work of art.[U] The true beauty sought in the tea ceremony, which also turns the observer into an artist, lies not only in the imperfection itself, but in a sphere in which the difference between the perfect and the imperfect is eliminated. *Wabi* goes hand in hand with the term *sabi*, which is derived from "sabishî" – "to leave" – and "sabiru" – "to mature". In the expanded meaning of "shivering", "exposed" or "withered", however, this principle, in contrast to the subjectivity of the *wabi*, refers to objective qualities inherent in the object. To find beauty in the patina of old age is *sabi*: The blunt shine of a teaspoon touched a hundred times in the same place, the tiny cracks of a coarsely glazed ceramic or the quality of the grain of the wood of a veranda that is given an incomparable polish by decades of walking.

I-CHING AND THE TEACHING OF THE "FIVE ELEMENTS"

Two old philosophical systems – the *I-Ching* and the teaching of the "five elements" – have also had a decisive influence on the design of tea rooms. The *I-Ching* is an ancient Chinese system of world explanation which, after its introduction in Japan in the 5th and 6th centuries, created the spiritual framework according to which life was organized for the following one and a half millennia. Much of this old knowledge was lost only during the modernization phase of the Meiji Restoration and the orientation towards Western rationalist models of thought. The primary existence in the *I-Ching* is the "great definite", which is called in Chinese *t'ai chi*, in Japanese *taikyoku*. From this, two fundamental original energies or principles arise. *Yin* and *yang* or *in* and *yô* in Japan. *Yang* corresponds to the sky and the sun, *yin* to the earth and the moon. Both are relative existences, which can unfold their effect only when combined. *Yin* and *yang* can be combined in four ways, and from these combinations follow the so-called "eight trigrams", each of which constitutes an "image" of a natural phenomenon: earth, mountains, water, wind, thunder, fire, swamp, and sky. Applied to a compass, they correspond to the main cardinal points. From this system the "five elements" are derived – the basis of everything that exists. Everything in the universe can be traced back to these substances – water, fire, wood, earth and metal. These are not absolute entities, but represent a temporary state that is constantly changing according to a fixed pattern of permutations. In pre-modern Japan, the systems of the *I-Ching* and the "five elements" in *chanoyu* occupy a fundamental place. Both the tea room and the ceremony itself are determined by these systems. One makes "fire" with charcoal ("wood"), boils "water" in an iron kettle ("metal"), while the tea bowls and the ashes represent "earth".

36   Geomantic compass

S   Quoted from Kôshirô Haga,
p. 197
T   Kakuzo Okakura, *Das Buch
vom Tee*, p. 70
U   A similar process is when a
master confronts his disciples with
Zen puzzles (*koans*) to break up
their habitual thought processes,
such as: "What is the sound of the
clapping of a single hand?"

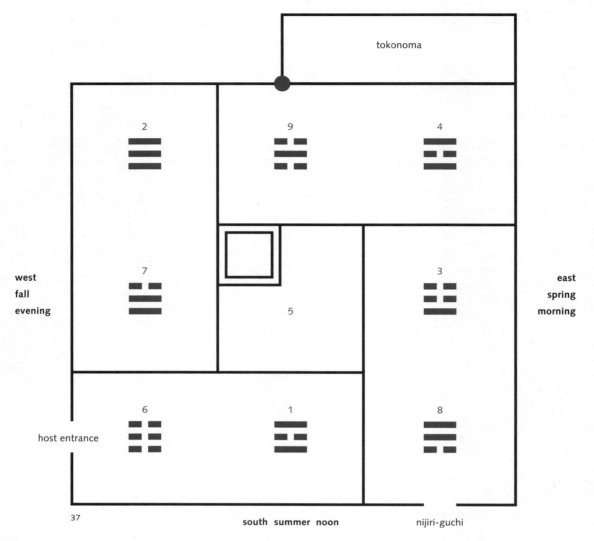

north winter midnight

tokonoma

2

9

4

west
fall
evening

7

5

3

east
spring
morning

host entrance

6

1

8

37

south summer noon

nijiri-guchi

44

The tea room was seen as a model of the universe and was organized according to principles that should harmoniously integrate all participants into this environment. A 4½-mat tea room can be divided into a magic square according to the model of the Chinese *Lo Shu*_v. In a square divided into nine squares, the numbers 1 to 9 are arranged in such a way that the sum of each line, row or diagonal always produces the same result. In the tea room these nine squares correspond to the "eight trigrams" with the neutral element *doyo* in the middle. The center thus remains without a trigram and becomes the dynamic emptiness of the Buddhist nothingness that sets everything in motion. The remaining areas will be integrated by the hosts and guests into the thus created universe. The teaching of the "five elements" is reflected not only in the structure of the entire space, but also in many other details. Sen no Rikyû points out the importance of the *yin-yang* principle for all aspects of the tea ceremony, too: "Even for an evening tea party, you don't use water scooped after lunch. From evening until midnight, the *yin* state prevails, and the water loses its vitality and is harmful. The water in the early morning, on the other hand, is in the *yang* state and still has the pure clarity of the water drawn first. Since it is the water that is so important for tea, the precaution of a tea connoisseur is crucial."_w

If one has finished an ash form in the *furo* or *rô*, one draws the symbol for water with the fire sticks in the middle of the surface. The arrangement of the utensils on the shelf (*daisu*) also follows the rules of the "five elements" by arranging the utensils on the "ground board" (*ji-ita*) and the "sky board" (*ten-ita*) in such a way that a *yin-yang* harmony of the left-right and top-bottom aspects is created.

v   The "Writings of the River Lo" originated in Taoist philosophy and was used 1,300 years ago by Princess Wu as the floor plan of the Ming T'ang temple ("Hall of Light").
w   Nampôroku, quoted from Horst Hennemann, p. 237

37 The tea room as an image of the universe (according to Gerhart Staufenbiel)
   1 The fire (*li*): In the south there is the window that illuminates the room.
   2 The heaven (*ch'en*): This is where the tea utensils are during preparation.
   3 The thunder (*chen*) symbolizes the new beginning, because everything great is introduced by the thunder. The second guest takes a seat here and expects the tea preparation.
   4 The mountain (*ken*): Although the outward appearance of the mountains changes with the season, they are calm inside throughout all changes. The first guest sits there expecting tea.
   5 The center (*doyo*) that initiates all transformations.
   6 The earth (*k'un*) is the center and basis of everything. This is where every tea preparation begins and ends. Here the host opens and closes the door, enters and leaves the room.
   7 The lake (*tui*): Here the host sits while preparing the tea for the guests, cheerful and clear as the lake.
   8 The wind (*sun*): In all Zen buildings the entrance is in the southeast, in the direction from which the wind comes.
   9 The water (*k'an*) represents the danger threatening from the north. That's why this place stays empty. Neither equipment is parked here nor do people take this place. Only the post of the *tokonoma* is given protection by this place.

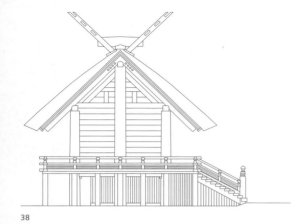
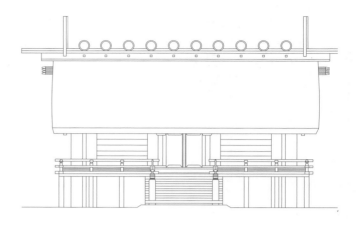

38

39

"While the enjoyment of art in the West is usually reserved for a few privileged people, in Japan everyone lives in the awareness that the esthetic quality of even the most ordinary object is just as important as its functions." [A]

FUNDAMENTALS

The abstract and unique beauty of Japanese buildings is based on the interdependence of structural, spatial and design elements, i.e. formal principles of order that are more subtle in nature than axes, symmetries or hierarchies. A clear geometry, resulting from simple wooden constructions and a system of measurements consistent down to the last detail create unity and a clear distinction of load-bearing and non-load-bearing parts. The design principle of structuring rooms solely by straight lines evokes austerity as well as elegance and purity. The horizontal and vertical lines of columns and beams, the patterns of the ceilings and the borders of the *tatami* mats dissolve all surfaces of the room into a rhythm of rectangles – everything seems to be covered in a "Mondrian pattern". According to the film theorist Noel Burch, this orthogonal composition of wall surfaces holds a kinetic potential:[B] Parts of the pattern like sliding doors (*shoji* or *fusuma*), can be pushed back to make a new, framed element visible – a person, an adjoining room, or even the garden. The design of the moving parts should not be decisive or stand out too strongly from the surroundings: Due to its formal specifications, a sliding door in a Japanese building stands in less clear contrast to the wall surface than doors and windows in Western architecture.

If it applies to everyday life in Japan that one moves in a sphere of hidden hints, subtle shades and ephemeral meanings, this applies all the more to the world of esthetics. In art as in architecture, the implicit meaning of a work has always been given greater attention than what can be read on its surface.[C] Simplicity and reduction of Japanese architecture are in this sense not only to be understood as an elimination of the ornamental, but rather as a concentration on the essential, as a "perfection to the point of inconspicuousness"[D]. Mies's dictum of "less is more" is thus expressed in Japanese. Already to be found in early Shinto shrine buildings, this tradition was certainly also formative for the esthetic preferences of Zen Buddhism. The absence of alignments, haughty frontality and superficial symbolism could also have its origin in the peculiarities of climatic conditions. Fog, frequent rain and high humidity soften the lines and contrasts of buildings and obscure their contours. The Japanese language reacted to the climatic peculiarities by producing a myriad of words to describe the different types and nuances of rain, fog and snow. The assumption that the architectural view could also be influenced by this is not entirely to be dismissed.

ASYMMETRY

"In some places one even preferred an intentional imperfection, such as we also encounter in nature, because only the unfinished was regarded as still belonging to life, symmetry as a symbol of perfection was reserved for the temple and the deity." [E]

Japanese esthetics is based on a dynamic concept of beauty, which always carries within itself the knowledge of the transience of all being.[F] The asymmetric order is a direct expression of this view: No static fact, but a sign of vital life processes – growth, change and interdependence – asymmetry is considered

38 Simplicity and reduction have always characterized the image of Japanese architecture. Inner shrine building (*naiku*) of the Ise shrine

39 Concentrating on the essentials produces its own kind of architectural beauty. Teahouse in the Koetsu-ji, Kyoto

A   Thomas Hoover, *Die Kultur des Zen*, quoted from Klaus Bosslet/ Sabine Schneider, *Ästhetik und Gestaltung in der japanischen Architektur*, p. 14
B   Noel Burch, *To the Distant Observer – Form and Meaning in the Japanese Cinema*, p. 200 f.
C   See chapter "Philosophical and religious background", p. 33
D   Werner Blaser, quoted from Karin Kirsch, p. 65
E   Walter Gropius, *Apollo in der Demokratie*, quoted from Klaus Bosslet/Sabine Schneider, p. 24
F   See chapter "Philosophical and religious background", p. 37

40

one of the most salient features of Japanese architecture. The architectural theorist Norman Carver regards the development of a formal system based on the perfection of asymmetry as Japan's most important contribution to architectural history.[G] Be it in the arrangement of individual buildings on a plot of land, the spatial organization within the house or in the floor plan of an individual room, only in the rarest of cases will one find the symmetrical and axial arrangements so familiar in Western architecture.

41

42

Japan's cultural development was closely linked to China for a long time. In the course of the construction of large temples of the Nara and Heian periods, formal aspects of Chinese architecture, and thus symmetry and alignment, were also adopted for the time being. However, they were soon abandoned in favor of a freer arrangement that was more in keeping with the esthetic preferences of the Japanese. With the construction of monasteries in remote mountain regions, a process of "Japanization" began, in which for topographical reasons straight axis systems were initially substituted by a pattern of several axes deviating from each other. Gradually symmetries and alignment were discarded in favor of more subtle arrangements, until they were finally used only in exceptional cases in individual temples and palaces. In the course of this the temples lost their strong colors; unpainted wooden structures are still a typical feature of Japanese architecture today.

Asymmetrical forms repeatedly challenge the viewer to rethink and arrange the relationships between the individual elements and to complete the forms in the mind that are unfinished in perception. From this point of view, asymmetry corresponds ideally to the idea of the tea ceremony, as the limited tea room is transformed into the infinite expanse of the universe during a tea gathering in the mind of the participants. It is therefore only logical that the principle of deviating from the regular form was perfected by the tea masters. Everything perfect was rejected by them for the reason that it could not change and grow and was therefore no longer part of living processes. Even objects of nature could never have geometrically exact shapes such as circles or straight lines. Starting with the irregularly shaped *raku* tea bowls with their rough surfaces, this preference spread throughout Japan. The starting point and highlight of this development is the architecture of the teahouse: Although the floor plans with 2 and 4½ mats were often square, the individual elements in the teahouse never obeyed a symmetrical order, and the same design pattern was never repeated. The striving for asymmetry manifests itself in the constant effort not to repeat any form or color in the tea room – tension is always sought between large and small, round and angular, light and heavy. In his investigation of the proportions of different teahouses, Masao Yanagi proves that even with square elements there is always a slight deviation from the exact geometric form.[H] The regularity with which this phenomenon occurs can not only be explained by tolerances of handcrafted production methods, but also refers to a conscious distancing from the perfect form.

40 In a process of "Japanization" of mountain temples, symmetry and alignment were abandoned in favor of more subtle systems of reference. Kiyomizu-dera, Kyoto

41 The principle of asymmetry was perfected by the tea masters: entrance facade of a teahouse

42 Imperfection as a design principle: *raku* tea bowl

G   Norman F. Carver, *Form and Space in Japanese Architecture*, p. 27
H   Masao Yanagi, p. 240 ff.

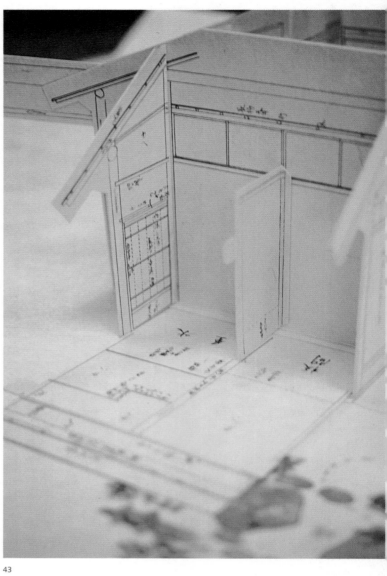

43

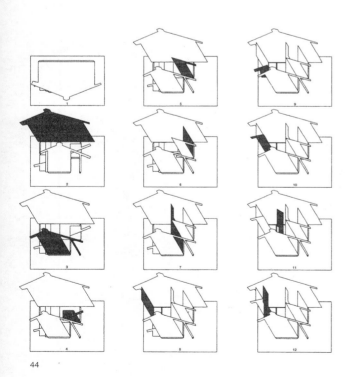

44

While in the countries of origin of Western architectural tradition, a plastic architecture of stone and brick evolved, which allowed lines to emerge with sharp edges and emphasized volumes, Japanese buildings evoke only a very slight feeling of physical solidity. The almost exclusive use of timber as a building material and the slow development of a concept for three-dimensional space led Japanese buildings to unfold their effect primarily through frontality. The space is perceived to disintegrate into independent two-dimensional units, which deny a direct spatial connection. The emptiness caused by the lack of furniture reinforces this impression even further.[I] The importance of frontality is also supported by the fact that all openings are closed with sliding elements that move exclusively within the wall layer. In contrast to tilting or oscillating mechanisms, the opening of which results in a trapezium in the frontal view and thus demonstrates the spatial dimension of the element, a sliding element – regardless of whether it is open or closed – always remains visible as a rectangle. The tendency to abstract walls until the feeling for their dimensions is lost and they appear as pure surfaces is also realized in the teahouse.[J] If one looks at two adjoining wall surfaces of a tea room, one has the feeling that each wall was designed separately, without consideration of the design of the adjoining surfaces. Two windows in adjoining walls do not seem to fit together in size, type and form. The independence of the teahouse design made it possible to break away from the usual rules of Japanese building and from the construction grid, and allowed a particularly free arrangement of the individual elements such as windows or doors. All areas of the teahouse that delimit the space are divided into smaller units, each of which is treated as an individual component. Although as a result all elements are subordinated to a uniform spatial effect, the main focus is on the second rather than the third dimension. The smaller the room, the more important were obviously the arrangement and size of the individual elements and the more complicated the interrelationship of all the parts determining the room. Despite – or, more precisely, because of – their small size, the buildings of the teahouses were so complex that the conventional method of depicting layouts and floor plans with annotations noted therein was no longer sufficient. Perspective was never common in Japan, so a method was sought that could serve as a graphic representation of the spatial effect in teahouses. Since the beginning of the Edo period, a form of representation developed in which the individual space-limiting surfaces were tilted into a plane. If one opened the wall surfaces, then one got a model of the tea room, in which the interaction of the individual elements was well readable. The effect of windows, pillars, doors etc. on the overall space could be checked in a simple way. The method of the "fold-out model" (*okoshiezu*) was used almost exclusively in the architecture of teahouses.[K] The individual surfaces of the model were labeled with detailed information regarding all dimensions and proportions. On a wall of a folding model of Sen no Rikyû's Taian teahouse, for example, the following information is noted: "[From right to left] [Lower wall section] Up to the upper edge of the lower strip 2.33 shaku[L], wall protection white paper. From the threshold to the upper edge of the window strip 2.6 shaku. [Right window] Lower strip 6.5 bu. Upper strip 6.5 bu. Distance between the strips 1.75 shaku. Frame 4 bu and 4.5 bu. Bamboo sticks. [Left window] Strip 6.5 bu. Hanging shoji 1.6 shaku. Hooks. Bamboo sticks. [Upper wall section] Upper wall 1.67 shaku. To top edge of beam 6.05 shaku. Bamboo 6.5 bu. Upper wall from the ceiling 1.75 shaku. [Ceiling] Underside of roof. Ceiling. [tokonoma] 2.32 shaku."[M]

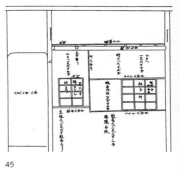

45

43   Fold-out model (*okoshiezu*) of a teahouse

44   Shunsôro, a teahouse by Oda Uraku; fold-out model by Vito Bertin

45   Eastern wall of the Taian tea room

I   This phenomenon can also be observed in Japanese painting, when the rules of perspective seeing are permanently disregarded, light and shadow are ignored, and the flatness so typical of Japanese paintings is achieved.

J   Tadao Ando, quoted from Robin Noel Walker, p. 3

K   The *okoshiezu* method also reflects the temporary aspect of Japanese construction: The room of the teahouse unfolded only temporarily and for a short period of time, while the model could be easily stored in its folded state for the rest of the time.

L   *Shaku, sun* and *bu* are traditional measures of length, where 1 *shaku* = 10 *sun* = 100 *bu* = 303.02 mm

M   Vito Bertin, "Ein Teeraum", in: *deutsche bauzeitung*, p. 23

46

47

In Western architecture, the aim is the separation of functions and living spaces to guarantee the highest possible degree of privacy for the individual. In Japan, borders are seen in less absolute terms. It is a long tradition to bring apparently contradictory circumstances into a mediating state. Continuity and synthesis are common principles that are placed above antithetic tendencies. The idea of the border (*kekkai*)[N] takes up this idea when it simultaneously acts as a separating element and as a link between the persons and spaces between whom it is erected, thus representing this specific dialectical relationship. Precursors of the *kekkai* can be found in Shintoism, where a "sacred straw rope" (*shimenawa*) enclosed a particularly important area or marked a certain object. Chang observes in his investigation of the Japanese space: "Enclosure is the result of surrounding an object or a space so as to 'inform' the contained space or object. An enclosure can be thought of as a wrapping and is quite a distinctive aspect of Japanese space."[O]

While early temples and palaces still applied principles of Chinese architecture in which a massive wall separated a certain district from its surroundings, emphasizing and distinguishing it, the indigenous measures of enclosing were of a more subtle nature. Although fences surrounded the shrines of the Shinto sanctuaries in several layers and removed the sacred district from the profane world, these fences always also formed a "soft", a permeable border. As a rule, they allowed at least a glimpse of the most holy, the inner shrine, without revealing a view of the whole. It is precisely this antithetical principle of simultaneous concealment and unveiling that was realized in Japanese garden design in later centuries. There massive walls separate the garden area from the outside space, but at the same time the landscape behind these walls is included in the garden design by the concept of the "borrowed landscape" (*shakkei*). Tea rooms are usually directed completely inwards and have only a few windows that are absolutely necessary for exposure.[P] Views into the garden are rarely granted, and a direct external view is usually prevented by covering the openings with translucent *shoji* screens and bamboo roller blinds (*sudare*). But even in these separating elements there is a mediating function: The *sudare* were already widespread in the Heian period, because they allow an effect similar to the one-way mirror. From the inside of the building, at least an inkling of what is going on outside is conveyed, whereas conversely no view to the inside is possible. This view through the *sudare* was so significant in the Heian period, known for its subtle insinuations, that the "half-seen form" (*sukikage*) was defined to denote a special, diffuse visual esthetics. The shadows, colored reflections and atmospheric hints reflected on the translucent *shoji* have a similar effect. Takarai Kikaku, disciple of the famous poet Bashô, illustrates the role of *shoji* as a mediating element in a *haiku*[Q]:

"suzumego ya	"Sparrow children – and
akari-shoji no	on the bright sliding door
sasa no kage."	Dwarf bamboo shadow."

The outside world enters the rooms only as a shadow, as an inkling of what lies behind it. Light, colors, images penetrate filtered into the interior, where they can be perceived poetically transformed. For example, maple trees are intentionally planted near the teahouse so that in autumn a red glimmer falls into the tea room. In rare cases, by shifting or hanging individual *shoji*, views from the tea room were allowed – for example to contemplate the moon; nevertheless, the view could not disturb the spiritual concentration within the room.

46   Subtle boundaries create a new quality of space. Kitamura residence, Kyoto

47   Bamboo roller blinds (*sudare*) filter light and colors and create a poetic, pure atmosphere.

N   Literally: "a marking that separates spaces". The word appears during the Heian period, although its use is initially limited to the temples of esoteric Buddhism. There it denotes a boundary line formed by low bamboo fences, hedges, and the like to prevent the entry of persons who could have disrupted the monastic order.

O   Chin-Yu Chang, "Japanese Spatial Conception", in: *Japan Architect*, p. 49

P   See chapter "Construction", p. 93

Q   Japanese poem form

48

49

"Light, natural or manufactured, floods to every corner of an architectonic form. Darkness, which is preserved, is what makes depth be seen. If light be called the life-blood of an architectonic form, darkness could rightly be called its soul." [R]

Just as the Taoist doctrine of nothing and the Buddhist principle of transience of all being have produced specifics of Japanese spatial perception, a concept deriving from Shintoism also forms a special spatial structure: The old Japanese word "yami", in addition to its literal meaning "darkness", speaks of a feeling for everything that lies hidden in the darkness of a room. According to Shintoist faith this world is populated by deities and spirits of the ancestors (*kami*). This ubiquitous and mystical darkness had a great impact on many aspects of construction and eventually became a determining factor. The writer Jun'ichiro Tanizaki emphasized this quality of Japanese architecture: "What is called beautiful is usually the result of the practice of daily life. So our ancestors, who had to live in dark rooms, whether they liked it or not, at some point discovered the beauty inherent in shadow, and they even managed to make shadow serve an esthetic purpose. In fact, the beauty of a Japanese space is based purely on the gradation of shadows. There's nothing else there." [S]

50

Here, too, a spatial concept deviates from Western architecture: For the people of Western culture, spatial experience is linked to the presence of light; light and space are interdependent and form an inseparable unity. If, on the other hand, you enter traditional Japanese buildings, you immediately become aware of the special quality of the light in these rooms. They do not have a bright, clear interior, but rather generate themselves from gradations of shadow and darkness. Beside the windows covered with *shoji*, a large roof with a wide overhang offers protection from rain and the summer sun. The mystical quality increases in those rooms in which certain parts, such as the niche (*tokonoma*), lie completely in the dark. As Tanizaki writes: "If the shadows crouching at every angle were to be chased away, the wall niche would immediately be nothing more than an empty room." [T] Even the entrance to the teahouse corresponds to a pilgrimage from the brightness of everyday life to the mysterious world of shadows. You pass through the tea garden, a plant tunnel, which becomes denser the further you approach the other end of the path. Inside the teahouse you are then surrounded by layers of darkness like in a cocoon. Only sparse light penetrates through the few openings freely distributed on the walls. The *shoji* have a special role to play in this context. The soft, subdued "light without a source of light" [U] is distributed in an inimitable way by the thick *shoji* paper made of the fibers of the mulberry tree (*kozo*) in a kind of blurred transparency, which makes the sliding windows appear not merely translucent, but even luminous by their own power. This impression is reinforced by the narrow frames of window and *shoji* construction that emerge as shadows against the light. Even at night *shoji* retain their illuminating power when the sparse light of candles or oil lamps is scattered and reflected by the rough white paper inside.

48 "Light without a source of light" (Ryôsuke Ôhashi): *Shoji* are not only translucent, but seem to shine by their own power.

49 Tea room in the Shôkintei, Villa Katsura, southwest of Kyoto

50 If all windows are covered, only the open *nijiriguchi* offers views into the garden.

R Amos Ich Tiao Chang, *The Tao of Architecture*, p. 16

S Jun'ichiro Tanizaki, *Lob des Schattens – Entwurf einer japanischen Ästhetik*, p. 33 f.

T Jun'ichiro Tanizaki, p. 38

U Ryôsuke Ôhashi, p. 108

Until the middle of the 16th century, strong, pure colors corresponded to the prevailing fashion, but with the advent of tea esthetics, subdued and calmer shades were preferred. From the reading of the *Choando Ki*, the tea writings of the main priest of the Kasuga shrine in Nara, the central influence of Sen no Rikyû for this development emerges:

"From the time that he came to serve as a tea master to Lord Hideyoshi, everyone began to learn Soeki's [Sen no Rikyu, 1522–91] way of tea. Thus did Soeki's distaste for colorful show achieve a widespread following, as did his verses advocating wabi *austerity. [Practitioners were instructed to] change the color of the collar of their underkimono, to wear cotton kimono dyed with ash to a neutral hue, and to outfit themselves with new sashes, footwear, and fans. Hosts were advised that it was befitting to serve simple dishes such as bean broth and vinegared shrimp and vegetables. From then on, the color gray enjoyed great popularity, and large quantities of gray cotton twill and broadcloth were imported from China."*[V]

This ash-dyed neutral shade has gone down in tea history as Rikyû gray (*Rikyû-nezumi*) and denotes a dark, greenish gray. Especially in the Genroku era (1688–1704), gray in all its shades was the most popular color: silver gray, indigo gray, pigeon gray, brown gray and, last but not least, Rikyû gray were fashionable and together with brown tones and indigo blue formed the esthetic color concept of the *iki*[W], which was extremely popular at that time. Bright or loud colors were regarded as vulgar and tasteless. In his essay "Rikyû Grey – A Culture of Greys", Kisho Kurokawa traces the entire Japanese culture back to a culture of "gray". No black-and-white contrast, but shades of gray prevail in the multidimensional Japanese culture loaded with ambivalent and multiple meanings.[X] Gray, synonymous with colorlessness, is in its appearance the negation of color, but at the same time carries all colors *in potentia* within itself and thus represents the actual reality of colors. While it is not perceived as a color, it is nevertheless "colorful".[Y] As an architectural example of the significance of gray, Kurokawa cites the covered veranda (*engawa*) of the Japanese house, which he regards as the pivotal point of Japanese spatial perception. The primary task of *engawa* is to protect the interior of the building from rain, wind and the strong solar radiation of the Japanese summer. At the same time, it is also the place where guests are welcomed and serves as a transition area from the garden to the house. "En" means "in between", and in this sense this multifunctional "gray" space separates the interior from its surroundings and at the same time connects it with them. The anteroom of the Japanese residential building (*genkan*) should also be mentioned in this context. Although it is already located inside the house, since it is still on the same level as the exterior, it is not a "real" interior, which is only entered when climbing up to the level of the *tatami*. With this concept of duality, a third spatial quality is created in Japanese architecture in addition to "inside" and "outside". *Genkan* and *engawa* can, depending on the point of view, be regarded as extensions of the house or the garden, both at the same time and neither of them – dual, "gray" spaces in between.

51 The outside world enters the interior only as a shadow, as an inkling of what lies behind it. *Shoji* in a residential house in Takayama

V   Kisho Kurokawa, p. 61
W   Most appropriately translated as "wealth in austerity".
X   Kisho Kurokawa, p. 62
Y   Amos Ich Tiao Chang, p. 13

52

53

52 Neither interior nor exterior: the
veranda (*engawa*) of the Japanese
house; drawing by Edward S. Morse

53 Color range of the *iki* color concept
(according to Design Exchange
Company, 2001)

"If Goethe could call architecture frozen music, we might call the Japanese architectural space the frozen Zen."
CHING-YU CHANG[A]

DIVISION OF SPACE

The teahouse (*chashitsu*) can in many respects be regarded as a focal point of Japanese architecture. A multitude of concepts, which were already used in the residential and palace architecture – the lifting of the floor from the ground, the perfection in the elaboration of the details, the distinction between load-bearing and space-dividing elements – were also used in the teahouses and received a special meaning in this context. These buildings had their own architectural style, and the effects of the so-called *sukiya* style[B] on the architecture of later times can still be seen today. Much of what is regarded as typically Japanese in the West has its origin in the architecture of the teahouses. On the other hand, the teahouses as an isolated phenomenon are in stark contrast to Japan's classical architecture. The complete orientation towards the inside, at least at the peak of the development, the rejection of any external reference and the radical-purist approach in the simplification of all elements, differs from the other buildings of the country and reveals the strong influence of Zen Buddhism on the tea masters.

The perfect synthesis of space, form and construction, which certainly contributes significantly to the unbroken fascination of the Western observer with Japanese architecture, has also been realized in the teahouse. The constructive system of traditional timber building is an essential factor in determining the spatial connections and many decorative elements can also be derived from the structure of the construction. Construction and design present themselves as dynamic processes that result in sequences of spatial units with similar meaning and no hierarchies. Since all dimensions are subordinated to a grid system, the individual element never loses its connection to the overall building. With the economical and simple construction of the wooden skeleton construction and the modular approach, rectangular rooms are created as the most rational ground plan form. The individual elements are combined to form larger units by adding them together in a horizontal direction, so that Japanese buildings often seem to have grown organically. Arthur Drexler describes this principle quite aptly in *The Architecture of Japan*, "like boxes of varying sizes packed unevenly in a carton."[C] The free choice of size, number and shape of the rooms leads to an assemblage of individual rooms, the complexity of which in its arrangement harbors tension, contrast and a playful approach to the expectations of the users. Since in Japanese buildings this basic structure is minimized to what is statically absolutely necessary and, moreover, virtually no furniture fill the rooms, one is very free in the design of the floor plans and can focus on the purely functional requirements. The load-bearing structure consists of slender, identically dimensioned elements that allow a maximum of two stories.

Internal access is provided either through the rooms themselves or through external verandas. Internal corridors can only be found in exceptional cases, and this minimization of internal access areas facilitates the extension of the houses in a horizontal direction. The building can be enlarged by simply adding new room units as needed. With the teahouse architecture, the diagonal becomes the determining design principle: Avoiding any symmetries, both the development and the organization of the building's interior follow this concept. The arrangement of the individual rooms along diagonal lines – called

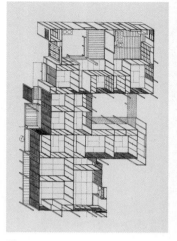

55

54 Iho-no-seki teahouse in the Kodai-ji, Kyoto

55 Axonometric projection of the Reizei-ke property in Kyoto: above the residential wing (*zashiki-bu*), in the middle the intermediate building (*toriai-bu*) with inner garden, below the kitchen wing (*daidokoro*).

A   Ching-Yu Chang, p. 32
B   See chapter "*Sukiya* architecture and the return of the *wabi*", p. 173
C   Arthur Drexler, *The Architecture of Japan*, p. 73

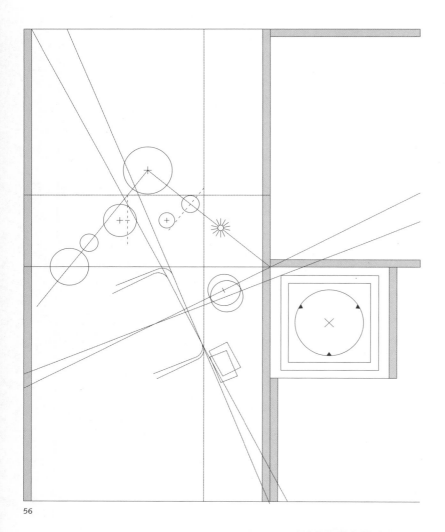

56

57

poetically *ganko-haichi* ("the flight formation of the wild geese") – ensures a varied external appearance, maximum ventilation in summer, and a complex interweaving of garden and house, of exterior and interior. Another special feature of the diagonal arrangement is that you can perceive other parts of the building from the inside of a room. Even the smallest teahouses feature this staggered arrangement of the individual spatial areas, which is so typical for Japanese architecture, since inclination and diagonal principles are also inherent to the tea ceremony: The tea utensils are always arranged along diagonal lines during the tea preparation process, and in the tea garden the bamboo ladle lies inclined on the water basin.

FLEXIBILITY

The individual rooms meet directly without corridors, whereby paper-covered sliding elements serve as dividing elements, which, depending on whether they are covered on one side with translucent or on both sides with opaque paper, are called *shoji* or *fusuma*. Since these elements are extremely light, they can also be easily removed from their guide rail. This makes it possible to combine adjacent rooms into larger units and to design the floor plans rather freely, as only a few elements such as supports or the *tokonoma* niche disturb this openness as unchangeable barriers. While this flexibility is a common principle in residential buildings, it was only used in exceptional cases in early tea rooms: The possibility of modifying the floor plan of the teahouse was obviously not desired by many tea masters in their designs. These principles began to contribute to the design of tea rooms only in the subsequent development, when more and more value was placed on opening the strict framework.

Thanks to this flexibility, the rooms are also available for different uses. While "absolute" spaces are created in the West through furnishing and exact functional definitions, the spaces of Japanese architecture are multifunctional. The rooms are not named according to their function, but according to their location within the house or in relation to other rooms. For example, *ichinoma* is the first room, *ninoma* the second and *okunoma* the innermost room of the house. One and the same room can become a living room, bedroom, dining area or working area. This requires empty rooms that are not furnished with fixed furniture. The existence of the traditional Japanese storage area (*kura*) built in the rear part of the property, facilitates this development: Light furniture and parts of the interior fittings can be stored in it, whereby the rooms retain the openness and emptiness necessary for the various uses. Already in the 14th century this preference for empty spaces is expressed in the *Tsurezuregusa* ("mixed remarks") of the poet Yoshida Kenkô: "Things that make you feel uncomfortable: a lot of equipment in the rooms, a lot of brushes in the ink box, many Buddha statues on the house altar, many stones and plants in the garden, too many words in conversation with others and too many vows in the prayers of supplication".[D]

The tea rooms are also part of this tradition, similar to what is omitted in a Japanese ink drawing or not voiced in a poem, this emptiness evokes a tremendously strong effect. The room, which is completely empty during the rest of the time, is only decorated with a hanging scroll or a flower arrangement in the *tokonoma* for the duration of the tea ceremony. The fact that the host only brings the tea utensils into the room at the beginning of the ceremony and removes them immediately afterwards emphasizes the temporary use of the tea room in the course of a tea gathering. Then the tea room is empty again, the tea bowls are drunk, the gathering is already a thing of the past.

56 During the preparation of tea, the utensils are lined up along diagonal lines.

57 Flexibility and openness are characteristic of Japanese buildings.

D   Yoshida Kenkô, p. 55

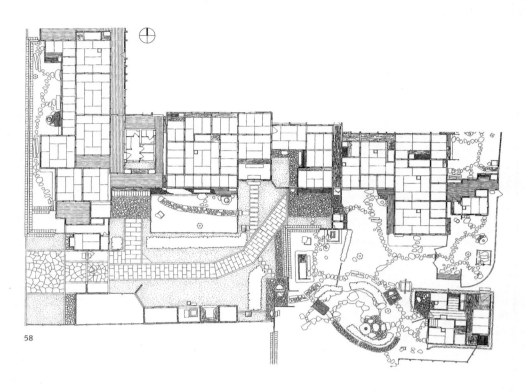

58

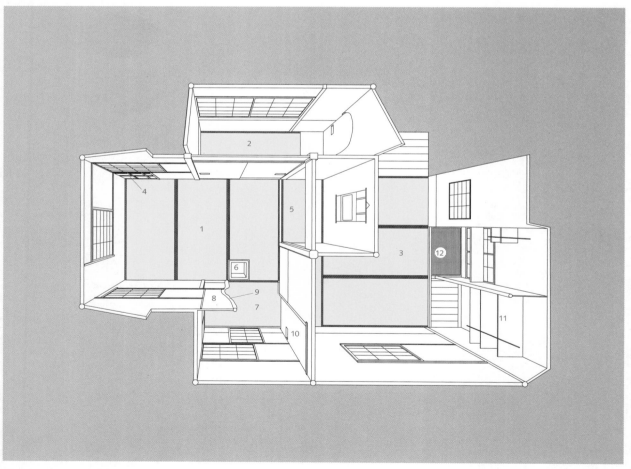

59

Teahouses can be differentiated by whether they are situated freely in the garden, attached to another building or integrated into it. Practical factors such as the size of the property as well as functional considerations play a role. If, for example, a teahouse is to be erected in a temple to hold Buddhist ceremonies in the form of tea gatherings, it is advisable to position it as close as possible to the temple building. On the other hand, if a tea master wants to take the guests as far as possible from the everyday world, a spatial separation makes sense: While walking through the garden, the visitors leave the concerns of daily life behind them. In some teahouses there are several tea rooms which differ in size and equipment and are used depending on the number of participants or the type of tea ceremony. Special structures can be found on the properties of the large tea schools: Over the centuries, various teahouses, gardens and preparation rooms were built, which today present themselves as a collection of nested rooms. Many of Japan's most important tea rooms are located within these complexes and will be discussed in more detail later.

60

Beside the actual tea room (*zashiki*) as the place of the tea ceremony, the area of the preparation room (*katte*) is an integral part of every teahouse. This room, which usually has a size of two to three *tatami* mats, is intended for storing and cleaning the utensils and contains all the necessary facilities for the preparation of the tea ceremony. Next to shelves and cupboards the "water room" (*mizuya*) is in this area: On several shelves, often placed in front of a window, the utensils necessary for the ceremony are arranged according to precise specifications. Under the shelf there is a drain for the wastewater covered with a bamboo grid, a large water tank with fresh water and hooks for ladle, bamboo broom and linen towels. The wall shelves are designed according to practical and esthetic guidelines, and all other elements of the room also follow this principle. It was precisely these exemplary conveniences when using this "tea kitchen" that drove forward and influenced the redesign of the uncomfortable and unhygienic kitchens of the old houses.[E] Depending on the size and type of the teahouse, there are various other anterooms and side rooms, e.g. a small kitchen in which the host prepares the meal (*kaiseki*) before the guests arrive.

Usually hosts and guests enter the tea room through separate entrances, which differ significantly in shape, size and material. The host comes from the *mizuya* and enters the tea room through the host entrance (*sadô-guchi*). This entrance is slightly lower than the height of a normal Japanese passageway, so that the host has to bend down slightly each time he or she enters the room. This movement expresses the respect for the guests and the humility before the ritual. In some cases the door has a round lintel, then it is called *katô-guchi*.

In some teahouses there is another entrance, from which an assistant of the host serves the food during the tea ceremony (*kyuchiguchi*). When the guests approach the teahouse from the inner garden, they walk over stepping stones to a high stone (*fumi-ishi*), from which they enter the teahouse. This large stone, as flat as possible on the surface, is carefully selected. After the sliding door has been pushed to the side, the guests crawl on their hands and knees through the small opening of the "crawl-in entrance" (*nijiriguchi*) into the interior of the tea room. There they turn around, bend outside of the teahouse and place the sandals, which they took off at the *fumi-ishi*, upright against the outer wall of the teahouse. This form of entrance is an invention of Sen no Rikyû, the most famous of the great tea masters. According to legend, Rikyû was influenced by the hatches on river ships he saw in northern Osaka. Chadô

58   The premises of the Omotesenke tea school in Kyoto meet directly without corridors.

59   Spatial organization of a teahouse:
  1   Tea room (*chaseki*)
  2   Anteroom
  3   "Water room" (*mizuya*)
  4   "Crawl-in entrance" (*nijiriguchi*)
  5   Niche (*tokonoma*)
  6   Sunken stove (*rô*)
  7   Host mat (*daime*)
  8   "Sleeve wall" (*sode-kabe*)
  9   Center post (*naka-bashira*)
 10   Host entrance (*sadô-guchi*)
 11   Shelf (*chigaidana*)
 12   Sink (*nagashi*)

60   All the tea utensils are arranged on the shelves of the *mizuya*: on the lower right is a large water container for washing the utensils, on the lower left the drain covered with a bamboo grid.

61   Following page: tea bowls in a *mizuya*

E   See also Heino Engel, *Measure and Construction of the Japanese House*, p. 68

62

Shiso Densho reports: "Finding it to be tasteful and interesting that one must crawl into and out of the boats at the dock at Hirakata in Osaka, Rikyû began to use such a passageway in the small tea room."_F_ The idea that boats, like the tea room, are a world of their own may have played a role in this.

The way in which the *nijiriguchi* forces the visitors to enter a tea room does not always arouse undivided enthusiasm. Dazai Shundai, a samurai from Shimano province and critic of the tea ceremony, comments: "[...] The entrance-way for guests is like one suitable for dogs. Obliged to crawl in on the belly, one has a suffocating feeling. In the winter it is unbearable."_G_ The low entrance forces every visitor to enter the tea room in a humble posture. At the same time, it is a sign that one crosses a threshold and enters another world. As in the Nô or Kabuki theater, where visitors have to squeeze their way through the so-called "mouse hole" (*nezumi-kido*) after they have paid admission, or the musicians only enter the stage through a narrow gate, there is also a separation between the profane and the sacred world in the tea room. In this context it is interesting to note the idea of Japanese Amida Buddhism, in which one can enter paradise only through a small opening. The *tainai-kuguri* rite of the Shugendô mountain religion, in which one has to squeeze through rocks in order to emerge purified, can also be seen in this context.

THE TEA ROOM

In contrast to the rooms of Japanese residential buildings, the use of the tea room is determined from the outset. The exact rules of the tea ceremony, which define the movements of the host and the guest, determine the position of the elements and the basic layout of the room. Nevertheless, and despite the fact that most teahouses have extremely small footprints, there is a surprisingly large number of variation possibilities in the layout of the floor plans.

The base room is the 4½-mat room (*yojôhan*). If the space is larger than *yojôhan*, then it is called "wide room" (*hiroma*), all other rooms are called "narrow rooms" (*koma*). *Hiroma* can have a size of up to 15 *tatami*, but usually tea rooms are not larger than eight mats. *Koma* are by far the most common; they are divided into eight basic types:

62 The *nijiriguchi* of a teahouse in the Koto-in, Kyoto

F   Quoted from Isao Kumakura, "Sen no Rikyû: Inquiries into his Life and Tea", in: Paul Varley/Isao Kumakura (eds.), *Tea in Japan – Essays on the History of Chanoyu*, p. 50
G   Quoted from Paul Varley, "Chanoyu: from the Genroku Epoch to Modern Times", in: Paul Varley/Isao Kumakura (eds.), *Tea in Japan – Essays on the History of Chanoyu*, p. 175

63

64

1   *yojôhan* with a square floor plan, in which the layout of the *tatami* mats changes according to the season

2   "long 4-mat room" (*naga yojô*), in which the four mats are placed next to each other with their long sides

3   "wide 3¾-mat room" (*hira sanjô-daime*), which is similar to the *naga yojô*. The only difference is that a full mat is replaced at the end by a ¾-mat (*daime*)

4   "deep 3¾-mat room" (*fuka sanjô-daime*), in which the three full mats meet as a T-joint

5   the "3-mat room" (*sanjô*) corresponds to the *fuka sanjô-daime* reduced by the *daime*

6   in the "2¾-mat room" (*nijô-daime*) the ¾-mat comes to rest on the narrow sides of the full *tatami*

7   the "2-mat room" (*nijô*), whose two mats are placed against each other with their long sides.

8   the "1¾-mat room" (*ichijô-daime*) corresponds to the *nijô* with a full mat replaced by a *daime* mat

In addition, however, a large number of other arrangements are possible and common.

Another type of classification is that of the "eight stoves", which differ according to the location of the stove in relation to the host's area. The four basic types are: *yojôhan*, "opposite stove", *daime*, and "corner stove". These can be in the "normal" position – the guests are to the right of the host – or in the "reverse" position – the guests are to the left – two variants that are also called "right-handed" and "left-handed" positions.

RÔ – THE SUNKEN STOVE

The sunken stove (*rô*) is the functional center of the tea room, as it describes the place of the ritual tea preparation. It is only used in the winter months, from November to April, during the rest of the year it is covered by a *tatami*. It serves not only to heat the tea water, but also for heating and is therefore located in the middle of the room, as close as possible to the seating area of the guests. In the warm season, on the other hand, a mobile ash pan (*furo*) is used, which is consequently situated as far away as possible from the guests in a corner of the room.

The *rô* is located in a very specific relation to the position of the two entrances and the *tokonoma*, a consequence that results from the exact rules of tea preparation. The square cutout of the *rô-tatami* has a side length of 43 centimeters; the depth of the *rô* is about the same. The ashes of past ceremonies – often mixed with the ashes of the mortal remains of former tea masters – are emptied into the sunken stove and a cast iron tripod (*gotoku*) is placed on top. The water kettle sits on this tripod, but in some teahouses the *gotoku* is dispensed with and the kettle is suspended from the ceiling by an iron chain. These rooms are also called "chain room" (*kusari-no-ma*). The elements of the *rô* are the sunken stove (*rodan*) and the stove frame (*robuchi*). The latter is considered to be a tea utensil and is available in various designs. A true to original *rodan* is made of clay and should be replaced annually by a specially trained craftsman. Today, however, *rodan* made of steel, copper, ceramics and stone are also available – materials that guarantee a longer working life.

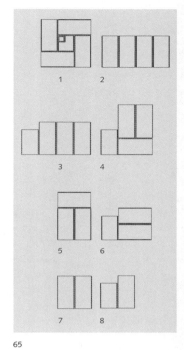

65

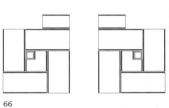

66

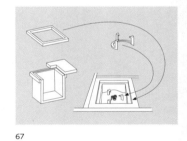

67

63   In the warm season one uses a *furo*

64   In the winter months the *rô* is used

65   The eight basic types of the tea room classified by number and location of *tatami*

66   Right-handed and left-handed position of a 4½-mat tea room

67   The components of the *rô*

TWO ESSENTIAL ELEMENTS – TATAMI AND TOKONOMA

TATAMI

Since Japanese houses have always been lifted from the ground to provide the necessary ventilation in the sultry summers, it was not necessary to use tables, chairs, beds and other furniture inside – elements that served to separate human activity from the cold or damp floor. Instead, the floors were made of wood and laid with rice straw mats, a fact that still characterizes daily life in Japan today. Only when one enters the platform of the raised floor in a Japanese house, one really has entered. Even if you have passed a door before, you are only inside the house when you climb up. The invitation to enter a Japanese house is therefore not "Please step inside" but "agatte kudasai", which means "Please step up". The importance of floor space for Japanese culture can therefore not be overestimated. The Japanese architectural theorist Yoshinobu Ashihara goes so far as to classify Japanese building as "architecture of the floor", while he sees "masonry architecture" in the Western buildings.[H] And so in Japan it is rather the floor, and not the wall, that separates the interior from the exterior. In addition, the floor-oriented way of life produces a multitude of special features and differences to Western architecture. It should be mentioned here that the view is thirty to forty centimeters lower than when sitting on chairs, and the fact that Japanese furniture is really "mobile" and is only be removed from the wall cupboards or the *kura* and set up according to the respective requirements.

Tatami mats consist of the so-called *toko* bottom layer, an approximately four-centimeter-thick core of pressed rice straw over which the front (*omote*), a rush mat, is stretched. This is woven in such a way that narrow parallel stripes (*me*) are created. On the long sides the *tatami* have fabric borders. The *tatami* mats are the visible expression of the constructive system: The *tatami* and the pattern of their mostly black borders reflect the structural elements of the buildings and link the floor and the system of wall surfaces to form a unit. In addition, the net pattern of *tatami* is also ornamental adornment. The number of mats used determines the size of the room, and despite the use of ½ or ¾ *tatami*, this rather large module significantly limits the number of possible variations.

HISTORY

The *tatami* probably were given their present form during the Heian period, until then thin grass mats fulfilled their function. These were easy to fold, a fact from which their name is derived, as *tatamu* means "folding" in Japanese. First mentioned in the poetry collection *Kojiki* (712 AC), *tatami* mats laid individually on the wooden floor in the *shinden-zukuri* palace style of the Heian period marked the seating area of the ruler and the highest guests. The colors of the border and the thickness of the *tatami* indicated the rank of the respective guest.

It was only with the *shoin* style that the custom of laying whole rooms with *tatami* became established. From the middle of the Edo period, *tatami* were also used in the houses of the lower classes, but in some rural areas *tatami* rooms were not to be found before the Meiji period. *Tatami* are widespread in Japan until today and shape the lifestyle of the population. The custom of taking off one's shoes at the entrance to the house is still maintained today, even though the modern apartment buildings of the big cities no longer have any *tatami* rooms at all. During the Edo period, principles were developed to lay out the mats in certain arrangements, with arrangements, in which the joints of the mats formed a T-shape (*kichi*), distinguished from arrangements with continuous joints (*kyo*). In the teahouse, primarily the first type of arrangement is used, where the *tatami* are placed so that there are no axes or continuous lines. The *tatami* in front of the *tokonoma* with its long side parallel to the ornamental niche serves as a base for the remaining mats. If there is no *tokonoma*, the *tatami* at the door acts as the basis for the rest of the layout. In the usual rules of Japanese architecture, the *tatami* narrow side must never point to the *tokonoma*, an arrangement called *toko-zasshi*. The only exception is the 8-mat tea room, where this form of arrangement is used for other reasons, including the location of the sunken stove.

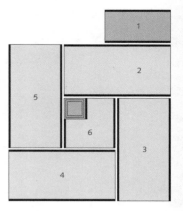

SIZE

The *tatami* mat is derived from the size of the human body and covers the area of one or two persons lying or sitting. It defines the smallest possible living space and can thus serve perfectly as a modular system for human dwelling. The sizes of the *tatami* were unified in the course of history, but the *tatami* measure varies depending on the region until today. The ratio of length to width always remains the same at 2:1. There are three different sizes: In the Kantô plain, the region around Tokyo, it is 176 centimeters long and 88 centimeters wide, which corresponds to a floor area of 1.54 square meters. These *tatami* are called *inakama-datami*. The *kyô-ma-tatami* of the Kansai region – around the cities of Osaka, Kyoto and Kobe – is somewhat larger with 191 x 95.5 centimeters and a floor area of 1.82 square meters. Between the two sizes there is the *ai-no-ma-* or "interspace" *tatami*. It is mainly found in the region around Nagoya and measures 182 x 91 centimeters for a floor area of 1.65 square meters. Throughout history, all sizes were used for tea rooms, but the *kyô-ma-tatami* was able to establish itself as the standard, presumably because of its larger dimensions, which guaranteed enough space even in the smallest rooms for the necessary activities of the tea ceremony. Besides the full *tatami* size (*maru-tatami*) there are the *han-jô-tatami* with the area of half a *tatami* and the *daime-tatami*. The latter is a ½-mat which results from the reduction of the full *tatami* by the width of the utensil shelf (*daisu*).

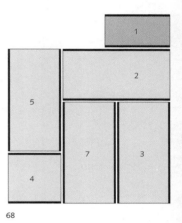

68

TATAMI IN THE TEA ROOM

The *tatami* occupy a fundamental position with regard to tea room organization: The *tatami* mats laid out on the floor further divide the surface into smaller subunits, each of which has its own meaning. Not only are tea rooms classified according to the number of mats (*jô*), each mat is also assigned a specific, irrevocable function.

The *toko-datami* 1 designates the *tatami* in the *tokonoma*, while the *kinin-datami* 2 located in front of the *tokonoma* marks the most prominent sitting area for the first guest. Depending on the size of the tea room, one or more *kyaku-datami* 3 form the area reserved for the other guests. The *fumikomi-datami* 4 and the *temae-* or *dôgu-datami* 5 mats have a special role to play: The former is located in front of the host's entrance, and as the host enters and leaves the tea room here, this *tatami* marks the beginning and end of each tea ceremony. The *temae-datami* is even more important, as it is the place where tea is made. The name of the *rô-datami* 6 refers to the stove cut out of it, and the *kayoi-datami* 7 is the mat crossed by the guests. The arrangements of the individual mats depend on the location of the sunken stove and may therefore differ between the *rô* and *furo* seasons: If in the *rô* season the half *tatami* of the 4½-mat room is placed in the middle, it functions as *fumikomi-datami* during the *furo* season – in which *rô* is usually covered.

But the relationship between *chanoyu* and *tatami* goes even deeper, as different rules for the location of tea utensils in relation to the *tatami* edges prove.

68 Each *tatami* mat in the tea room is assigned a specific function. The arrangement of the mats varies according to the *furo* or *rô* season.

H   Yoshinobu Ashihara, *The Hidden Order – Tokyo through the Twentieth Century*, p. 33

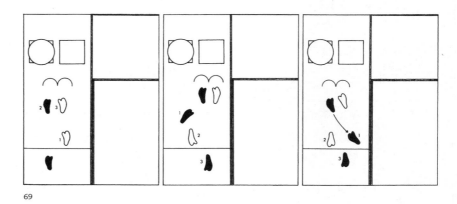

69

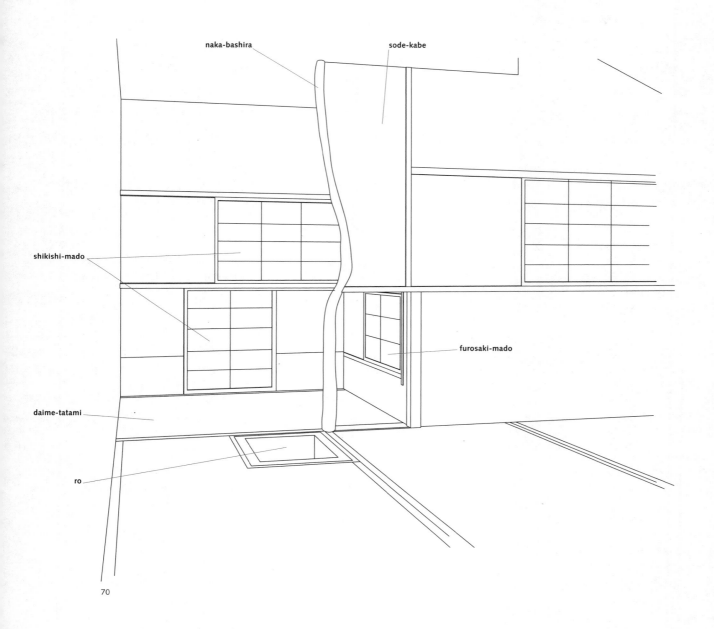

naka-bashira

sode-kabe

shikishi-mado

furosaki-mado

daime-tatami

ro

70

These distances are counted by the *me* on the *tatami*. In the book *Chadô Benmôshô* (*The Way of Tea at a Glance,* 1680) published by Yamada Sôhen one reads for example: "...The tea caddy (*chaire*) is forward of the position of the waste-water receptacle (*kensui*). It is placed about 3 or 4 woven lines from the edge of the tatami. However, consideration must be given to the size of the tea caddy...",

The regulations for step sequences in the tea room – when to cross which edge with which foot – also prove the close connection between the *tatami* layout and the tea ceremony. Illustrations in textbooks, which are reminiscent of dance steps, illustrate the "choreography" in the teahouse, which is guided by the position of the *tatami* mats.

Although there is a variety of designs of the *tatami* border, it is always kept in an almost black dark blue in tea rooms. Only the border of the *tokonoma* can be patterned. The size of the pattern depends on both the size of the room and the *tokonoma*. In *koma* the single-colored dark blue border is also used for *toko-datami*.

DAIME MATS

The introduction of a ¾- or *daime* mat as the host's seat marked a new stage in the development of the tea room. The use of a smaller mat for the host's area is a direct result of a change in the procedures within the tea ceremony. With the elimination of the *daisu* and the folding wall (*byobu*) behind it, the *temae-datami* could be reduced by exactly this amount. In addition, the *daime* mat is separated from the rest of the tea room by a center post (*naka-bashira*) and a narrow "sleeve wall" (*sode-kabe*). The host seat was thus established as a separate area in the tea room, its location in a subordinate position in relation to the *tokonoma* even allows later tea masters to speak of the host seat as an anteroom, a spatial concept that is entirely dominated by *wabi* tea.

The lower two fifths of the *sode-kabe* are usually left open so that the guests can follow the movements of the host. When Sen no Rikyû's son Sôan built a replica of a tea room built by his father in Osaka in 1582, he extended the sleeve wall to the floor without leaving the usual area in the lower part of the wall free. This refers to the original idea of the *daime* as a separate space for the host. In the form known as *Doan-gakoi*, this concept reaches its climax: Here the host seat is even separated from the guest area by a sliding door with a curved lintel. The guests cannot follow the beginning of the ceremony, because they are only involved after the host opens the door and connects the two areas after bringing the utensils into the room.

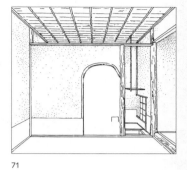

71

69 The given sequence of steps in the *furo* season is reminiscent of dancing steps: entering the *temae-datami*, leaving the *temae-datami*, leaving the *temae-datami* with the wastewater container (*kensui*).

70 *Daime* arrangement: The shortening of the host mat resulted from the omission of the *daisu* shelf in small rooms.

71 Special form of a tea room structure: Doan-gakoi

ı   Satô Osamu, "A History of Tatami", in *Chanoyu Quarterly*, p. 15

ı   See chapter "The development of the *sôan* teahouse", p. 135

72

TOKONOMA

The wall surfaces of the Japanese house are not decorated with paintings or other decorative elements like the houses of China or the West. If the sliding doors (*fusuma*) or other architectural elements themselves are not painted, the room remains without decor. Instead, the rooms with the *tokonoma* possessed a place that could be decorated with a hanging scroll or a flower vase. Before the Second World War, practically every Japanese house still had a *tokonoma*, even if they were sometimes only mobile or rudimentary.

ORIGINS

The *tokonoma*, however, did not serve exclusively as a place for the exhibition of a work of art, but since the feudal period it has also marked the most important area in the room called *kamiza*, from which the rest of the seating arrangement was defined. The highest guest sat with his/her back to the *tokonoma*, and this seating arrangement was modified during the tea ceremony, to allow every guest to admire the decoration objects of the day.

The exact origin of the *tokonoma* is controversial, most likely it developed from a combination of different elements: First of all, there is the *jodan-no-ma*, an elevated area of space developed in the late Muromachi period in the palaces of *shoin* architecture in response to the need to create a particularly distinguished place for the ruler and the guests of honor. This area, which was previously identified by individual *tatami* mats laid on the wooden floor, disappeared as soon as all the rooms were covered with *tatami*. Raising a part of the floor was a tried and tested means of redefining the lost place of honor. The fact that the *tokonoma* is now the only area with an elevated level in the tea room, and that this also determines the location of the most important guest in the room, indicates the *jodan-no-ma* as the forerunner of the *tokonoma*. The fact that the ruler Toyotomi Hideyoshi often took a seat in the *tokonoma* himself and Sen no Rikyû is said to have repeatedly offered this seat to his highest guests also fits in with this.

The second potential forerunner of the *tokonoma* is the *oshiita*: a wooden board about 25 to 30 centimeters above the floor, which was attached to the wall. It was placed in front of hanging pictures, and decorated with a decoration set (*mitsugusoku*), consisting of a candleholder, holder for incense sticks and a vase. While the early *oshiita* were still transportable, over time they became a fixed fixture in a niche. The similarity with the arrangement of a *tokonoma* is so obvious that the *oshiita* can also be assumed to be the origin of the *tokonoma*.

ELEMENTS AND TYPES OF TOKONOMA

A formal *tokonoma* in a tea room is called *hondoko*. It should face south and receive light from its right side. The elements considered constitutive for a *hondoko* are the *tokonoma* post (*toko-bashira*), the lower and upper *tokonoma* frames (*toko-gamachi* and *otoshi-gake*) as well as a floor covered with a *tatami* mat. If one or more of these elements are missing, it is called "*tokonoma* in informal style" (*ryakushiki-toko*). The *kabe-doko* represents the most rudimentary form of a *tokonoma*. It simply provides an area of a wall to hang a scroll, but it does not have any of the *hondoko* elements mentioned above. The *oribe-doko* marks the *tokonoma* room by a wooden board (*oriba-ita*), which is mounted on the wall in the ceiling area. The *oki-doko* and *tsuri-doko* forms are modifications of *kabe-doko*. In the former, a transportable wooden board is placed in front of a *kabe-doko*, while in the *tsuri-doko* the space of the *tokonoma* is defined by a wall projection suspended from above.

72 Flowers and a picture scroll decorate the *tokonoma* of a 4½-mat tea room.

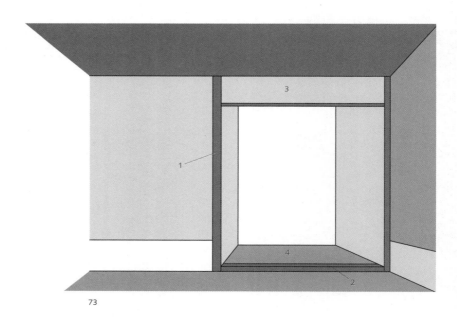

73

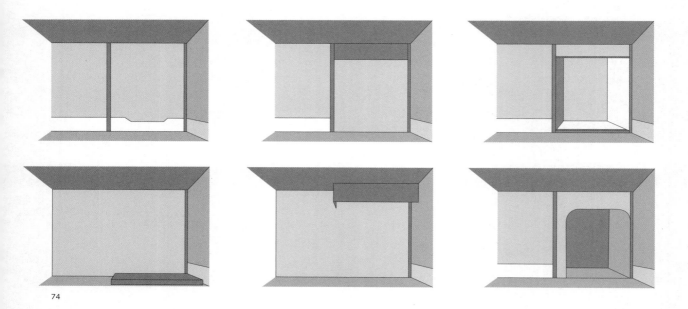

74

If a *tokonoma* has all the elements of a *hondoko*, but is different in shape or size, it is called "modified" *tokonoma* (*henkei-doko*). Examples are the *fumi-komi-doko*, which is at the same height as the floor level, or the *kekomi-doko*, in which the *tokonoma* floor does not consist of a *tatami* mat, but of a wooden board protruding like a step. A *tokonoma* plastered on all sides, including the ceiling, in which only the floor is covered with a *tatami*, is called *muro-doko*, and the *tsuchidoko*, *fukuro-doko*, *hora-doko* and *ganwari-doko* are special forms of this type.

Tokonoma can also be classified according to their width, whereby they are usually described according to their *tatami* size: For example, the *masu-doko* has the width of a half *tatami*, the *daime* or *genso-doko* the width of a ¾-*tatami* and the *ikken-doko* the width of a full *tatami*. If the *tokonoma* is wider than a *tatami*, its measure is given in *shaku*$_K$: The "seven *shaku* size" (*nanashaku-doko*) is then about 212 centimeters wide, the "eight *shaku* size" (*hasshaku-doko*) 242 centimeters wide, and so on. There are a lot of other *tokonoma* forms, but they only add insignificant new aspects to the ones discussed here and only differ in their details. Despite the abundance of different expressions, the *tokonoma* variations are strongly standardized.

Since the *tokonoma* usually did not cover the entire width of the room, the space next to it is usually occupied by a second niche, in which staggered shelves (*chigaidana*) are often arranged. Since they appear almost exclusively in combination with a *tokonoma*, they are more a part of the *tokonoma* than an independent spatial element. They are called *tokiwaki*, literally "*tokonoma* side", which further underlines their dependence on *tokonoma*. They are rarely to be found in tea rooms, as these rooms had generally been rid of all the usual elements of residential architecture except for the *tokonoma*. Only in tea rooms that were equipped like the *shoin* reception rooms you can find the *chigaidana*.

With the tea master Sen no Rikyû, the *wabi* ideal of teahouses in grass hut style reached a climax. With a strong emphasis on the spiritual aspects of the *chanoyu* and a completely inward orientation, the *tokonoma* became the absolute center of space. All other elements had only a subordinate function in relation to this. Rikyû arranged the *nijiriguchi* and the *tokonoma* along an axis in such a way that the first thing a guest saw when entering the room was the ornamental niche with the picture scroll and flower arrangement displayed therein. The discontinuation of the philosophy of Rikyû in the later history of the tea ceremony is due to a large degree in the changed importance that was attributed to *tokonoma* by later tea masters. They increasingly moved themselves into the center of the action and designed the tea rooms in such a way that the host seat attracted all attention. The *tokonoma* was thus also physically moved from the center of the tea room.

73 A formal *tokonoma* (*hondoko*) with all defining elements:
  1 *Tokonoma* post *(toko-bashira)*
  2 Lower *tokonoma* frame *(toko-gamachi)*
  3 Upper *tokonoma* frame *(otoshi-gake)*
  4 *Tatami* mat *(toko-datami)*
74 Forms of informal (*ryakushiki-toko*) and modified (*henkei-doko*) *tokonoma*

K *Shaku* corresponds to the length of 0.303 meters

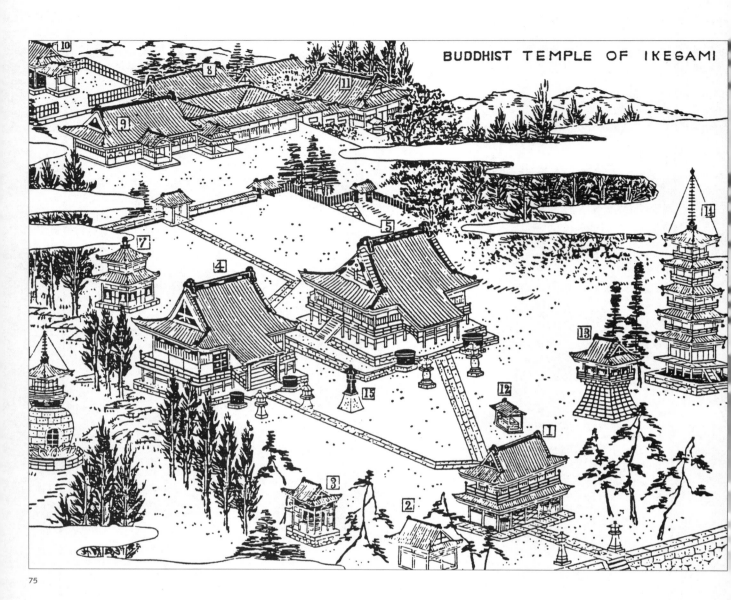

BUDDHIST TEMPLE OF IKEGAMI

75

"Pine pillars, bamboo joists, left as they are, curved and straight, square and round, up and down, left and right, new and old, light and heavy, long and short, broad and narrow, repaired where chipped, patched where torn. Everything at odds, nothing matching."

ZEN CHA ROKU[A]

TIMBER CONSTRUCTION

Japan has always been a country of timber construction, and until the 19th century there were hardly any stone buildings to be found. Simple procurement possibilities, easy processing and manufacturing techniques, static earthquake resistance and, last but not least, lower costs were the decisive factors in Japan's preference for wood – in contrast to stone construction in China – as the predominant building material. These advantages and the special relationship of the Japanese to nature, especially to plants, far outweighed the disadvantages of the material's easy flammability and limited durability. The temple forms adopted from China and Korea, which were built in their countries of origin solid structures, were made in Japan as wooden constructions set on stone platforms. Even with the fortified, multi-story castles, only the mighty stone base was erected, the rest of the building consisted of a plastered wooden construction. Only when the wave of westernization associated with the Meiji Restoration took hold of architecture did brick and stone become common building materials and the necessary construction methods were adopted at the same time.

The teahouses are entirely dedicated to this tradition of wood construction, even if they have some special features. The teahouse differs from temples and residential buildings in the use of as natural and diverse materials as possible. While only one type of wood is used for the latter – mostly Japanese cypress or Japanese cedar – the teahouse was built from natural materials that were available on hand or from beams of old residential buildings. The architect Kisho Kurokawa describes this aspect in more detail in his description of teahouse architecture: "Originally, tea rooms were constructed of materials that could be found easily and near at had. Rare and expensive materials were avoided. A log or branch from a nearby grove of trees, a stone by the roadside – materials such as these were collected and incorporated into the final design. But of course the aesthetic perceptions of the tea masters were operating in the selection process. Their ability to discover the beauty of such commonplace objects was crucial. They were alert to the aesthetic interest of these trees and stones which, to the average person, were just like any other. And they possessed the skill to incorporate these objects into the design of a tea room."[B]

A large number of different types of wood are used in the construction of tea rooms. The predominant part comes from conifers; wood from deciduous trees is rarely used. Japanese cypress (*hinoki*), Japanese pine (*matsu*), larch (*akamatsu*), Japanese cedar (*sugi*) and cryptomeria (*suginoki*) are the most important softwood species, among the hardwoods are chestnut, camphor, oak and Zelkova (*keyaki*), the latter due to the wild grain and the hardness particularly suitable for carving. As the color and texture of natural materials were appreciated, they were mostly used with unpainted surfaces, but rarely were they really untreated. Special pillars and beams were made of Japanese cedar from the forests of Kitayama or Yoshino, a wood famous for its high quality. First the rough outer bark was removed and the wooden surface was directly rubbed with fine sand or sand wrapped in the leaves of the hemp palm, a final

75 Illustration of Honmon-ji, Tokyo; from an English-speaking travel guide to Japan, ca. 1900

A   Quoted from Kôshirô Haga, p. 198
B   Kisho Kurokawa, p. 56

76

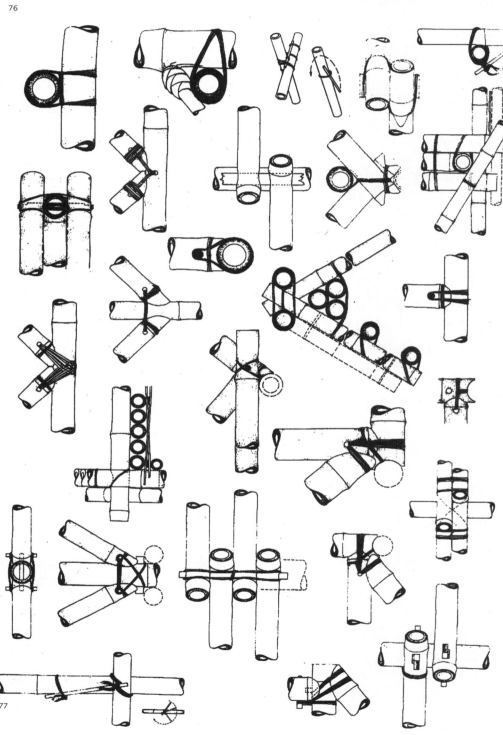

77

polish was then done with a rough straw rope. For certain supports, especially the *tokonoma* post (*toko-bashira*) and the central column (*naka-bashira*), trunks with special curvatures or surface structures were preferred. With the increased demand, this preference for unusually grown wood led to the artificial production of growth anomalies. Today, for example, hard plastic pieces are bound around the trunks of young cedars in order to force the desired, extremely unstable surface. Sometimes a dyeing technique was used in which dark brown pigments, mainly from ash, dissolved in tannin or vegetable oil, were applied to the wood. The surface took on an almost blackish hue, while the grain, knots and other natural elements of the trunk stood out particularly well. The juice of the kaki fruit was also used to stain wooden surfaces.

BAMBOO

Bamboo (*take*) became one of the most important building materials in the teahouse. As an easily obtainable material in rural Japan, it has always been used in farmhouses in a variety of ways in the construction of buildings. Since the time of the great tea master Sen no Rikyû, who liked to be influenced by objects of rural origin and architecture, bamboo was also used in the construction of teahouses. Starting with structural elements such as supports or rafters, via window types such as *shitaji-* or *renji-mado* to decorative use as *toko-bashira*, this material determines the appearance of a large number of teahouses. The fact that many tea utensils are also made of bamboo points to the great importance the tea masters attach to this material. This originates from a tradition spread throughout East Asia that ascribes fundamental ethical and esthetic values to bamboo. Thus its straight growth is compared with the upright character of a human being; its hard, regular, flexible trunk stands as a symbol for an inner straightness that remains steadfast despite all flexibility. The hollow space of bamboo also refers to the principle of the "emptiness" of Zen Buddhism – the immersion in the essence of bamboo was considered by some Zen monks to be the ideal of meditation. Early on, bamboo paintings adorned the monasteries of the Zen orders, since it is considered – together with plum blossom, orchis, and chrysanthemum – to be one of the "four nobles" representing the four seasons.

The biggest disadvantage of bamboo is its susceptibility to insect and fungal attack, which is why procedures were developed early to make the material more durable and lasting. The preferred harvest time is November and December, months when the sugar content in fresh bamboo is as low as possible. The fresh bamboo is steamed, a method to reduce the natural oil and starch content. It is then polished several times before being stored for about a year and left to age until it takes on a yellowish color. Together with the use of bamboo, a connection technique was also adopted that used to be exclusively applied in rural *minka* architecture: The binding of bamboo sticks is often practiced in teahouses and used as a decorative element – for example in *shitaji-mado* or ceiling design.

78

76 Bamboo in the wind; ink drawing
    by Shin'etsu (1639–1696)
77 The artful binding of bamboo
    has been perfected in teahouse
    architecture.
78 Specially worked wooden post;
    Manshu-in, Kyoto
79 Following page:
    With the teahouses, bamboo gained
    in importance as a building material.

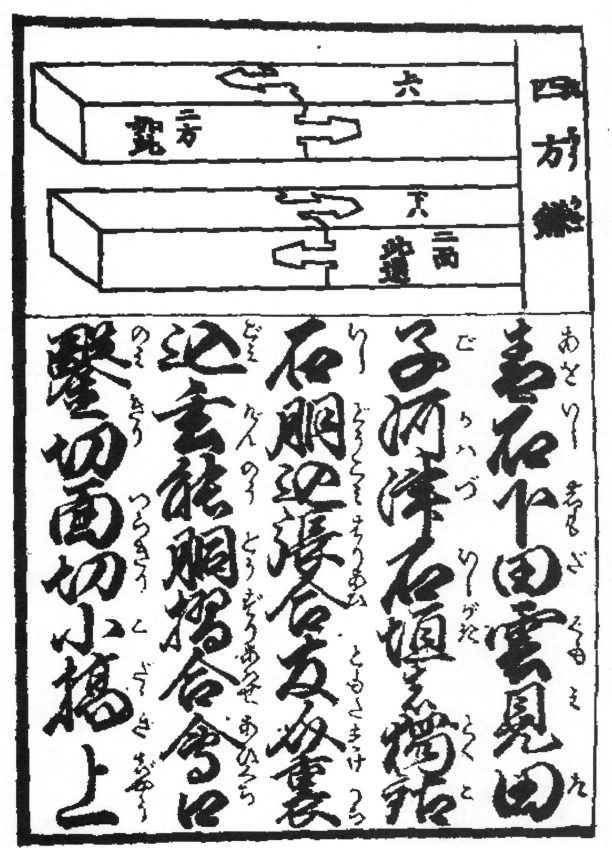

四方鎌

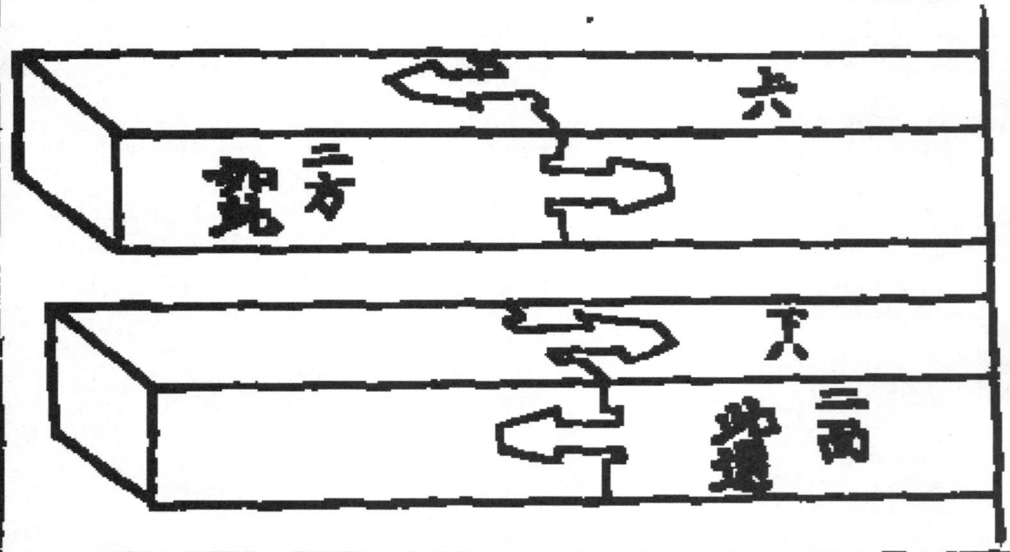

青石下田雲見田
子浦津石垣擂鉢
石胴込張合友谷重
込素稜胴擂合
鑿切面切小橋上

80

Like all traditional Japanese architecture, the teahouse is based on a simple supports-beams system consisting exclusively of vertical and horizontal elements. The use of reinforcing diagonals is completely dispensed with, not least in order to guarantee the elasticity required during earthquakes. It is also statically more advantageous to install the timber in its full length, which results in a large number of crossings of different construction elements. Since no metal parts are used in the construction of Japanese wooden buildings, the traditional wood joints are highly complicated. The connections must guarantee part of the structural stability, and the individual elements must be connected to each other in a tension- and compression-resistant manner. Special wooden dowels (*sensen*) and spigots (*hozo*) were developed for this purpose. A distinction is made between longitudinal connections of elements with the same function (*tsugite*), such as two columns or beams, and transverse connections of elements with different functions (*shiguchi*), such as supports with beams or purlins. Since naturally shaped woods are preferred in teahouses, new techniques were developed to master the connection between purlins and logs.

The great complexity of all these connecting forms also holds great esthetic appeal. In Japan, the technical necessity of protecting end-grain wood in corner joints becomes an esthetic principle: The point where two constructive parts meet should remain as hidden as possible, no more than a straight line should remain visible to the observer at the joint, no matter how complicated the construction's interior design may be. The carpenter designs the connections in the context of the building as a whole, thus fulfilling the functions of the architect in the West as well as the execution. Even today, a good craftsman still masters about two hundred different wood joints, even if twenty joints were sufficient in modern residential building due to the techniques adopted by Europe and America.[c] Since the separation between carpenter and joiner is unknown in Japan, no distinction is made between the design of traditional building constructions and interior finishing: The same construction methods and principles are used in both cases.

In the Japanese architectural tradition, the carpenter was usually also the designer of a building. Only with the advent of the teahouses did a paradigm shift emerge in this respect: Unlike the rest of the architectural work, the tea master who designed the building is not identical with the carpenter who built it. Japanese architecture thus only became familiar with the concept of authorship in architecture with the advent of the teahouse of the Momoyama period. Although there were individual buildings that were closely connected with the name of the client, clients never designed the building. The tea masters are thus among the first architects in Japan. It is symptomatic of this change that, from this point on, a connection between buildings and styles bearing the designers' names – such as *Rikyû-gonomi* or *Oribe-gonomi* – appeared for the first time. Last but not least, the creative originality and individuality of the tea masters (*sakui*) is one of the most important driving forces in the development of the tea ceremony.

80 Wood joints from a handbook for carpenters

c   Wolfram Graubner, *Holz-verbindungen – Gegenüberstellung japanischer und europäischer Lösungen*, p. 36

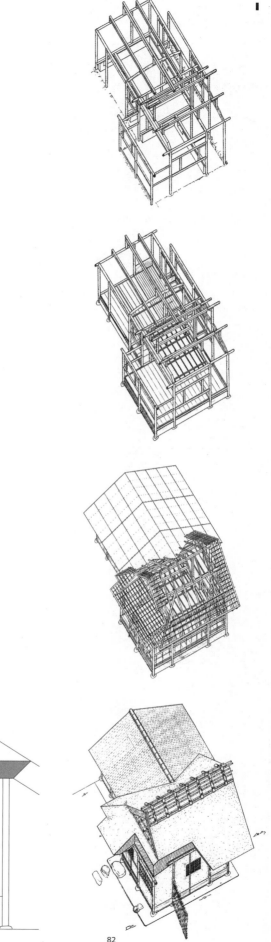

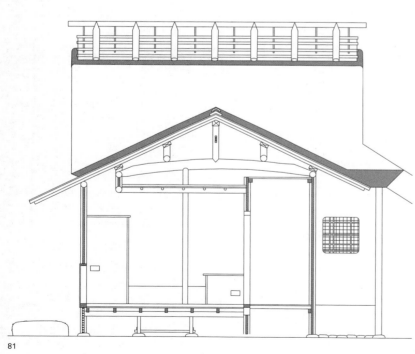

81

82

"Here, apart from the standard dimensions of the mats, all other strict rules of taste with which the delicate sense otherwise tends to test the work of the carpenter and his comrades [...] cease. The height of the room is little more than that of the normal sliding door and often little more than the head height of a European, maximum to about 2 m. Windows are arranged quite freely without the slightest rule [...]. Since the builders are not bound to their rules here, everything, the ceiling, the treatment of the wooden posts, the plaster, in short the whole style, is extremely free."[D]

The beginning of the teahouse architecture was still strongly influenced by the style of the *shoin* buildings[E]. Only when the strong formalism of the *shoin* style could no longer satisfy the freedoms of the tea ceremony, lighter and more natural construction systems were sought. Therefore, the use of round, often untreated supports is typical for the construction of the teahouse. However, the general structure follows the Japanese building principles: It is formed from a simple sequence of overlapping horizontal and vertical elements, whereby a larger unit is repeatedly divided into individual subunits. All constructive elements are dimensioned in such a way that they appear light and fragile; the proportions of the individual parts to each other are given the greatest attention. Since the construction system is regarded as unchangeable for various reasons, the construction details in particular are constantly being refined. In this way a peculiar contradiction develops between a quite simple system of construction and an extremely complicated execution of details.

Since the floor of the Japanese house is elevated about 70 to 80 centimeters from the ground, the primary function of the foundation is to isolate the structural elements of the skeleton structure from the damp ground. Since the walls only carry their own load, deep foundations under the main columns are sufficient. The building is not firmly anchored in the ground and does not receive any additional stabilization from the foundation. In former times the supporting columns and posts were put directly into the earth, only in the 8th century the technique of placing supporting columns on buried foundation stones was adopted from China. No deep ditches had to be dug, and since there were no cellars either, the surface of the earth remained as untouched as possible so that "the veins of the dragon are not damaged", as an old geomantic commandment from China dictates.[F] The foundation stones are called "round stones" (*tana-ishi*) or "flat stones" (*narashi-ishi*), according to their shape, and have cylindrical recesses that accommodate dowels cut from the underside of the columns. In contrast to the formal, hewn stones of *shoin* architecture, teahouses almost exclusively use naturally shaped foundation stones. If today traditional teahouses are built, it is however quite common to erect concrete foundations, whereby depending upon requirement from deep via strip up to plate foundations all forms can occur.

The construction of the floor follows the general method of systematic superposition of individual construction elements: Beams arranged between the supports form a frame, which is additionally supported by individual posts placed on their own foundation stones. In between there are also floor beams supported at regular intervals (*obiki*), on which crossbeams (*neda*) lie at modular distances. The floor boards are mounted on these, and on top of the floor boards the *tatami* mats are finally laid, protected by a separating layer of paper.

81 Horizontal and vertical elements are stacked on top of each other: section of a teahouse

82 Axonometric projection of the construction phases of a teahouse

D Bruno Taut, p. 161 f.

E See chapter "The development of the *soân* teahouse", p. 131

F Manfred Speidel, "Das japanische Wohnhaus und die Natur", in: Manfred Speidel (ed.), *Japanische Architektur – Geschichte und Gegenwart,* p. 14

WALL

In cultures in which stone construction predominates, the walls are built first, as these have to absorb all structural loads and transfer them to the ground. In Japanese buildings, on the other hand, the wooden skeleton construction meets all static requirements and supports the roof, which is completed as soon as possible in order to protect the rest of the project from rain and sun. The infill of the walls only takes place at the very end.

The walls recede behind the elements of the construction. They have no supporting function whatsoever. They can therefore be thinner than the column and beam cross sections. In this way, all wall surfaces are dissolved into rectangles of different sizes, thus avoiding the feeling of heaviness and massiveness of the surrounding components. This lack of solidity of Japanese walls is already evident from their name – shinkabe: kabe means wall, while shin means the middle of the columns. A shinkabe is therefore only a thin layer that connects the centers of the supports. In the teahouse, the wall thicknesses can be particularly thin due to the small distances between the supports: At only four centimeters thick, they are about a third thinner than the mud walls of residential buildings. Only in exceptional cases in Japanese buildings do fixed walls serve as room dividers or as architectural means to interrupt viewing axes; all other wall surfaces are designed as sliding elements.

This is different in the teahouse, where all four sides are bounded by solid clay walls. Only a few constructive parts are left visible if formal reasons or the importance of an element require it. But the wall surfaces of the teahouse are also divided into rectangles, even if the pattern generated in this way has detached itself from the strict grid of the construction: It consists of individual elements of the construction and the freely distributed windows and shoji rails and offers the designer much greater freedom in the design – freedom that was welcomed by the tea masters. A basic sleeper frame is stretched between the supporting columns (hashira), on which the remaining upright supports of the wall construction rest. On their upper side are beams (noki-geta), which lead to the horizontal alignment of the roof. They often have a round cross section, which requires a correspondingly complicated design of the support heads. The nageshi – horizontal bands that run across all wall surfaces and form continuous lines – used in temple and residential architecture is generally dispensed with in the teahouses. The supports are usually arranged at a distance of one ken$_G$ and are held in their upright position by latches and horizontal elements (nuki) at a distance of about 60 centimeters. The individual fields of the grid formed in this way are filled with a bamboo weave. This consists of a primary frame of stronger bamboo sticks (mawatashi-dake) and a grid of narrow bamboo strips (komai-dake), which are connected to each other with rush or rice straw strings. Once the skeleton is finished, clay is applied on both sides in several layers, resulting in the so-called rough wall (arakabe). Once this has dried, the top layer (uwa-nuri) of fine clay is applied. There is a choice of countless types of clay in different color nuances, in addition the clay plaster is mixed with sand in different color hues or seaweed and mother-of-pearl pieces are mixed in. The top layer of clay is often dyed using soot, ink, rusty nails or squid ink. The darkening of the surfaces creates lighting conditions in which the hanging scrolls and flower arrangements are accentuated particularly well with rich contrast. In some teahouses, the top layer is omitted in order to obtain a particularly rough and natural texture.

The connection of the mud walls to the supporting columns is not embellished by decorative or cover strips, so that even for these elegant and precise details the highest level of craftsmanship is required. The clay plaster on the exterior walls is usually not colored, which is why most teahouses blend into their natural surroundings. The lower wall end in the outside area is often formed by a wooden board, which, however, does not reach to the floor. The remaining space is filled with flat stones lying next to each other, which from the outside are almost the same size and shape as the foundation stones. On the outer wall of some teahouses, between two posts of the construction, a bamboo post (*chikara take*) is visible in the wall. Located exactly in the middle, it is a common element of the wall structure that reinforces the construction. The *chikara take* is originally clad in clay, provided it does not pass through a window. In this case it remains uncovered along its entire length. Later tea masters, however, took the liberty of making this bamboo post visible in any case. The first known example of such an arrangement can be found in Sen no Rikyû's Taian tea room, where a *chikara take* runs near the crawl-in entrance next to a *shitaji mado*.

Another element typical of teahouse architecture is the so-called toothpick post (*yoji-bashira*) a corner post covered with clay in the lower section and only visible from the upper half. The wall corner, which is clad in clay and thus rounded off, does not provide any point of reference for the eye at seated height, thus visually expanding the room.

Walls and sliding doors (*fusuma*) remain unpainted in the teahouses, unlike in *shoin* architecture, but often the lower part of the walls is covered with paper up to a height of 30 to 45 centimeters: Depending on the desired effect, light, cream-colored or white *torinoko* paper or black or gray *minato-gami* paper is used. Sometimes also old letters or diary sheets are used. Sen no Rikyû, aware of the inadequacy of the written word for the transmission of the tea rules, gives the following advice to his student Nambô Soeki, who recorded the conversations with his teacher: "Since you have written down many of my conversations with you, I should regret them afterwards. Still, I didn't know where to find fault. Use the same for sticking on walls or sliding doors."[H] In the Kon'nichian and Joan teahouse a beautiful *wabi* effect is created from old calendar sheets, in the Zangetsutei tea room a paper printed with a Pauwlonia pattern is used.

OPENINGS

In Japanese homes, the same sliding elements – the translucent *shoji* and the opaque *fusuma* – always perform the function of doors, windows, and partitions between rooms. In the teahouse, on the other hand, each element is treated separately. A clear distinction is made between the individual entrances and windows and each component is designed according to its specific function.

ENTRANCES

a) Host's entrance: The host's entrance (*sadô-guchi*) allows the host to enter the tea room from the preparation room. The opening is closed with a single *fusuma*. The use of a solitary sliding element is one of the special features of teahouse architecture. In the rest of Japanese architecture, sliding doors always appear in pairs and, in order to facilitate the sliding of the two *fusuma* elements, have a mostly black lacquered wooden frame. With Sen no Rikyû a new element appeared in Japanese architecture – the so-called "drum" *fusuma* (*taiko-busuma*). In this form, which is used exclusively in tea rooms, the paper covering extends beyond the frame. *Shoji* and *fusuma* are already extremely easy to open due to their construction and can usually be opened with only one finger. The *taiko-busuma*, a single white surface, which additionally stands in strong contrast to the dark clay walls, visually conveys a special feeling of lightness and weightlessness. Consequently, there are no door handles like on the normal

83

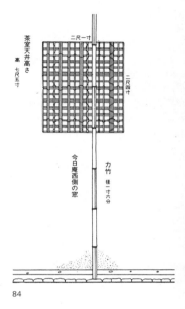

84

83 Wall structure before it is covered with clay.

84 Bamboo post (*chikara-take*) in the Kon'nichian teahouse of Sen no Sôtan

G   1 *ken* = (1.81813 m)
H   Horst Hennemann, p. 261

85

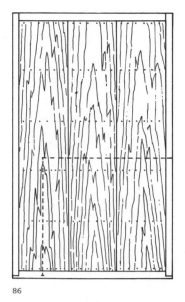

86

87

fusuma. Rather, by folding a part of the covering diagonally inwards, a recess is formed, which makes it possible to grasp the door to open and close it.

b) nijiriguchi: According to Artur Sadler, the word *nijiriguchi* derives from a slang expression used by carpenters and has only been used since Furuta Oribe's time. Before that, the term *kuguriguchi* was in use. Before Sen no Rikyû's time, the entrance was large enough for the guests to walk through it in an upright posture, although certain sources say that the entrance to the tea room of Sen no Rikyû's teacher Jôô had already been lower than usual, or that one had to enter it on hands and knees from the veranda. Today, however, the entrance to the Taian tea room of Rikyû is considered the first classical *nijiriguchi*. With a size of 79 x 72 centimeters, it is slightly larger than the later standard size of 66 x 66 centimeters. The *nijiriguchi* of Taian is cut out of the lower right corner of an old wooden door, a technique often copied by other tea masters and later used in teahouses. The intention to build the entire teahouse from used materials could have been the background for this. Later, the *nijiriguchi* were made from old posts and boards and a narrow piece of fresh wood, with the simultaneous use of worn-out old and high-quality new wood providing an attractive contrast.

Both the lower rails (*hasamishikii*) and the *nijiriguchi* door itself are cleaned by the host before the guests arrive. He or she takes the door out of the rails and wipes it off, giving the guest who touches the still damp door a feeling of freshness. The last guest closes the door and locks it with a simple hook that symbolizes isolation from the outside world rather than offering real protection against intruders. Closing is done with an audible click – the sign for the host that the guests are fully assembled.

When in the course of history the equality of all guests in the tea room was abandoned and attention was again paid to social hierarchies and differentiation, the highest ranking guest is allowed to enter the tea room in an upright position through a separate entrance closed with a *shoji* – the so-called *kinin-guchi*.

WINDOWS

The window openings of teahouses do not only have the function of lighting and ventilation, they are also determining elements of the formal appearance. The atmosphere of a tea room is therefore decisively influenced by its size, arrangement, design and number. The Japanese word for window is composed of the terms *ma* and *do*: Ma denotes a space-time interval, and *do* means "door". This refers on the one hand to the idea of viewing windows and doors as equivalent elements, and on the other hand to the fact that components in Japanese architecture can only be understood in relation to the overall structure. A *mado* is therefore not an independent element, but something that is inserted into the *ma* – the interval between two columns. Wall openings are traditionally made by stretching a beam (*shiki kamoi*) between two posts and turning the entire width of the surface down to the floor into a window or door opening that is always closed with the same sliding elements. In the early teahouses, this conventional method was still used, but gave way to new techniques when the atmosphere in the tea room required a different type of lighting. The windows were detached from the construction grid and cut into the wall wherever they are needed. Larger and freer window types are realized in this way. Some of them are borrowed from the architecture of the farmhouses (*minka*), which is in keeping with the philosophy of naturalness and simplicity of the "grass hut style". In terms of design and workmanship, however, the teahouse windows were much more elaborate and sophisticated than their predecessors. The windows are mostly covered with white paper *shoji* on the inside. The light dampened by white paper gained in importance as soon as Sen

88

85 Area of the *nijiriguchi* in the Taian teahouse
86 The *nijiriguchi* was mostly sawn out of the lower right corner of an old door.
87 A sliding door (*fusuma*), which was covered with paper sheets with writing
88 The door of the host's entrance forms a single white surface; teahouse in the Daitoku-ji
89 Following page: washbasin (*tsukubai*) and *nijiriguchi*: The woman in the tea room puts her sandals upright against the teahouse. Woodcut by Foshikata Mizuno (1866–1903)

I See chapter "Spatial principles", p. 15

90

91

no Rikyû introduced dark clay walls, which form a strong contrast to the white surfaces of the *shoji*.

Teahouse windows are usually rectangular, but in some buildings round windows in the form of flower blossoms (*hanagata*) are also used. Circular windows are often arranged next to the entrance, for example in the Joan teahouse, where the round of the window and the square of the *nijiriguchi* face each other in a tension-filled way. In some cases, they are also cut into the back wall of the *tokonoma*. Possibly round windows at this point serve as a replacement for the picture scroll, which often contains a circle. In Zen Buddhism, the circle (*enso*) was regarded as a symbol of "emptiness" and thus belongs to the central images of the religion.

*"The circle is like the great emptiness, nothing is missing and nothing is super-fluous. That is, the great emptiness becomes the realm of freedom. Here the emptiness means an untouchedness of at the same time infinite extension and without any extension, but in no case does it contain a negation."*ⱼ

Although the shape and arrangement of the windows seem completely free, certain window types and standards have developed in the design prin-ciples:

1) *shitaji-mado*: Literally "under the earth window", are wall openings that are created by omitting the clay cover and exposing the bamboo substructure. The shape of the window is in most cases a rounded rectangle, but round windows are also produced in this way. *Shitaji-mado* are a fixed component of the Japa-nese *minka*, which provides adequate ventilation for the farmhouse.

The production of the *shitaji-mado* in the early teahouses is carried out according to this old method, but later the wickerwork structure of the win-dows differed from that of the wall. The *shitaji-mado* are manufactured sep-arately, receive their own frame and are used only after completion of the walls. These windows are designed with special care in order to preserve the impression of the substructure, which is exposed as if by chance. The bamboo sticks are placed in an irregular pattern single or double next to each other and linked by thin tendrils.

Inside the windows are covered with *shoji*, on the outside bamboo roller blinds (*sudare*) or wooden shutters regulate the lighting. The host removes them during the break (*nakadachi*), in which the guests leave the tea room, which they find on their return under completely new conditions. The *shoji* are either removable and hang as *kake-shoji* with hooks on the wall or are sliding elements (*kadohiki*). Since the clay covering in the tea room hides almost all constructive elements, the white surfaces of the *shoji* and the narrow wooden strips in which the sliding elements move are among the essential dividing ele-ments of the interior.

2) *renji-mado*: Lattice windows with diagonally twisted woods arranged in a square, vertical, or horizontal cross section are found early in Japanese architec-ture. Since the Heian period they have been regarded as a status symbol and may only be installed in the homes of certain population groups. When Rikyû first used the *renji-mado* in the Taian teahouse, he replaced the wooden strips with bamboo sticks, because no element of the teahouse should be understood as a status symbol. Rather, they are used for their practical use, since their size allows good control of the various lighting effects by opening and closing

90 Round window in a tea room in the Sesshu-ji, Kyoto
91 Ink drawing (*ensô*) by Bankei (1622–1693)

J   Kurt Brasch

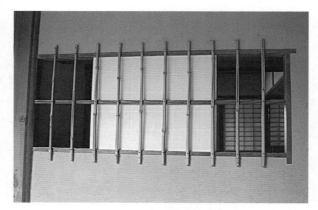

the *shoji* or *sudare* on the outside. In general, *renji-mado* is the name for any barred window or door opening. In teahouse architecture, however, only windows with bamboo sticks are called *renji-mado*. If other types of wood are used it is referred to as *koushi-mado*.

3) furosaki-mado: rectangular windows on the side of the host's seat in front of the ash pan (*furo*). A frequently used standard size is 55 x 42.5 centimeters, with the lower edge of the window about 20 centimeters above the floor. This type of window is often used in small rooms (*koma-seki*), where the *shoji* light dissolves the cramped feeling on the wall of the host side. The *shoji* can also be either designed as sliding elements or attached to the wall with hooks. In contrast to other window types, the *shoji* of the *furosaki-mado* are never opened or hung up, because the utensils arranged in front of the window are more effective in subdued light.

4) shikishi-mado: This window type consists of two windows arranged one above the other, whose *shoji* resemble two paper squares used as poetry cards (*shikishi*). This window form is often found in rooms with a ¾-*tatami* (*daime-seki*), as a window on the host side. The upper window is usually transversely rectangular and designed as a *renji-mado*, the lower window is set upright and designed as a *shitaji-mado*. But this arrangement is not binding; two *shitaji-mado* can sit on top of each other or the *shitaji-mado* on top of the *renji-mado*.

5) tsukiage-mado: The *tsukiage-mado* is a skylight through which the rapidly changing light of the morning or evening penetrates into the tea room at sunrise or sunset. In a size of about 40 x 55 centimeters it is usually placed in an inclined roof area above the *nijiriguchi* or in the ceiling above the host side. It is kept open with a pole (*tsukiage-bo*), which is available in four lengths – corresponding to the different window heights. Only the long *tsukiage-bo* have a special metal hook at one end, the shape of which is reminiscent of the head of a bird.

6) bokuseki-mado: The scrolls of Zen monks are called *bokuseki*. The window of the same name in the side wall of the *tokonoma* has the task of illuminating and accentuating the scrolls suspended in the *tokonoma*. In the further development of the teahouse, as more and more value was placed on decorative elements, a flower vase was hung here by means of a hook. Mostly designed as *shitaji-mado*, they are sometimes also covered in *shoji* when the lighting conditions require it.

92   Clockwise from top left:
shutters, *shitaji-mado*, *renji-mado*,
shikishi-mado

93

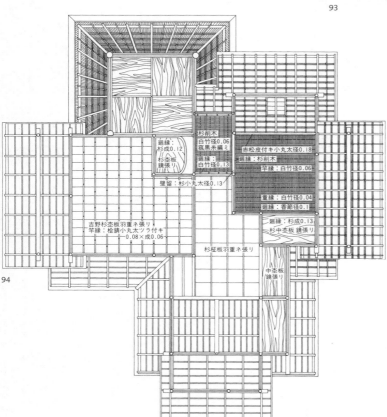

94

迴縁：
杉成0.12
杉杢板
鏡張リ

杉削木
白竹径0.06
菰黒糸編ミ

迴縁：
白竹径0.13

壁留：杉小丸太径0.13

赤松皮付キ小丸太径0.18
迴縁：杉削木
竿縁：白竹径0.06

重縁：白竹径0.04
迴縁：香節径0.1

迴縁：杉成0.13
杉中杢板 鏡張リ

吉野杉杢板羽重ネ張リ
竿縁：桧錆小丸太ツラ付キ
0.08×成0.06

中杢板
鏡張リ

杉柾板羽重ネ張リ

The Japanese feudal society under the rule of the Tokugawa shoguns was subject to strict regulations. Since the end of the 16th century, the shogunate determined daily life in every detail, and the design of a residential building was inseparably linked to the social status of its inhabitants. Even within the houses, an extremely fine differentiation was necessary in order to do justice to the fine social gradations. As a consequence, different floor levels and ceiling heights emerged as important indicators of a person's status: The floor levels are graded into a ground floor area for the lowest ranks, a wood-floored area, a normal *tatami* area, and one or more elevated *tatami* areas for the guests of honor. Not only the heights of the individual levels, but also the used materials are of decisive importance.

95

Since all guests are to be treated equally regardless of their class in the tea room, the usual flooring levels in residential buildings are deliberately avoided. Nothing during the tea ceremony should be reminiscent of the status symbols so important in the outer world. The tea room must meet other requirements: Although there is also a hierarchy of guests in the context of a tea ceremony, this does not usually depend on their social status. The role of the first guest can be taken over by any member of the tea gathering, the only condition for this is his/her exact knowledge of the ceremonial procedures since he/she should lead the other guests and conduct the highly ritualized communication with the host. In order to characterize this subtle differentiation of status, the ceiling design is used as a new architectural means: Individual ceiling elements are arranged at different heights, whereby the ceiling height indicates the status of the guest: the higher the ceiling, the more important the person seated below it. The room height of the *tokonoma* is therefore usually somewhat higher than the rest of the room, while consequently the ceiling above the area of the host has the lowest height.

In the smaller tea rooms in particular, the different ceiling levels, inclinations and designs are intended to create an exciting atmosphere in order to counteract the physical confinement of the room. The result is a variety of differently worked ceilings, unique in Japanese architecture, in a very confined space.

While the room heights in the houses of that time were regulated by the *kiwari-jutsu*ₖ, a measurement system for timber construction, and depended on the room size – a room in the size of three mats is about 2.19 meters high and a 4½-mat room is 2.30 meters high – then the teahouse is detached from these specifications and the ceiling height is reduced to a minimum. Already in the 4½-mat tea rooms of Jôô, one of the pioneers of the classical teahouse, the room height was limited to 2.12 meters, a measure which was even lowered to 1.80 meters with Sen no Rikyû. This ensures that nobody in the tea room can ever stand up. If something is out of range, you slide on your knees to reach it.

Unlike the finely crafted ceilings of the *shoin* rooms, the ceilings of the tea rooms are kept very simple. The suspended slatted ceilings known from residential architecture are often found, but other materials such as shingles, wickerwork, bamboo and reeds are also used, forming a strong contrast to the magnificent coffered wooden ceilings of the *shoin* architecture. The great importance attached to ceiling design can be seen in the teahouse designed by Emperor Gomizunoo in the Minase shrine in Osaka. The intersecting ceiling beams made of Japanese cedar form a coffered ceiling whose individual fields are not richly decorated as is usual in *shoin* architecture, but filled with stems

93 Different ceiling areas in the narrowest space in the Shôkô-ken; Koto-in, Kyoto
94 The ceiling view of a contemporary teahouse shows the variety of different constructions.
95 Skylight *(tsukiage-mado)*

K   See chapter "The development of the *soân* teahouse", p. 131

of various types of grass and reeds. The result is a cross-over pattern over the entire ceiling surface, which dominates the room and gives the building its name: When the fibers of those plants were used as lamp wicks in oil lamps, the tea room was called *tooshinseki*, which means "lamp wick room".

In many teahouses there are inclined ceiling areas, which usually rise from the entrance of the guests to the middle of the room and contribute to the visual expansion of the room. These ceilings, called *keshoyaneura-* or *kakekomi-tenjo*, are no more than the underside of the roof surface, with the bamboo rafters offset at a distance of about 60 centimeters left visible and decorated with thin bamboo poles and wickerwork.

The suspended ceilings are simply constructed: The ceiling boards (*tenjo-ita*) lie on slender slats (*sao-buchi*), which are fastened with nails to a second set of slats at right angles. These lie above the ceiling boards and are suspended from the roof girders above with vertical bands. Depending on the size of the room, the center of the ceiling is usually raised by two to three centimeters to take account of any yielding of the beams under the roof load. Since both the secondary set of the support grid and the suspensions remain invisible, the feeling of extreme lightness is evoked – especially in larger tea rooms – since the ceiling seems to rest completely on the narrow *sao-buchi*.

The *ajirotenji* and the *gamamushirotenji* are other types of ceiling designs that are often used in tea rooms. In the first type, thin strips of wood are interwoven to form a herringbone pattern, while the second type consists of straws that are fixed in position by sewing and thin bamboo sticks.

ROOF

The roof of Japanese buildings is the defining visual element that has always shaped the country's architecture. Due to the wide roof overhang and the weight – the buildings are often covered with tiles – the roofs of the Japanese buildings appear very dominant. Teahouses are no exception in this respect, as can be seen especially in buildings covered with straw or grass, whose extremely thick roof cladding in relation to the size of the building gives the buildings a tremendous plasticity. But the roof is also a special functional feature of Japanese architecture. The writer Jun'ichiro Tanizaki compares the roofs of European houses with hats, while assigning the Japanese the function of an umbrella: "So when we build a dwelling, above all we spread out the shield of a roof, shade a measured area on the ground with it, and construct the house into this dusky shadow district."[L]

The roof is completed first; all interior work is then carried out under its protection. In Japan, four roof forms have established themselves, all of which are also used in teahouse architecture: the simple saddle roof (*kirizuma*), the pyramid roof over a square ground plan (*hôgyô*), the hipped roof (*shichû* or *yosemune*) and a combination of saddle and hipped roof (*irimoya*). The special form of the leaning *hisashi* roofs so typical of Japanese architecture, which usually cover the veranda space, is rarely found in teahouse architecture. They are only sometimes found above the *nijiriguchi*, and also above the window openings to protect the paper *shoji* from the effects of weather.

The roof construction is kept as simple as possible: On the beams of the wall construction (*noki-geta*) lie heavy, often only roughly hewn roof beams (*hari*), which carry the entire roof load. If larger buildings require several *hari*, these are simply placed on top of each other at their ends. At regular intervals vertical supporting elements (*koya-zuka*) are distributed on these roof beams, which carry purlins (*moya*) and rafters (*taruki*) of the roof structure. Even in the roof area, there is no need for any diagonal bracing.

The roof cladding is placed on a layer of boards – previously bark was also used – which is mounted on the rafters. Roof tiles are either hung on a roof batten or embedded in mortar, which gives the construction additional stability, but gives the roof an enormous weight. Although the teahouse is designed to look as natural as possible and therefore reeds, zebra grass and wooden shingles are often used for roofing, other roofing materials commonly used in Japanese architecture, such as bricks and copper plates, are also used. The roofing of different parts of the building – tea room, anteroom, *mizuya* – is often different and covered with varying materials. A change of the materials is also seen frequently in the area of the roof overhang, if for instance the area of the interior is covered with bricks, the area projecting beyond it features wooden shingles. The gutters are halved bamboo poles, with the esthetic factor playing a greater role than the function to be fulfilled. The gutters are attached to every second rafter by means of a wooden element and held in position with copper wire.

96

97

98

96   *Ajirotenji* ceiling with herringbone pattern
97   The most common roof shapes in Japan
98   Bamboo gutter; Shugakuin Villa, Kyoto

L   Jun'ichiro Tanizaki, p. 33 f.

"Roji wa tada
Ukiyo no hoka no
Michi naru ni
kokoro no chiri wo
nado chirasuran."
SEN NO RIKYŪ[A]

"Since the tea garden is nothing else
as a way off
of the worldly way of life,
it'll have the heart
rid of its impurity."

Tea gatherings take place in spaces that differ from the places of everyday human activity. The garden (*roji*) is the transitory place between the busy everyday life and the loneliness of the tea hut. Walking through the *roji* is the spiritual equivalent of a journey from the city to a hermitage in the depths of the mountain forest. In the course of this "journey", visitors have to overcome a number of thresholds; some barriers are physical, others rather abstract in nature. At each threshold, the guest is encouraged to leave worldly affairs behind and step by step reach the spiritual state of tranquility that is indispensable for participating in a tea ceremony.

The classic tea garden evolved in the 16th century at the same time as the concept of the *wabi* tea and, like the grassy hut of the *sôan* teahouses, is an integral part of this tea style. Tea gardens represent a new prototype in the history of Japanese garden design: Unlike the gardens of palaces, monasteries and residences, which were viewed from a fixed position in the reception room or veranda, the tea garden is a place of movement. It is thus the first garden in the history of Japan with such a function, and in the course of its development an almost religious rite of passage with fixed, recurring elements developed.[B] The original meaning of the word "roji" is "path", and its predecessors were nothing other than that: They were designed by city dwellers as paths to their teahouses, which could thus be reached via a separate entrance without disturbing the household. Towards the end of the 17th century, a new combination of signs appeared in the writings on the tea ceremony as a designation for the tea garden: Also read as "roji", it nevertheless has a completely different meaning: Literally translated, the tea garden is now called "dew-covered ground" or "dew earth", a term derived from the Buddhist *Lotus Sutra*. It says, "Escaped from the fiery abode of the Three Worlds[C], they sat down on the dew earth." It describes the place where people are born again after they have been able to escape the temptations of the world. This reading of the word underlines the great importance that Buddhism has within the tea ceremony, and the poetic name "dew earth" also reflects particularly well the atmosphere of the moist, mossy tea gardens. In order to underline the purity and freshness, the host sprinkles the garden with water before the guests arrive. The time of the ceremony must also be taken into account: If the ceremony takes place during the day, a wet garden would not have the desired effect. The garden must therefore be sprinkled a long time in advance, so that by the time the guests arrived the moisture is about a third dry again. The situation is different at night, when the tea garden illuminated by candles in stone lanterns and freshly moistened with water turns into an unreal fantasy world far removed from everyday reality.[D] In general, *roji* can be described as the least "artificial" garden form in Japan. Since the tea masters wanted to imitate the atmosphere of a forest path to a remote temple, trimming and pruning the plants was taboo, contrary to other gardening styles. When selecting plants, trees from the urban area or the plain were avoided in order to reproduce the nature of the mountains as perfectly as possible. Evergreen shrubs and trees were given preference over flowers and flowering bushes. Fragrant, poisonous plants or plants with thorns

99 When you enter the tea garden, you enter another world.

A   Quoted from Horst Hennemann, p. 225
B   Günter Nitschke, *Japanische Gärten – Rechter Winkel und natürliche Form*
C   The Buddhist "three worlds of this life" are:
1. desire,
2. objectivity,
3. non-objectivity,
cf. Horst Hennemann, p. 224, note 151
D   Teiji Itoh, *Die Gärten Japans*, p. 85

100

101

were very rarely used. The moss carpet often found in tea gardens grows naturally – at least in Kyoto – and makes a significant contribution to the mood and atmosphere of tea gardens.

HISTORICAL DEVELOPMENT OF TEA GARDENS

Already in the Muromachi period (1333–1467), the gardens played an important role in the course of a tea gathering: After the banquet, the guests went to the garden adjacent to the *shoin* room to take a break next to a pond. Afterwards the tea was taken in a garden pavilion. With the development of the *chanoyu* to an independent art form and the change of the teahouse to an independent structure, the task of the tea garden also changed. It had to shield the building from the hustle and bustle of everyday life and ensure a slow approach in keeping with the ceremony. The building was initially surrounded by a veranda and several courtyards. Since neither plans nor drawings exist of the surroundings of early teahouses, the size and exact arrangement of these elements remain unknown. Contemporary descriptions, however, provide at least an atmospheric picture: The visitor Washinoo Takayasu writes about the Shimogyo teahouse of Sôju: "In the very heart of the city I have the impression of being in the country."_E And in the records of Yamanoue Soji one reads that in the garden of Shukô there was "a large willow in the front courtyard and several pines visible beyond the garden wall" and that at Jôô's tea garden were "many large and small pines in the courtyard and beyond it"._F The illustrations of Jôô's garden around his 4½-mat hut depicted in the same work show the situation: The veranda upstream of the teahouse was both the entrance to the tea room and the location for the break (*nakadachi*) between the individual parts of the tea ceremony. The space in front of the veranda was divided into two sections that had different functions: The courtyard area near the hut, oriented towards the veranda, was an inner courtyard (*omote-no-tsubo-no-uchi*) surrounded by walls without an eye-catcher, since the guests were to remain completely concentrated on the tea. A second outdoor area or side courtyard (*waki-no-tsubo-no-uchi*) provided access to the veranda. Also surrounded by walls, sometimes even roofed over, before the introduction of the *roji*, it played the role of a transitory element: By crossing the side courtyard and climbing onto the veranda from there, one entered the tea room. In subsequent development, the veranda and the front yard assigned to it were eliminated. The side courtyard, on the other hand, became more and more important, it was extended and eventually developed into the tea garden known today. The function of the veranda was taken over by a waiting bench (*koshikake-machiai*) in the garden, which from now on served as a waiting area for the guests during the tea ceremony break.

The new function also changed the design of the tea gardens. In the tea book *Senrin*, written at the time of Jôô, it was stated that the garden of a 4½-mat hut should contain neither plants nor stones or gravel; in order not to disturb the concentration of the guests on the tea by too varied a design, only a little green was permitted around the stone washbasin. The danger of distraction was hardly any longer present in the later, more closed tea rooms. Bushes, trees and stepping stones, which allowed the guests to wander around comfortably, have since been used in the tea garden. Techniques were developed to guide guests through the garden and emphasize the *roji's* passage function. The most important of these is the so-called *miegakure* technique, which allows visitors to wander through various scenes. In the literal translation of "hiding and revealing", *miegakure* plays with the expectations of the visitors:

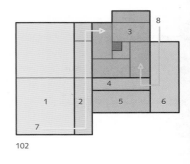

102

100 In the past, gardens were viewed from a fixed point of view. Reiun-in, Kyoto; woodcut from the *Miyako Rinsen Meisho Zue*

101 The courtyard (*omote-no-tsubi-no-uchi*) in the reconstructed Taian in the Zuiho-in, Kyoto

102 Diagram showing the structure of early tea gardens:
 1 *Shoin* room
 2 Corridor
 3 Tea room
 4 Veranda
 5 Courtyard
  (*omote-no-tsubo-no-uchi*)
 6 Side yard
  (*waki-no-tsubo-no-uchi*)
 7 Host's path
 8 Guests' path

E Tatsusaburo Hayashiya/Masao Nakamura/Seizo Hayashiya, "Japanese Arts and the Tea Ceremony", in: *The Heibonsha Survey of Japanese Art*, p. 167
F Tatsusaburo Hayashiya/ Masao Nakamura/Seizo Hayashiya, p. 167

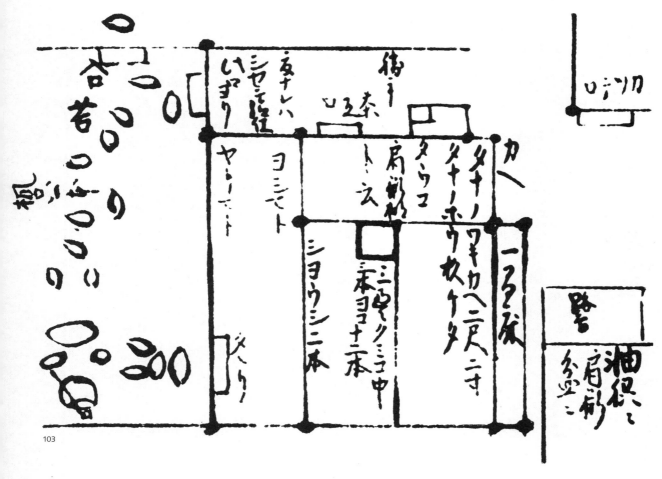

103

104

By repeatedly bending the paths, the axes of vision are interrupted again and again, the view of the whole is obscured, so that a state of increased concentration and attention is built up as one passes through the garden.

With the adoption of the tea ceremony by samurai and aristocrats, the tea gardens became larger and divided into an outer and an inner tea garden – *soto roji* and *uchi roji* – separated by bamboo fences. If the tea gardens of Sen no Rikyû still had primarily a path function, with the tea masters of the samurai aristocracy the *roji* became again a "real" garden in the sense of the Japanese garden tradition. Elements such as small hills, brooks and ponds were added to the environment, which had previously only been designed with plants. As with his teahouses, Furuta Oribe attached great importance to the selection of the individual elements and developed a varied scenery with different plants. While Rikyû's stepping stones were formed as naturally as possible, Oribe chose large, unusually shaped stones, with a preference for large, rectangular-hewn stepping stones. This development was continued by Kobori Enshu. He is regarded as the one who introduced the straight line into Japanese garden art with his precisely cut stepping stones, an element that had previously been reserved for architecture and frowned upon within the near-natural design of Japanese gardens. Oribe and Enshu were pioneers of a new garden prototype with their preference for the use of scenic elements: Under their influence, the tea garden was to develop into the large promenade garden, in which visitors wandered through various parts of the garden depicting famous landscapes of China and Japan. Unlike the *roji* with its spiritual roots in Zen Buddhism, this type of garden, which flourished during the Edo period (1603–1867), is a purely leisure garden. The tea garden also inspired another development: As an area surrounding warrior and merchant class residences or Zen temples, the garden was often established in free corners of plots with existing buildings. The primary act of garden design was thus a densification in a very small space. The techniques used resulted in the tea garden serving as a prototype for the small house interior garden (*tsuboniwa*) from the 17th century onwards. Mostly built on a small area and surrounded on all sides by building sections, the *tsuboniwa* took over many elements from *roji*. However, although constituent elements of the tea garden were used in the form of water basins, stone lanterns and stepping stones, the function of the *tsuboniwa* was different: It was not entered, but viewed from inside the house; it was a supplier of light and served to ventilate the rooms.

103 The plan of Matsuya Hisayoshi's teahouse, built in 1587, already shows the essential design elements of the *roji*.

104 The small inner garden of the house (*tsuboniwa*) serves as a light source and ventilation for the rooms.

105

106

In the course of time, certain elements of the *roji* emerged that are essential for the sequence of a tea gathering. Depending on the possibilities – the size of the tea garden and the available resources – these can be present in different forms:

OUTER GATE – SOTMON OR ROJI-MON

Even if the teahouse is built in conjunction with the main building, usually only the host enters the teahouse via a corridor from the house. Guests enter the tea garden via a separate gate. This leads either from the street or from part of a larger garden into the *roji* and is thus the first step from everyday life into another world. Behind the gate is the building where the guests can take off their outer wear (*yoritsuki*) and put on their *tabi*G as well as the straw or wooden sandals provided.

WAITING BENCH – KOSHIKAKE-MACHIAI

The path through the outer garden (*soto-roji*) leads to the *koshikake-machiai*, where the guests sit down and wait for the host. Although there is no reason for him or her to let the guests wait – everything in the tea room has long been prepared – this period of contemplation has a deeper meaning, as the guests should leave the hectic everyday world behind them and get in the mood for the upcoming tea ceremony. In the past, the veranda in front of the teahouse was used as a waiting and sitting area. With the development of the tea garden, the *koshikake-machiai* became an independent element that took over the functions of the veranda. In front of the bench there are stepping stones on which the guests can rest their feet. The stone for the first guest can differ from the others in height, arrangement or design. In some *koshikake-machiai*, a single long stone is available for all guests.

THE STEPPING STONES – TOBO-ISHI

The stepping stones divide the space of the tea garden and guide the steps of the guests. Initially used as crossing aids on muddy ground, the *tobo-ishi* found their artistic perfection only in the *roji*. It is not completely clear when stepping stones were first used in the tea gardens. Hayashiya, Nakamura and HayashiyaH date the first use in a teahouse designed by Rikyû in the Daitoku-ji temple to 1584. The stones used in the garden paths can be roughly divided into two groups according to their size: stones with a diameter of about 40 centimeters – just big enough to be walked on with one foot – and stones that are twice as big and allow standing with both legs. The paths generally consist of the smaller stones, which are laid about ten centimeters apart, corresponding to the stride length of people in a kimono, which is smaller than in Western clothing. The larger stones are only used at certain strategic points. This results in about four stones over a distance of two meters. Generally, rather larger stones are laid at somewhat further distances in the outer *roji*, while smaller, narrower set stones were preferred for the path through the inner *roji*. In front of the teahouse, the stepping stones move even closer together, so that the guests' pace slows down the closer they get to the teahouse. Some stones are intended for special purposes (*yaku-ishi*); these include the stones in front of the sword shelf (*katanakake*), the stone washbasin (*tsukubai*) and the *nijiriguchi* or the host's stone. In order to achieve a harmonious arrangement, special attention is paid to the shape of the individual stones. Contours and the side surfaces facing each other are particularly important. If two stones placed next to each other do not offer a satisfactory design solution, one uses small intermediate stones (*sute-ishi*) as a visual link. No fixed rules have been specified for the distance between the upper edge of the stone and the ground. Here the personal taste

105 Overview of the garden of the Yabunouchi tea school from the *Miyako Rinsen Meisho Zue*

106 The guests sit on the waiting bench (*koshikake-machiai*) until they are greeted by the host.

107 Following page:
The stepping stones in the Kitamura residence in Kyoto divide the tea garden and guide the steps of the guests.

G   White socks with detached big toe

H   Tatsusaburo Hayashiya/ Masao Nakamura/Seizo Hayashiya, p. 174

108

109

110

111

114

decides, a height of three to six centimeters is usual. In general, however, the stepping stones are sunk deep into the ground; under no circumstances should the impression be created that they lie on the ground; they should appear as if they emerged from the ground. When moving, the stones are first laid at strategic points – in front of the teahouse, in front of stone lanterns and the *tsukubai*, as well as on both sides of the gates – and thus a rough framework of corners is set out. Only then are the remaining stepping stones inserted. In the course of time, patterns were developed for the laying of the stepping stones, which differed in size and arrangement of the stones. In some cases, people relied on chance: Sen Sôtan threw a handful of beans from the *nijiriguchi* of the Yûin teahouse into the garden area in front of the building, thus determining the position of the stepping stones – an arrangement that became famous as *mame-make-ishi* ("scattered beans").

Initially, only untreated stones from the mountains were used, but later river stones and pebbles from the sea were also included in the design. Stones with unusual shapes were particularly in demand. Parts of the *roji* were also designed as paved paths, with the interplay between the cut and natural stones providing an attractive contrast. If a path, for example at a fork in the road, is closed off or if it is directed in a certain direction at an intersection, a small stone (*tomeishi* or *sekimori-ishi*), wrapped with a black hemp rope, is placed on a stepping stone. Although small and inconspicuous, it indicates an insurmountable barrier for the initiated.

MIDDLE GATE – CHÛMON

The middle gate is situated between the inner and outer garden, a symbol for having taken the next step on the way to tea and thus reached a deeper state of consciousness. Accordingly, the gate did not usually form a strong physical barrier. An exception is a middle gate in the tea garden of the Omotesenke tea school, which is formed as a crawl-in gate similar to a *nijiriguchi*. A *chûmon* could be designed in many different ways, and examples exist from the rudimentary branches stuck into the ground (*shiorido*) to the sophisticated *baikemon* of the Mushano kôji tea school in Kyoto, a bamboo gate between peeled cypress pillars with a roof of cedar shingles.

STONE WASHBASIN – TSUKUBAI

The washbasin (*tsukubai*), literally "the place where one has to kneel down", is used for ritual hand washing and mouth rinsing of guests as an act of purification before attending a tea ceremony – a custom that goes back to purification rituals of the Shinto religion. Forerunners of the *tsukubai* were water basins in the reception rooms (*kaisho*), which were brought to the veranda when needed and could thus be used without having to enter the garden. The water basins were large and high and corresponded to the custom of the nobility to be poured water over their hands by servants with a ladle. As an integral part of the *roji*, the *tsukubai* became lower and smaller, so that the guests had to sit down to wash their hands. A fixed arrangement, which is still in use today, was developed, with *tsukubai* referring to the entire arrangement and *chôzubachi* referring to the washbasin itself. Initially left in its natural form, it was only later that a formal design for this stone emerged. To the right of it was a flat stone (*yuoke-ishi*), on which a kettle with hot water was placed in winter, and on the left side there was the large lamp stone (*teshoku-ishi*). One or two flat stones (*mae-ishi*) were placed in front of the sink to sit on when washing hands.

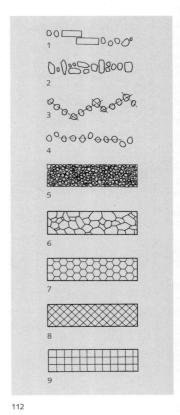

112

108 Stepping stones in the Kitamura residence, Kyoto

109 A single stone wrapped in black hemp rope (*tome-ishi*) blocks a path in the Kitamura residence, Kyoto.

110 The middle gate (*chûmon*) is situated between the inner and outer garden.

111 Although the middle gates usually do not form a strong physical barrier, the *naka-kuguri* middle gate of the Omotesenke tea school is formed like a *nijiriguchi*.

112 Configurations of stepping stones and paths
1 Raft (*ikada-uchi*)
2 Seven-five-three (*shichigosan-uchi*)
3 Goose flight (*gan-uchi*)
4 Triple arrangement with single stones in-between (*sannen-uchi*)
5 Hail stones (*ô-arare-jiki*)
6 Cracked ice (*hyômon-jiki*)
7 Turtle shell (*kikkô-jiki*)
8 Diamond (*shihan-jiki*)
9 Chessboard (*ichimatsu-jiki*)

113

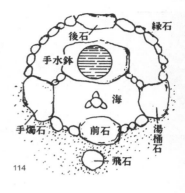

113 The washbasin (*tsukubai*) is used
for ritual hand washing before the
tea ceremony.

114 Illustration of a *tsukubai* from a
Japanese garden book

115

116

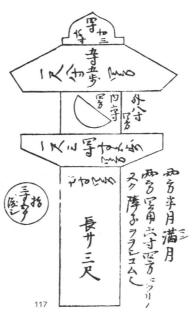

117

Between these and the basin was the water gate (*suimon*), a depression in the ground filled with pebbles or broken roof tiles to collect the excess from the basin.[

STONE LANTERN – ISHI-DÔRÔ

Stone lanterns were introduced by Buddhism from China and Korea to Japan, where they were used as votive lamps in Buddhist temples from the 13th century and later also in Shinto shrines. Around 1580, stone lanterns on the cemetery of Toribeno in Kyoto were said to have made such an impression on Sen no Rikyû that he put them in his tea garden. During the Momoyama period, tea ceremonies often took place during the night. The usual lighting for this was wood fires in suspended iron baskets, but their excessive brightness was not in harmony with the gentle atmosphere of the tea garden. As an alternative, stone lanterns were used in which oil lamps and later candles were placed. The openings of the lamps were then closed with small paper doors. The use of lanterns for practical reasons soon became a question of esthetic considerations. While old, mossy lanterns from temples were initially used, the growing demand quickly led to new ones having to be made. Old designs were copied and given the name of the temple from which they originated. Later, the tea masters created their own shapes that bore the name of their designers, such as the Oribe-style stone lanterns, which stand directly on the floor without a formal base.

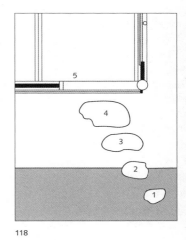

118

AREA OF THE NIJIRIGUCHI

The last threshold before entering the tea room is the area in front of the *nijiriguchi*, which is usually protected from rain by a roof overhang. In front of this area the garden path divides: One path leads towards the waste pit (*chiri-ana*), another towards the *katanakake-ishi*, a stepping stone to place your sword on the shelf. The shelf is a simple wooden frame construction consisting of approximately ten-millimeter-thick strips suspended from the roof overhang. Under the overhang of the roof, several stepping stones are set into the ground made of crushed clay: Immediately in front of the *nijiriguchi* is the high *fumi-ishi*, from which one can reach the interior of the teahouse. Somewhat deeper lie the *otoshi-ishi* and the *nori-ishi* before the last ordinary *tobi-ishi*. The three stones are arranged so precisely that the *nori-ishi* can be used to catch raindrops from the eave of the teahouse.

Beside the *nijiriguchi* there is another entrance for special guests in some teahouses. This opens with *shoji* to the tea room, and the stone in front of this entrance is higher and wider than that for ordinary guests.

WASTE PIT – CHIRI-ANA

Originally a small pit for garden waste, it later became a symbol of purity in ritualized use. It is the place where the guests can deposit the worldly affairs that burden their hearts and minds. Before the guests arrive, the host fills the pit with leaves and needles, demonstrating the purity of the garden, for the same reason a broom has been left at a place in the garden. For decorative reasons, an arrangement has been developed in which a stone is placed on one side of the pit: A pair of fresh bamboo sticks used to collect the leaves are placed in the *chiri-ana* and leaned against the stone. The shape of the *chiri-ana* depends on the size of the teahouse. Larger teahouses have a square *chiri-ana*, smaller ones a round *chiri-ana*.

115 Stone lantern and *tsukubai*
116 The stepping stones lead to the *nijiriguchi*.
117 Oribe-style stone lantern without base
118 Area in front of the *nijiriguchi*
  1 *Tobi-ishi*
  2 *Nori-ishi*
  3 *Otoshi-ishi*
  4 *Fumi-ishi*
  5 *Nijiriguchi*

[There is reason to believe that the origins of the cleansing on the *tsukubai* are to be found not only in the principles of Shintoism and Zen Buddhism, but also in the baptismal ritual of Christianity, which exerted a strong attraction on many tea masters.

雪隠門之事

一 隠之門深サ九寸下ニ三寸ホト白砂ヲ入ルヘし

一 角之唐穴指渡シ六寸深サ九寸ブチヲ丸ミヲ付テ

ヨリ土ニテヌルヘし

杉葉ヲ六寸ホト入ル

此雪隠ハ亡雪

隠好ハ古人ハ

寸ハ有ヘし

119

Two different types of toilets are built in combination with a tea room: In addition to an ordinary toilet (*kafuku setsuin*), which is usually located near the *yoritsuki* building at the entrance to the tea garden, some *roji* also have a decorative toilet (*kazari setsuin*), which is never used and is kept meticulously clean by the host. It is inspected by the guests as they wander through the tea garden. In Zen monasteries, cleaning has always been regarded as part of the spiritual discipline, and in this sense, *chiri-ana* and *kazari setsuin* embody the purity and immaculateness of the tea ceremony. Ideally, the *kazari setsuin* is set up somewhat apart from the other buildings and is half covered by bushes or bamboo. While used beams and bamboo are often used for the construction of the tea rooms, the *kazari setsuin* is made exclusively of fresh wood.

119 Illustration of a toilet (*setsuin*) in a
Japanese garden book

J   A. L. Sadler, *Cha-no-yu,
The Japanese Tea Ceremony*, p. 32 f.

"Around 300 BC there lived a pharmacist in China who knew the effects of 84,000 medicinal herbs. Before his death he could teach his son the benefit of 62,000 plants, the remaining 22,000 seemed lost forever. But from his grave grew a plant that combined the strengths of the 22,000 species – tea." A

THE BEGINNING OF JAPANESE TEA CULTURE

A long time had to pass before tea drinking in Japan could develop into the traditional form of tea ceremony. The starting point of the historical development was the ritual drinking of tea in the Buddhist monasteries of China. Its shape was completed by the work of great tea masters in the 15th and 16th centuries. The tradition passed down through the *iemoto*B system has kept this heritage alive to this day. Japan's cultural development was closely tied to China for centuries, and tea drinking in the imperial palaces was also taken over from the Chinese court. The first evidence of tea enjoyment in Japan dates back to the Nara period (710–794), but little is known about the environment in which tea was drunk in that period. If one follows poem anthologies from the early Heian period such as the *Ryoun Shu* or the *Bunka Shurei Shu*, in which tea drinking is described as a leisure activity of the nobility, the preferred setting for this was outdoors: Folding armchairs were set up for this purpose at a pond in an extensive garden, and the music of the *koto*C might have been constant accompaniment.

During the early Heian period, Buddhist monks who traveled to China to study new aspects of Buddhism played an important role in the spread of tea at the Japanese court. Monks such as Saichô, Kûkai and Eichû learned about a tea ritual in the Zen monasteries of the southern dynasties, where they gathered in front of the image of the cult founder Bodhidharma. Horst Hennemann describes a tea gathering of that time: "At the Bodhidharma commemoration a table with incense, flowers and candles was placed in front of the picture of the patriarch. After the abbot had entered the room, he sacrificed incense, bowed three times before the Bodhidharma image and took his place. Now pastries and tea were offered to the Bodhidharma. A monk then took the pastry from the table and handed it to the abbot, who took a piece and then passed it on to the assembled monks. After each of them had eaten, the tea sacrificed to the Bodhidharma was offered to the abbot. The abbot drank from the bowl and passed it on; every single monk tasted the drink. Then the abbot rose and was the first to leave the room." D

When the rule of the T'ang dynasty came to an end and Japan ended the system of mutual diplomatic relations with China (*kentoshi*) in 895 AD, the Heian aristocracy lost interest in tea. It did not fall completely into oblivion, but the custom of drinking tea was initially reserved for monasteries and temples. It was used by the Buddhist monks as a medicine, or to counter the fatigue that arose during the long hours of meditation. But also the spiritual aspect continued to play a role when tea was served at formal banquets after religious ceremonies (*naorai*). The weakened imperial court and court nobility paved the way for the samurai, the class of warriors and soldiers, to seize power. In 1185 AD Minamoto no Yoritomo established his military government in Kamakura and thus escaped the control of the emperor and the court in Kyoto. In 1192 he was awarded the highest military title of shogun by the emperor. This gave rise to the model of a dual system of rule that was to remain typical of the distribution of power in Japan until the second half of the 19th century: emperor (*tenno*)

121

122

120　Cherry blossom festival
121　Picture of the Bodhidharma of Shunsô (1750–1839)
122　Tea utensils for the *yotsugashira-charei* tea ceremony; Kennin-ji; Kyoto

A　Chinese legend about the origin of the tea plant
B　Heads of tea schools are called *iemoto*.
C　Japanese string instrument
D　Horst Hennemann, p. 43

123

versus warrior nobility, with actual power lying in the hands of the shoguns and their vassals.

Within a short time, the tea ritual became known among the up-and-coming class of samurai who appreciated the strictly regulated life in Zen monasteries. In their search for a cultural basis that differed from that of the courtly aristocracy, they copied elements from the Sung dynasty of China: The legal systems, political values, religious currents, and not least the tea ceremony were adopted. The text *Kissa Ôrai* ("Letters about drinking tea") from the second half of the 14th century describes the secular preparation of tea in close imitation of those of the monasteries. The guests ate a light meal of sake and tea in a meeting room then went for a walk in the garden before going to a pavilion for tea. "The building is a magnificent pavilion with two superimposed, tribune-like floors, which are open on all four sides for the sake of a good view. It's a tea pavilion, but is also used for watching the moon[E]."[F]

On the upper floor of this pavilion (*kissa-no-tei*) there was a gallery that offered a beautiful view all around. Buildings such as the Golden and Silver Pavilions in Kyoto – Kinkaju-ji and Ginkaku-ji – may have been built for this purpose. The Shiguretei teahouse in the Kodai-ji temple in Kyoto gives an idea of what a simpler type of pavilion might have looked like. However, the samurai began to detach tea from its religious context and adapt it for their rituals and competitions. In this way, tea competitions (*tocha*) developed, which represented a remarkable contrast to the quiet pleasures of the Heian aristocracy. The winners were awarded valuable prizes held in a magnificent setting.

"When the guests entered the tea room, a Buddha picture hung on the main wall and on its sides pictures depicting the Buddha's teaching interpretation by well-known painters. Or a picture of the holy Kwannon occupied this place. From a table in front of it hung a gold brocade on which stood a Chinese bronze vessel for flowers. Incense pots were set up as well as tea urns. On decoration boards on the west side of the room rare fruits were shown, on the north side the prizes were shown. In between stood the kettle of water, in which the water simmered. The guests sat down on seats over which leopard skins were spread. The sliding doors of the room were decorated with various Chinese paintings."[G]

However, these competitions did not always take place inside a building, as is reported in *Taihei-ki* ("The Story of the Great Peace") about a cherry blossom festival: "In the shade of the blossoming trees, curtains are stretched, chairs are lined up, various rare dishes are prepared, a hundred bowls of tea are tasted for their origin and variety, and gifts are piled up in mountains".[H]

The *tocha* games not only appealed to the rich samurai, they were also extremely popular with soldiers and the poorer classes. The consumption of tea was therefore no longer reserved to the nobility, clergy and the rich warrior class, but spread to all classes of the population. The chronicle of the To-ji temple in the south of Kyoto mentions a stand outside the gates of the temple in 1403, which offered tea in cups, and from 1433 further stands along the temple walls are reported. The custom soon spread to all the great temples of the city, and in this way more and more people became familiar with the drink. Merchants with tea stalls in public places were very popular, and in the middle of the 15th century such stalls were a common sight in the cityscape of Kyoto. Tea was sold for "Ippuku issen", "a bowl of tea for a *sen*", the smallest coin currency at that time.

123 The Shiguretei teahouse in the Kodai-ji, Kyoto

E   In Japan, observing the moon has always been regarded as an expression of a special closeness to nature.
F   Horst Hennemann, p. 47
G   Horst Hammitzsch, p. 39
H   Horst Hennemann, p. 45

124 Kinkaku-ji, the "Golden Pavilion", Kyoto

125

126

いづれをしも拍悲乃茄の茶ます思わひたるもあまれよき出極わ持小ゆへし

一圓く一ゃ茶

こ茶乃汇茶とめ色

おもやく

茶一わし色

THE KAISHO

During the Ashikaga shoguns, the residences of the upper classes were predominantly decorated with Chinese art objects, and only porcelain of Chinese origin was used in the tea collections. This "preference for objects from the continent" (*karamono suki*) was obviously influenced by the formal tea services in Zen temples and the frequent journeys of Zen monks between Japan and China. Objects brought to Japan by monks for religious purposes – portraits and calligraphies of Zen masters, monochrome landscapes, tea bowls, and other ceremonial items – were alienated from their religious significance and became objects of esthetic contemplation. They were appreciated by connoisseurs and were highly sought after by collectors. Some collections became so extensive over time that monks who had acquired knowledge of the art of the continent during their numerous trips to China were hired as specialists (*dôbôshû*). Their task was to catalog the collections and filter out the most valuable from the large number of imported works of art. As Zen monks, they were familiar with the ceremonial use of tea utensils, so the ritual of making tea was also their responsibility. They dealt intensively with the course of the tea ceremony, set rules for the behavior in the tea room and determined in which way the art objects should be presented. They reacted to the new architectural conditions, as the tea ceremonies, but also the *waka*₁ and *renga*ⱼ meetings were no longer held in the pavilions in the garden, but in the reception buildings (*kaisho*) in the villas and palaces. These buildings were usually divided into a public southern and a private northern part, whereby the three southern rooms together formed the guest area (*kyakuden*), in which the tea ceremony and also *tocha* competitions were held. In the north was the tea preparation room (*chanoyuma*) with a shelf (*chanoyu-dana*) on which the tea was prepared for such gatherings. Since there was a fireplace in the room above which a water kettle was suspended from the ceiling by means of a chain, it was also called a chain room (*kusari-no-ma*). Situated in a secondary position, it was sometimes even placed a step below the floor level to underline its use by members of lower classes. Here the *dôbôshû* prepared the tea and served the host and guests in the reception room. This absolute separation between the rooms of the tea preparation and the tea ceremony was known as "serving already beaten tea" (*tatedashi*) and is regarded as a key feature of the early palace tea.

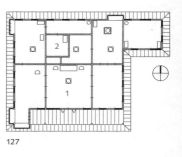

127

125 Chinese-style tea gathering in a
kaisho; Sarei-zôshi picture scroll
about ceremonies and festivals,
15th century
126 Tea merchants; picture scroll by
Kano Osanobu, 1846
127 Minamimuki-kaisho of the Muro-
machi-dono Palace of Ashikaga
Yoshinori:
 1 South-facing guest room
 2 Tea preparation room

I Poem form with 31 syllables
J Poem form, literally:
"connected verses"

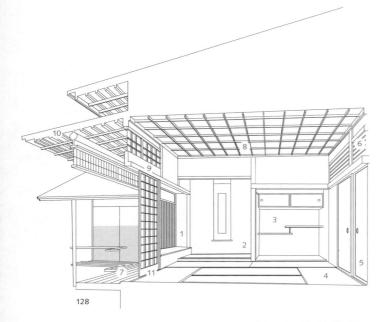

128

129

Since the early Muromachi period_K, a new architectural style developed from the adaptation of the *shinden* palace buildings of the Heian period: The *shoin* style was accompanied by fundamental changes in construction, and many elements were introduced that characterize Japanese buildings to this day. The *shoin* rooms succeeded the *kaisho* of the *shinden* residence. They became the most important rooms within the samurai residences where the guests were welcomed and entertained; tea gatherings also took place in this setting. The *shoin* architecture got its name from an element called *tsuke-shoin*, a table-like board installed in a niche in front of a translucent sliding window. Also known under the name *idashi-fuzukue* ("desk for spreading out writings") and actually originating from the monks' writing room, the *tsuke-shoin* became a fixed part of every *shoin* room and gave the style its name.

Fundamental differences to the predominant *shinden* style are already evident in the construction system: While round columns were still used in the *shinden* buildings, the posts were now square in cross section, often with chamfered or ground corners. Together with horizontal bands (*nageshi*), they structured the wall surfaces and formed a grid that clearly expressed the construction system of the building. A further change concerned the introduction of suspended, richly decorated coffered ceilings, which were missing in the rooms of the *shinden* palaces, most of which were open towards the roof. Opaque paper-covered sliding doors (*fusuma*) divided the interior into individual sub-units, while translucent sliding elements (*shoji*), which could be protected from wind and weather on the outside by heavy wooden sliding panels (*amado*), closed off the *shoin* rooms. The wall areas above the *fusuma* were designed as permeable lattice windows (*ranma*) and sometimes provided with elaborate carvings. In the *shoin* style, *tatami* mats covered the entire floor of a room for the first time, and since then it has also been customary to indicate the room size by the number of mats. The *tokonoma* is another element that evolved with the *shoin* style: a slightly elevated niche used to display incense, flowers or hanging scrolls; a shelf with offset shelves (*chigaidana*) was often placed next to it.

With the advent of the *shoin* style, a rational planning process began to manifest itself in Japanese architecture. Step by step, drawings, cost calculations and tenders were prepared on the basis of technical planning material. Until then, construction drawings included nothing more than simple floor plans with comments on the construction work. Sections, elevations and detailed plans were never drawn in advance, the dimensioning of the constructive elements was mainly based on the experience of the contractor. The first step towards a more comprehensive presentation was the use of elevations and this coincides with the introduction of the so-called *kiwari jutsu*_L: This is a dimensional reference system for timber construction that indicates the dimension of each individual element from the ratio to a certain basic dimension, which varies depending on the size and purpose of the construction. Towards the end of the Momoyama period, the system was already well advanced, and the proportions were laid down in numerous compendia (*kiwari-shô*).

With the *shoin* style and the development of elements such as *tokonoma* and *chigaidana*, new space was created for decorations. New arts such as ikebana flower arranging and ink painting replaced the picture scrolls (*e-maki*) of the Heian period. "In the picture niche two or three picture scrolls with an inner connection are hung up. The incense burner, the flower vase and the candlesticks are placed in front of them. Opposite the window of the reading oriel is a table with ink writing stone, ink, brush and water container. The wall boards

128 The innovations of the *shoin* architecture
  1 *Tsuke-shoin*
  2 *Tokonoma*
  3 *Chigaidana*
  4 *Tatami*
  5 *Fusuma*
  6 *Ranma*
  7 Veranda *(engawa)*
  8 Coffered ceiling
  9 *Nageshi*
 10 "Leaning" roof *(hisashi)*
 11 *Shoji*
129 The *shoin* style created a new space for decoration: ikebana and ink painting replaced the picture scrolls of the Heian period.

K   Muromachi period
(1333–1573)
L   *Ki* = wood, *wari* = division,
jutsu = system

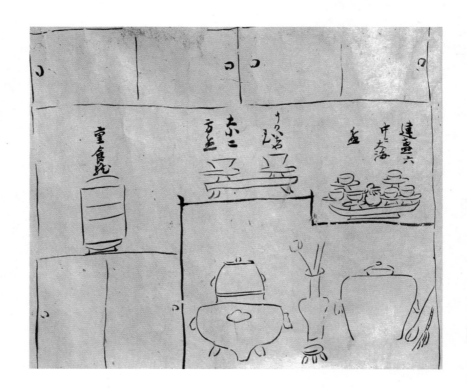

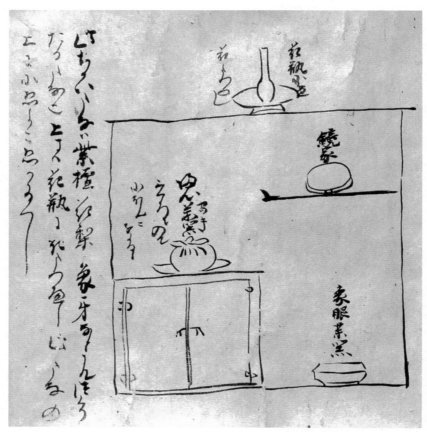

130

show incense containers of various kinds and other objects of taste and value."[M] After tea gatherings were also held in the *shoin* rooms, these innovations were to have a great influence on later tea rooms. Both the use of flower arrangements and calligraphy in the *tokonoma* of the teahouse goes back to the design of the *shoin* rooms.

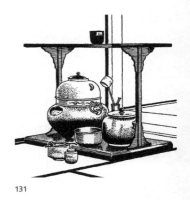

131

The tea ceremony was constantly gaining new followers and was able to establish itself as an independent social art form. From the synthesis of the formal tea etiquette based on the rules of tea service in Zen monasteries, the preference for Chinese utensils, and the interiors of *shoin* architecture emerged the oldest and most formalized form of *chanoyu* – the *shoin*-style *chanoyu* practiced by high-ranking members of the samurai class predominantly on the premises of the Ashikaga shoguns. The tea utensils used, all of which came from China, were placed in a fixed arrangement on a special portable lacquer shelf (*daisu*), which was designed in Chinese style, and presented to the guests. The use of the *daisu* has been identified by subsequent generations with the *chanoyu* in *shoin* style, and a *daisu* is used in the most formal form of tea ceremony to this day. While every reception room could previously be used for drinking tea and preparing tea, the increasing importance of the ritual led to the furnishing of certain rooms specifically for the purpose of the tea ceremony. One of the most important elements that indicate the use of a room as a tea room is the sunken stove (*rô*). In the past, these charcoal stoves were only cut into the floors of living rooms, but never in rooms where guests were received. Mobile charcoal basins were brought there in the cold season and could be removed again after use. The cutting of a stove into a guest room, the replacement of the fixed *chanoyu-dana* shelf by the mobile *daisu* and the decoration of the room with tea utensils dedicated the space for a certain use and was a decisive step in the further development of teahouse architecture. With the elements *tokonoma*, *daisu* and *rô* a new environment was created for the tea ceremony.

The first example of a specialized tea room is the Dojinsai in the Togudô hall of the Higashiyama Villa of shogun Yoshimasa, today part of the Ginkakuji temple in northwest Kyoto. The room with a size of 4½ mats was built in 1486, at a time when the *shoin* rooms were becoming more and more magnificent and richer decorated. But Dojinsai is equipped in a simplified *shoin* style, still with *chigaidana* and a *tsuke-shoin*, but without *tokonoma*. Recent repairs have revealed an inscription identifying it as a "room with a sunken stove", which would make the Dojinsai the first tea room and the forerunner of the teahouse. The Dojinsai is also important for another reason in Japan's architectural history, as it is the first room whose size is defined by half a *tatami* mat. Up to this point only whole mats were used. The introduction of a smaller unit than the surface of a *tatami* (*ken*) indicates that a refined sense of space developed in 15th-century Japan.

The great popularity of the tea ceremony among the ruling classes also influenced other classes. Although they could not afford the same setting, they wanted to imitate the etiquette developed by the samurai nobility. They held their meetings in smaller, less lavishly furnished rooms that corresponded to their social status and economic possibilities. But wealthy samurai also used smaller, less formal rooms to entertain only a few guests or to create a more intimate atmosphere, as some *shoin* rooms had a size of more than 18 *tatami* mats. By separating partial rooms with mobile partitions, smaller, five to six *tatami*-sized areas were created. Starting from this separate room, the rustic teahouse (*chashitsu*) was able to develop as an independent structure. The name of the partition walls – *kakoi* – was retained as the name for those tea rooms that were

130 Arrangement of tea utensils; *Kuntaikan Sochoki* (textbook on interior design and utensils), 1559

131 The mobile shelf (*daisu*) is still used today in the most formalized tea ceremony.

M Horst Hammitzsch, p. 43 f.

133

132

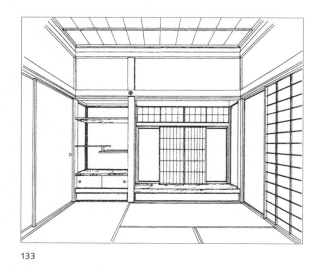

133

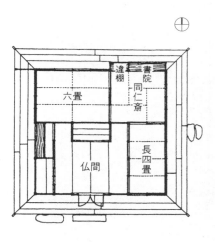

六畳

違棚

書院
同仁斎

長四畳

仏間

134

not integrated into freestanding buildings, but into a residential or temple building or attached to it.

THE DEVELOPMENT
OF THE SÔAN TEAHOUSE

MURATA SHUKÔ AND THE BEGINNING OF THE WABI TEA

"The worst thing on this path is to carry arrogance and obstinacy in your heart. And it's unbecoming to envy an expert and look down on a beginner." [N]

Murata Shukô (1422–1502) is regarded as the actual founder of the Japanese tea ceremony. He grew up in a rich merchant family in Nara and, through the mediation of dôbôshû Nôami, learned about the tea ceremony in the form in which it was practiced in the palaces of the Ashikaga shoguns. At the age of twenty, he became a disciple of Ikkyû Sôjun (1394–1481), the abbot of the Daitoku-ji-Zen temple in Kyoto, who, according to his credo "Buddha lives in the tea ceremony" [O], taught him the techniques of making tea as was customary in the monasteries of Zen Buddhism. Under this influence, Shukô simplified the formalized tea ceremony. He criticized the lavish celebrations in which the tea ceremony was embedded and railed against the focus on valuable utensils. Instead, he advocated a ceremony in the spirit of Zen philosophy and repeatedly emphasized the unity of Zen and tea. He came up with the idea that it was no longer a servant, but the host himself who prepared the tea and served it to the guests in order to create a bond between all the participants – in contrast to the ceremonies in the large shoin rooms, which took place like a performance in front of an audience.

In the famous Kokoro no fumo ("Letter of the Heart") to his favorite student Furuichi Harima, he presented his concept of chanoyu and his views on esthetics. He saw tea as a way (do), as an art form that shapes the human being as a whole and can only be practiced with devotion, a pure heart and free of selfish feelings. According to Shukô, the host should dedicate his entire personality to the well-being of the guest. This concept of the kokoroire – literally: "the insertion of the heart" – is still the focus of the Way of Tea today. With the changed processes of the tea ceremony there was also a fundamental change in tea esthetics. Shûko emphasized that not only Chinese but also Japanese utensils were used. He noted this in Kokoro no fumo: "It is important for this path to blur the boundaries between Japanese and Chinese things; one should keep that in mind above all." [P] For him, the bringing together of contrasting Chinese and Japanese objects brought to light a new kind of beauty, a harmonization of different esthetic tendencies. With rustic Bizen and Shigaraki-style ceramics, a trend began away from richly decorated Chinese objects towards an appreciation of the restrained, semi-hidden beauty of simple local objects. This new, so-called wabi esthetics not only influenced all elements of the tea ceremony – from the tea bowl to the teahouse – but generally became a determining element of Japanese esthetics. Shukô preferred the atmosphere and intimacy of smaller structures, because only in these did he see the possibility of communication through the medium of tea. This preference became a fundamental rule for all later developments: The 4½-mat room, which he created as a quieter setting for the ceremony, was to become the standard. Shukô was the first to design rooms for exclusive use as tea rooms. While rooms such as the Dojinsai could also be used as waiting or guest rooms, Shukô's tea rooms could no longer be used for other purposes. In the Nampôroku ("Notes of Nambô"), a "bible" of chanoyu, Nambô Sokei [Q] describes a tea room of Shukô:

132 Togudô hall in the Ginkaku-ji, Kyoto
133 The Dojinsai in the Togudô hall is regarded as the first tea room: floor plan and perspective drawing

N   Horst Hammitzsch, p. 52
O   Teiji Itoh, p. 132
(own translation)
P   Horst Hammitzsch, p. 53
Q   Nambô Sokei was a rich merchant from Sakai and a student of Sen no Rikyû.

134

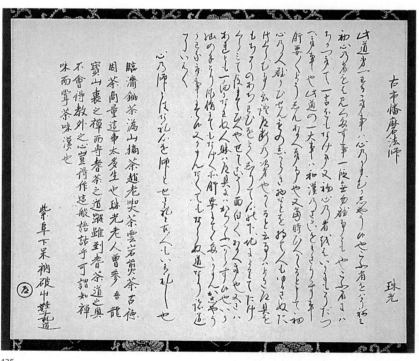

古市幡磨法師　珠光

此道第一もわろき事は心の我慢我執也……

臨済の茶潙山の茶趙老喫茶雲巌喫茶古徳……
因茶商量造車太多生や珠光老人曽参吾龍……
寶山裏之禅而専春茶之道雖到春茶道之奥……
不會得教外之心宣得作遮般語話于可謂知禅……
味而嘗茶味漢也

紫阜下呆祚破門参和道

135

136

"For tea drinking, Juko made use for the first time of a 4.5-mat room. He used glossy light-yellow paper to cover the walls, installed a joistless ceiling made of pine boards, and constructed a pyramidal roof covered with small wooden shingles. On the wall of the six-foot tokonoma he hung a rare and treasured calligraphy scroll by the Chinese Zen priest Yuan-wu [c. 1063–1135] and on its floor displayed a tea-utensil stand [daisu]. Then he provided a sunken hearth, the rims of which were decorated with a fine wooden frame [kyudai]."[R]

In the layout of the tea room tatami the strong influence of Buddhism became visible: The mats were arranged in such a way that they form the swastika symbol, which is widespread in Buddhism as a sign of the "wheel of teaching". By moving the tea ceremony from the shoin rooms to the teahouses modeled after the hermit huts, Shukô created the original form of the wabi tea. Thus a tea ceremony could develop, independent of material conditions, in which only the acquisition of knowledge and skills was of importance. While the tea ceremony created by Shukô had little influence on the tea ritual of the upper class; it was, however, enthusiastically received by the merchant class, which became wealthy towards the end of the Muromachi period.

SÔJU AND THE SHIMOGYO-CHANOYU

The growing prosperity of the merchant class and their need to meet to discuss business and politics led to the establishment of rooms for the reception of guests in merchant houses. These were either separate rooms within the main building or separate buildings in the garden at the back of the property. The models for these buildings were small huts that had been built since the 15th century by wealthy merchants on their property. Separated from the main buildings, they were used to hold memorial services and other Buddhist ceremonies. An early example of such a small retreat is the hut of Sanjônishi Sanetaka, one of the most important individuals in the cultural life of his time. He bought a 6-tatami hut in 1502 and had it transferred to his estate on Mushanokôji Street in Kyoto. He reduced it to a 4½-tatami hut, arranged stones, planted trees, surrounded it with a wooden fence and used it as a retreat to pursue his studies. It was named corner hut (sumiya) after its location on the property. The floor was covered with tatami and the wall behind the decoration board (oshiita) and the shelves was covered with paper with a regular wood print pattern in Chinese style (karakami). With buildings like these, erected far from the distractions of daily life, a place was created where the tea ceremony could unfold undisturbed.

Shûko's disciple Sôju (1421–1502) was the central figure of the so-called Shimogyo-chanoyu, which developed in the bustling Shimogyo district of southern Kyoto. He shared his master's preference for small tea rooms and built a teahouse in the back of his property on the north side of Shijo Street, reminiscent of a hermit's hut, consisting of a 4½-mat room and a 6-mat room. After his visit to the teahouse, Washinoo Takayasu, Sôju's contemporary, reports: "I am deeply impressed by this scene: Here, in the very heart of the city, I have the impression of being in the country. Sôju deserves to be called a hermit and is undoubtedly a driving force behind the suki of today."[S] This teahouse, which was called Gosho-an ("hermitage to the pine tree of the late afternoon"), is considered the prototype of the so-called sôan or grass hut style. This atmosphere of the secluded hut became the trend among the wealthy and cultivated townspeople. Toyohara no Muneaki, for example, a well-known musician and poet, built the 4½-mat hut Yamazato-an ("mountain village hermitage") under a large pine tree on his property and in one verse conjured up the longing for loneliness in the middle of the big city:

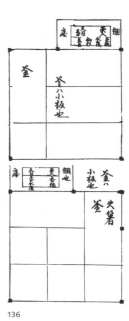

136

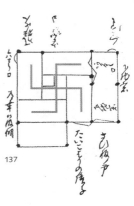

137

134 Portrait of Murata Shukô
135 In Kokoro no fumo ("Letter of the Heart") to his favorite student Furuichi Harima, Shukô presented his concept of chanoyu and his views on esthetics. Copy of Konoike Do'ku from the Edo period
136 The drawings of early 4½-mat tea rooms from the Cha Donsho ("Writings to Tea") are attributed to Soami.
137 The layout of the tatami shows the Buddhist swastika symbol.

R   Hayashiya et al, Japanese Arts and the Tea Ceremony, p. 29
S   Tatsusaburo Hayashiya/ Masao Nakamura/Seizo Hayashiya, »Japanese Arts and the Tea Ceremony«, in: The Heibonsha Survey of Japanese Art, p. 29

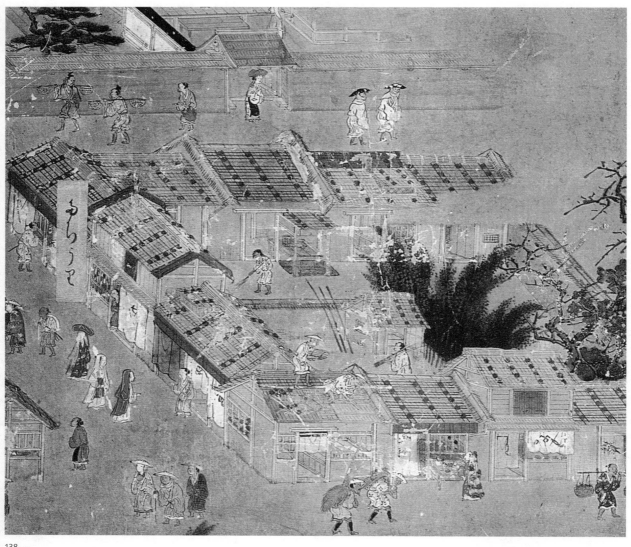

138

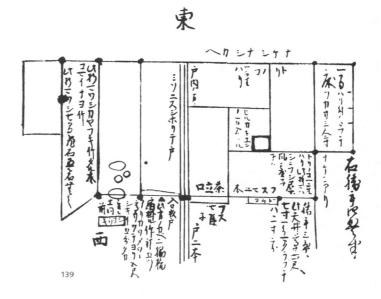

東

西

139

"Yama nite mo
Ukaramu toki no
Kakurega ya
Miyako no uchi no
Matsu no shita io."

"When even in the mountains
my sadness does not give way
is my hiding place
in the middle of the capital
the hermitage under the pine tree." [T]

The intention is clear: The hut served as a refuge from the concerns of everyday life, as a seemingly remote hiding place and an opportunity to retreat – a longing that has long existed in Asia. Hermits who turned their backs on the world to live in the mountains were a familiar image. The city dwellers, on the other hand, never really wanted to give up the sociable city life. Instead, they tried to create a place with the atmosphere of the mountains, while at the same time not missing out on the amenities of city life. Shukô's aphorism to the *wabi* philosophy, "Even the moon is disliked without clouds", refers to the necessary contrast within the *wabi* esthetics: The "mountain hut" only became meaningful in contrast and in the opposite coexistence to rich city life. A real, remote hermitage would have been meaningless. Later, this esthetics was also adopted by military rulers: The contrast between the grassy hut on the premises of a fortified multi-story castle (*dojon*) was probably much greater.

138 In the center of the busy Shimogyo district in Kyoto there is a "hermit's hut".
139 Plan of the teahouse of Matsuya Kyuei; *Cha-no-yu Hisho* ("Secrets of the Tea Ceremony"), 1738

T Quoted from Horst Hennemann, p. 81

TAKENO JÔÔ AND THE SÔAN TEAHOUSE PROTOTYPE

The arrival of Portuguese merchants around 1550 led to a further strengthening and expansion of the middle class. The merchants, who profited greatly from trade with Europe, enjoyed a reputation that had previously been reserved for the nobility and the upper samurai class. In the middle of the 16th century, *chanoyu*, carried by members of the merchant class, developed into a mass movement, and for the first time it became possible for tea masters to earn their living through education. Apart from Kyoto, the center of trade was the port city of Sakai near Osaka, which had developed from a small fishing village into a prosperous trading town in the approximately 200 years of the Muromachi and Momoyama periods. Sakai became a trading center for foreign goods and ideas, and the inhabitants known as *machi-shû*$_U$ were known for their exquisite taste and the sumptuous furnishings of their townhouses. Against this background, the grass-covered Shimogyo hut also found its way into Sakai, where it was to mature into the prototype of the classic teahouse. The Portuguese Jesuit João Rodrigues recorded his observations in the *Historia da Igreja do Japão* ("History of the Church in Japan"):

"Certain Sakai men versed in cha-no-yu *built the* cha *house in another way. It was smaller and set among some small trees planted for the purpose, and it represented, as far as the small site allowed, the style of lonely houses which are found in the countryside, or like the cells of solitaries who dwell in hermitages far removed from people and give themselves over to the contemplation of the things of nature and its First Cause ... In order that the furnishings might be in keeping with the smaller hut, they did away with many of the utensils and items required by* cha-no-yu, *together with the order and arrangement of these things, and in everything they did what seemed most fitting and appropriate for their purpose.*
So they entertained each other with cha *in these small huts within the city itself and in this way they made up for the lack of refreshing and lonely places around the city; indeed, to a certain extent this way was better than real solitude because they obtained and enjoyed it in the middle of the city itself. They called this in their language* shichu no sankyo, *meaning a lonely hermitage found in the middle of the public square."*$_V$

Takeno Jôô (1502–1555), Shukô's successor as an advocate of the *wabi* tea style, was instrumental in the next stage on the path to the completion of classical tea art. He came from a merchant family in Sakai and initially devoted himself entirely to poetry, which allowed him to come into contact with courtly culture. Initially, he held the tea ritual according to Shukô's teachings, and since his tea teacher practiced Zen, Jôô also immersed himself in the teachings of Zen Buddhism. He placed value on mutual reverence and respect between host and guest and formulated the still valid principle of the *ichigo ichie*$_W$ – "here and now" – in the tea ceremony, the awareness that every single gathering in the tea room is unique and unrepeatable. In a letter to his student Sen no Rikyû he explained this as follows: "The behavior of the host shall truly show reverence to the guest in his heart [...] even in an ordinary tea ceremony, if one has entered the garden path to the last end, one shall approach the host with reverence as if it were a single and unique meeting."$_X$ In his search for a beauty in keeping with the philosophy of the *wabi*, he went even further than his predecessors: Endowed with an extraordinary artistic sense, he discovers beauty in things with a poor and unpretentious exterior: According to Jôô, any tea utensil that is too "loud" should be rejected, because everything in the tea room must stand in balance and harmony with each other. In rejecting richly decorated tea utensils of Chinese origin, he followed his role model Shukô: "Only using famous Chinese tea utensils at tea gatherings is highly inappropriate. The tea lover selects utensils discarded by others and uses them as tea utensils; all the more so for my followers. Anyone who is a tea lover should strive above all for the *wabi* mentality of a hermit, understand the meaning of the Buddha teachings and have a feeling for the mood of poems. Loneliness is appropriate and corresponds to this way; who strives for beauty weakens it, who strives for the coarse pollutes it; both inhibit it, it is to be well considered."[Y]

He applied the esthetic principles of the *wabi* in his 4½-mat room and simplified the teahouse and the used utensils more and more. Three sides of the room were enclosed by windowless walls, the fourth side opened over a *shoji* onto a veranda and a garden to the north. The square posts of Japanese cypress were chamfered at the corners, and a fireplace was set into the floor in the middle of the room. It is noteworthy that in the description the height of the lintel is described as "lower than usual", other sources even say that Jôô's tea room had to be entered from the veranda on hands and knees. This reduction of the door opening became one of the essential characteristics of the teahouse, and was later further emphasized by the introduction of the crawl-in entrance (*nijiriguchi*). Roll-up bamboo blinds were installed in front of the entrance to regulate the lighting of the room. The spatial concept of Jôô's 4½-mat room became a model for later tea masters through the careful coordination of all dimensions, proportions and materials. Written records testify that it was often copied in Sakai. Although elements of the *shoin* tea room such as square posts or paper-covered walls were still used, many of Jôô's innovations already referred to the new architectural style. With the use of clay and bamboo – building materials that came from the rustic architecture and had never been used before in the houses of the upper classes – the *sôan* teahouse, which was to be completed by Jôô's disciple Sen no Rikyû, already existed as a rough draft.

140

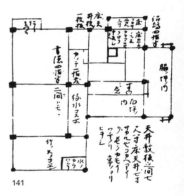

141

140 Portrait of Takeno Jôô
141 Tea room of Jôô; records of Yamanoue Soji, 1588

U *Machi-shû* was originally used to describe the inhabitants of a self-governing city, later it became a general term for city dwellers.
V Sen Sôshitsu XV, p. 15
W Literally: "A time, a meeting"
X Horst Hammitzsch, p. 64
Y Franziska Ehmcke, *Der japanische Tee-Weg*, p. 47

"Since Rikyu is a master of *chanoyu*, he can say the mountain is the valley and the west is the east. He can break the traditional formality of *chanoyu* and create it by himself. He can do it and it is interesting. Only a nobleman or an expert can do that. Such a tearoom has meaning for an expert like Rikyu. For ordinary people, it is useless."

YAMANOUE SOJI, A DISCIPLE OF RIKYÛ[A]

TEA CEREMONY AND POWER STRUCTURE

In the middle of the 16th century numerous civil wars raged in the country. The Muromachi shogunate disappeared and was replaced by the power struggles of numerous local warlords and powerful feudal lords (*daimyô*[B]) who fought fiercely against each other. With the *daimyô* Oda Nobunaga (1534–1582), Toyotomi Hideyoshi (1536–1598), and Tokugawa Ieyasu (1542–1616) the empire was unified and an era of lasting peace began. Nobunaga was a passionate supporter of the tea ceremony, which is why he hired three tea connoisseurs from the Sakai merchant class as tea masters. Thanks to his commitment, the tea ceremony became a national ritual and a means of reaching political consensus for his hegemonic aspirations. After the basis of the *chanoyu* had already been laid in the time of the Ashikaga shoguns, it was given a decidedly power-political dimension with this renewed promotion. Many *daimyô*, among them the most famous tea masters of later epochs – Kobori Enshu, Katagiri Sekishu, Matsudaira Fumai or Ii Nasosuke – saw in the tea ceremony the optimal prerequisite to form the necessary behavior of an exemplary leader and citizen. Tea was regarded as an ideal of human communication and as a medium for cultivating the mind. Nobunaga's successor, Toyotomi Hideyoshi, shared his passion for the tea ceremony and placed it even further at the center of cultural life. Shortly after his enthronement in 1585, Hideyoshi had a transportable golden tea pavilion built for him: Although this was only a small 3-mat room, the interior was completely covered with gold. All utensils were also made of gold or gilded, with the exception of a white linen cloth, a bamboo tea broom and a wooden water ladle. The *tatami* were covered with a red carpet, which gave the interior a strangely "un-Japanese" quality. The structure made of Japanese cypress was constructed without nails and in such a way that the tea room could be easily assembled and dismantled. It was kept in the castle in Osaka and only erected on special occasions. In 1586, for example, it was transported to the imperial palace in Kyoto, where Hideyoshi served tea to the emperor; and at the big Kitano tea gathering (*Kitano-dai-chakai*)[C] the "Golden Tea Room" was erected as the most important building in the center of the shrine. The tea room was destroyed around 1615; today a replica is exhibited at the Osaka Castle Museum and the Museum of Art in Atami. The importance Hideyoshi attached to the tea ceremony can be seen in the *Kitano-dai-chakai* of October 1587. Tea lovers of all social classes were invited to the event. Throughout the country, the population was made aware of the large-scale event by placards: "For ten days, depending on the weather, a big tea ceremony will take place in the Kitano wood from the first day of the 10th month, and according to the rules, valuable tea utensils will be gathered there without exception and presented to tea lovers. If someone has a love for the tea ceremony – whether he is a young servant or a merchant or a farmer – he should bring a kettle, a ladle, a water container and something to drink. If you don't have tea powder, you will not be blamed if you bring roasted barley powder [...] If anyone is particularly impecunious, however far he may have come, he will also be offered tea by prince Hideyoshi's own hand."[D]

142 Reconstruction of the "Golden Tea Room" in the Osaka Castle Museum

A   Quoted from Teiji Itoh, "Sen Rikyû and Taian", in: *Chanoyu Quarterly*, p. 9
B   The literal translation means "big name".
C   The event was named after the location of the event, a shrine in Kyoto.
D   Franziska Ehmcke, p. 40

143

Around 800 tea huts were built, so that a contemporary remarked: "Between the lecture hall and the Shobaiin, no open space was to be found."[E] In addition to various *chashitsu* variants, radical approaches to teahouse architecture were also noted: The tea master Hechikan set up an umbrella, with the shadow of which he demarcated the room of the tea ceremony to the extent of about two mats. Hideyoshi exhibited his most valuable tea utensils, and after the opening formalities, the ruler and his three tea masters went to their tea huts, where they served about 800 guests during the morning. For no apparent reason, the ten-day event was cancelled after the first day on the official grounds that Hideyoshi had to rush to the aid of an ally. Besides his preference for the opulent and power-political aspects of the tea ceremony, Hideyoshi also became a true follower of the *wabi* tea, a merit that may be attributed to his origins in poor circumstances, but certainly to his tea teacher Sen no Rikyû.

After the death of Hideyoshi began the political rise of the Tokugawa family, who were to hold sway over the country until the second half of the 19th century. The Tokugawa shogunate was founded by Tokugawa Ieyasu, who received the shogun title from the emperor in 1603. When he died in 1616, he had laid the foundations for an inner and outer peace that would last over 250 years. Unlike his predecessors, Tokugawa Ieyasu was not a follower of the philosophy of *chanoyu*. In terms of power politics, the tea practice was linked to the hostile Toyotomi family; an expression of interest in the *chanoyu* could have been seen as a political manifestation. This led to a short-term break in the history of the *chanoyu*, which opened the way for a new tea practice and philosophy – free of the political and symbolic associations of the *sôan* tea ceremony. Not only the method of preparation was new, but also the type of tea – dried and roasted tea leaves (*sencha*). The use of *sencha* spread rapidly throughout the country, and even today this type of green tea is the national drink of Japan.

SEN NO RIKYÛ

Sen no Rikyû was born in Sakai in 1522 as the son of one of the most influential merchant families. His grandfather, Dôetsu Sen'ami, served as tea expert (*dôbôshû*) at the court of Ashikaga Yoshimasa, and through him Rikyû came into early contact with the art of tea ceremony. His first teacher, Kitamuki Donchin, who introduced him to the Ashikaga tradition of formal *shoin* tea style, recognized Rikyû's extraordinary talent and recommended him to Takeno Jôô, the most famous tea master of his time. From Jôô he learned the basics of *wabi-cha* and the importance of Zen philosophy for the tea ceremony. Rikyû then began Zen studies with the master Shôrei Shûkin in the Daitoku-ji temple, where he received his Buddhist name Sôeki. After his apprenticeship in Sakai he was called together with his tea friends Imai Sôkyû and Tsuda Sôkyû to Oda Nobunaga's court in 1570, where he led a life as a dedicated tea master.

After Nobunaga's death he also served his successor Toyotomi Hideyoshi in the same position. Initially only engaged as a tea master (*sadô*), Sen no Rikyû gradually rose to become Hideyoshi's closest confidant and became one of Japan's most influential men of his time. At the beginning of 1591 Hideyoshi ordered the ritual suicide (*sepukku*) of Rikyû for no apparent reason, and so Rikyû died on 25 February at the age of 70[F] by his own hand.

Although as Hideyoshi's tea master he was committed to the formal tea style of the ruling class, *shoin-chanoyu*, his ideal was the *wabi* tea, in which Zen philosophy and tea ceremony merged into one spirit. In the *Nampôroku*, his ideas are recorded this way: "The basis of the *cha-no-yu* is the *daisu*, but if we look for the heart of the *cha-no-yu* we will find it nowhere other than in

143 An umbrella symbolizes the tea room; detail from a picture scroll of the Grand Kitano Tea Gathering by Ukita Ikkei, 1843

E   Louise Allison Cort, "The Grand Kitano Tea Gathering", in: *Chanoyu Quarterly*
F   Age was then counted by calendar year; at birth, man was one year old, and with each New Year's day grew one year older.

144

the small 'informal' room."_G Rikyû introduced a new kind of *chanoyu*, in which the objects were brought from the preparation room to the tea room during the ceremony and placed directly on the *tatami*. He thus disposed of the *daisu*, one of the essential characteristics of the formal tea ceremony. Step by step he continued to make the ceremony less formal, and during the time as Hideyoshi's tea master the completion of his *wabi* ideal progressed rapidly: He eliminated all unnecessary activities in the tea room in order to reduce the art of drinking tea to its essence. While the tea ceremony used to be only part of a banquet and festivity that could last all day, it now received undivided attention and was limited to a maximum of four hours. When a student asked him about the most important rules to follow during a tea ceremony, Rikyû replied:

145

"cha wa fuku no joki jo ni
sumi wa yuno waku jô ni oki
fuyu wa atataka ni natsu wa
sukushiku

hana wa nô no hana yo ni ike

kokugen wa hayamani
furasutomo ame no yôi
eikyaku ni kokoro seiyo."

"Make a satisfying bowl of tea;
Lay the charcoal so that the water
boils efficiently;
Provide a sense of coolness in the
summer and warmth in the winter;
Arrange the flowers as though they
were in the field;
Be ready ahead of time;
Be prepared in case it should rain;
Act with utmost consideration toward
your guests."_H

In the *Shuun'ann-hekisho* ("seven rules of Rikyû") an ethical-moral code is defined in simple words, which made the Way of Tea more than just a leisure activity: The host was required to spend all his energy to create the most pleasant atmosphere possible for the guest. This corresponds to the principle of the *kokoroire*_I, valid since the time of Shukô. Rikyû selected everyday objects, often of rural origin, for use in the tea room with great care, and his choice has remained an esthetic standard to this day. He was the first to design his own tea bowls for use in the tea room and instructed the Korean potter Chojiro to make a new type of tea bowl: As simple pottery, shaped by hand and fired at low temperature, they later became famous and widely used as *raku* ceramics. Rikyû chose red and black as colors for the glaze because they seemed to harmonize best with the green of the tea. Weight and shape as well as the shape of the rim were produced according to his specifications.

144 Black *raku* tea bowl (*shunkan*)
by Chojiro
145 Portrait of Sen no Rikyû

G   Tatsusaburo Hayashiya/
Masao Nakamura/Seizo Hayashiya,
p. 87
H   English website of the Urasenke
tea school: www.urasenke.or.jp/
texte/index.html
I   See chapter "The development
of the *soân* teahouse", p. 123

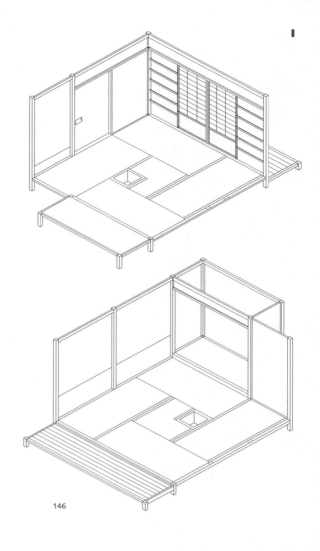

146

147

Like his predecessors, Sen no Rikyû placed the tea room at the center of his esthetic considerations. Starting from the buildings of Shûko, Sôju, and Jôô, he modified the teahouse and introduced a number of new elements. The transformation from his early teahouses, in which many elements of *shoin* architecture can still be found, to the small, undemanding *sôan* hut, will be traced in the following by means of a tea room in Nara and the Taian teahouse, Rikyû's best-known building.

148

THE TEA ROOM IN NARA

The exact date of the construction of the tea room in Nara is not known, but is probably between 1555 and 1572. The teahouse was located in the Shisei-bo, a part of the Tôdai-ji temple. The 4½-mat room followed the general concept and proximity to the *shoin* architecture of the Jôô tea rooms and also had a veranda through which the tea room was entered through translucent sliding doors (*shoji*) – i.e. still in an upright posture. An essential step in the development of the completed *sôan* teahouse was to be the redesign of this entrance area for the guests, whereby the external appearance was also subject to major changes. The transition area of the veranda was removed, heralding a complete break with the *shoin* architecture. In the beginning it was replaced by an inner courtyard surrounded by walls, but finally there was no transitory space between the tea room and the tea garden: The stepping stones led directly to the crawl-in entrance (*nijiriguchi*), which marked a sharp border between the *tatami* of the tea room and the tea garden. The tea room in the Shisei-bo did not have any windows, as was usual in the tea rooms at that time, so that only the *shoji* of the entrance acted as a light source. All wall surfaces of the room were divided by regularly arranged square posts and covered with white paper. However, Rikyû's later teahouses remained uncovered and unrendered, with the result that the rooms looked much darker without the reflections of the white paper. The floor – unlike the *shoin* rooms – no longer had a raised area (*iodan-no-ma*): All guests sat at the same level. Only the elevated *tokonoma* still referred to the place of the guest of honor. The ceiling height was generally lower, and the materials used in the ceiling design were lighter than the finely crafted and richly decorated beams of the coffered ceilings of the large *shoin* rooms. In the tea room in Nara, the ceiling was done horizontally over the entire surface, later design approaches by Rikyû were more differentiated in this aspect.

In further development, Rikyû increasingly detached himself from the requirements of *shoin* architecture and gradually approached his ideal of the *sôan* teahouse. Two buildings, which were associated with Rikyû for a long time, but which according to recent findings do not originate from him, show the design variety of early teahouses in the *wabi* style: The Karakasatei ("umbrella hut") and the Shiguretei ("hut of the fine late autumn rain"), both situated in the temple complex of Kodai-ji in Kyoto and connected by a roofed corridor, are said to have been designed for the Fushimi castle and only later transported to their present location. Supposedly they were situated at a pond and could be entered directly from a boat. The Karakasatei got its name because of its unusual roof shape, which inside resembled an umbrella, while the Shiguretei was the only known two-story teahouse in Japan. The ground floor was equipped with a fireplace where food could be prepared, and the stove on the upper floor also had a special shape: A brick fireplace (*kudo*) was an element still used by Jôô, but soon replaced by the sunken stove (*rô*). In front of the *kudo* a precursor of a sleeve wall (*sode-kabe*) can be seen; the place of the center post (*naka-bashira*) is occupied by a bamboo post.

146 With its general concept and proximity to the *shoin* architecture, the tea room in Nara still followed the example of the Jôô tea rooms and had a veranda through which the tea room was entered through *shoji* sliding doors.
Axonometric projection

147 The Karakasatei teahouse in the Kodai-ji, Kyoto, got its name from its unusual roof shape, which resembled an umbrella stretched out inside.

148 The Shiguretei in the Kodai-ji, Kyoto, was the only known two-story teahouse in Japan. Upper floor view

149

150

Although Sen no Rikyû had built a large number of teahouses, the Taian teahouse in the Myoki-an temple in Yamazaki south of Kyoto is the only one still existing that can be attributed to him with great certainty. This building occupies a special position in the history of the *chanoyu*, as it is considered to be the early highlight of a teahouse in the *wabi* style and the crystallization point of Rikyû's work. The first reduction of a tea room to a size of only two mats – until then these were always at least 4½ mats – and a multitude of architectural innovations make Taian one of the most important buildings in Japanese cultural history, with an enormous impact on the architecture of later buildings. Recent architectural historical findings do not locate the original site in the Myoki-an temple, but in Hideyoshi's Yamazaki fortress.ⱼ However, Hideyoshi moved to the fortress in Osaka without ever using the Taian tea room. As a result, it was dismantled and rebuilt at its present location in the Myoki-an, a practice that was quite common at the time. Various speculations were made about the name "Taian". The word has the meaning of "waiting" in it, so that depending on the interpretation "waiting for the return of Hideyoshi" while he was in Osaka can be considered, or the "hut to expect the moon". This second interpretation is also supported by the fact that the temple building next to the Taian was called Meigetsudô ("hall of the pure moon"). The area of the actual tea room took up only two mats, which corresponded to a floor area of 3.70 square meters, the entire building was no larger than 8.70 square meters. On the west side there was an annex room (*tsugi-no-ma*) in the size of a *tatami*, which was separated from the main room by two "drum" sliding doors (*taiko-busuma*). The *tsugi-no-ma* was extended by a narrow board on the west side. The service room (*mizuya*), also with the surface area of a *tatami*, was connected to the north, and the building was connected to the main temple via this room. The reduction of the room size brought structural problems with it: The constructional elements such as posts, beams and window elements standardized for the 4½-mat room could not simply be adopted for the 2-mat room – they would have looked too clumsy – and could also not be reduced to scale, since a supporting post can only be reduced in diameter up to a certain static limit. This necessitated new elements adapted to the size of the room. Rikyû resorted to posts at whose corners the natural curvature of the trunk was still visible, making them more elegant and fragile. Rikyû liked the mud-blasted walls in the houses of the poorer classes and used this technique for the first time in the Taian teahouse. A layer of clay with straw as a binding agent was applied over the basic structure of the wall, but Rikyû dispensed with the usual covering layer of fine clay. Thus the straw of the rough wall remained visible, giving the walls a rough, rustic-looking structure. In order to achieve a special effect of isolation and introversion, the interior walls were additionally blackened with soot. For the protection of walls and kimonos the lower area was covered with white paper. The wood was also dark colored, but the exact techniques used by Rikyû are unknown. He also covered the interior of the *tokonoma* with clay, thus creating the new element *muro-doko*. He took advantage of the material properties by covering the inner corner posts with clay and rounding off the corners. He applied the same technique to the *rô* in the northwest corner of the host mat, thus achieving an indefinite depth and a visual expansion of space, as the human eye cannot find support in the curves. Access for the guests was via an area protected by a roof overhang on the south side of the building. As an entrance Rikyû created the crawl-in entrance (*nijiriguchi*), probably the first in the history of the teahouse. In front of the teahouse there was a sword shelf (*katana-kake*) on which the guests had to put their weapons, because nobody was allowed to enter the tea room with a sword. While the openings in Rikyû's early teahouses still followed the grid of

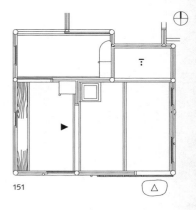

151

149 A multitude of architectural innovations make Taian one of the most important buildings in Japan's cultural history – the only remaining teahouse that Sen no Rikyû can certainly be credited with. Illustration from the *Miyako Rinsen Meisho Zue*
150 The western wall of Taian
151 Taian, floor plan
 ⊤ *Tokonoma*
 ▷ Guest's entrance
 ▶ Host's entrance

ⱼ   Toshinori Nakamura, "Reconstructing the Taian Tearoom", in: *Chanoyu Quarterly*

152

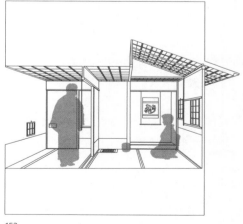

153

the construction, in the Taian windows of different sizes were distributed freely on the wall surfaces and set in such a way that the light came in from behind above the seated guests. Above the *nijiriguchi* there was a large window with bamboo grilles (*renji-mado*) cut into the wall, on the east wall there were two *shoji*-covered *shitaji-mado*, windows created by omitting the clay cover. One of the *shoji* was movable, while the other one was designed as a hanging *shoji* (*kakeshoji*). The extremely slim bars of the *shoji* made of split bamboo and the structure of the *shitaji-mado* overlapped against the light, thus forming an esthetically extremely attractive abstract composition. A vertical bamboo stick reaching up to the ceiling next to the window became the optical focal point of this wall surface. The ceiling was no longer flat throughout. It was kept very low and never measured more than 180 centimeters anywhere. Despite its small surface area, it had several differently structured sub-areas: Two sections were designed as horizontal suspended ceilings made of narrow wooden boards, the third part was the underside of the sloping roof, where the bamboo poles of the construction had been left visible. The ceiling in front of the *toko-noma* marked the seating area of the guest of honor. It was a little higher than the one above the host mat and indicated the special position. The other guests sat under the sloping roof. With these means it was possible to define a finely differentiated spatial hierarchy even in the 2-mat room.

In general, the development of Sen no Rikyû's teahouses shows a process towards a freer handling of the wall surfaces, which were each treated as independent elements and no longer had to follow the general specifications of the construction grid. The window and door openings were freely distributed in the wall surfaces, the rules of the *kiwari jutsu*$_K$, valid for the buildings of the *shoin* architecture, were suspended. However, Rikyû's changes in teahouse design did not exclusively concern design principles; rather, they were accompanied by a qualitative change that had repercussions right to the essence of the *chanoyu*. Through the internalization and spiritualization that accompanied the minimization of space, Rikyû finally detached himself from the formal rules of the *shoin* tea. There was no place for a *daisu* here, nor did the atmosphere of the straw hut allow other tea utensils than those in the spirit of the *wabi* philosophy. With the reduction of the tea room and the associated restriction of freedom of movement, the Zen principle that true freedom can only develop in self-restriction was expressed. A Zen verse speaks of the fact that mighty mountains can find their place in a tiny poppy seed, and this precisely describes the teahouses of Rikyû: The infinite finds space in a limited building. This idea was so convincing that even Japan's most powerful man, Toyotomi Hideyoshi, was impressed: His "Golden Tea Room" was splendid in design, but only three mats in size. And also in his residence in the Osaka castle he had a 2-mat tea room built in the *sôan* style.

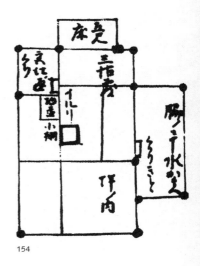

154

152 Rikyû covered the interior of the *tokonoma* in the Taian with clay, creating the new element *muro-doko*.

153 Taian, perspective of the interior

154 A 3¾-mat tea room (*sanjô-daime*) in Osaka ascribed to Rikyû; records of Yamanoue Soji, 1588

K   See chapter "The development of the *sôan* teahouse", p. 123

"The oil in the only lamp is burned,
the white of the flower shimmers slightly.
The water in the kettle dries out and the tea
loses its green color.
The tea hermitage abandoned by the master
seems like a dream of triple enlightenment.
The east wind announces dawn,
and tears flow in vain."

FROM THE *NAMPÔROKU*, ON THE THIRD ANNIVERSARY OF RIKYÛ'S DEATH[A]

THE BEGINNING OF THE DAIMYÔ-CHA

Three disciples of Sen no Rikyû had a decisive influence on the further development of the tea ceremony after his death: Furuta Oribe, Oda Uraku and Hosokawa Sansai came from the class of ruling princes (*daimyô*), and with them the center of the *chanoyu* shifted away from the trading classes of Sakai and Kyoto to the samurai aristocracy in Edo, today's Tokyo. Under the influence of the ruling class, Rikyû's successors adapted the *wabi* tea style as well as the architecture of the teahouse. Their creative approach to the elements of the *sôan* style had an impact not only on the teahouse design, but on the entire Japanese architectural tradition. But already Rikyû foresaw the inherent dangers of the *daimyô* tea style:

"What worries me is that the more tea lovers there are among the people, the more tea masters there will be, who all teach differently, or the sôan *tea hermitage, whose actual meaning is no longer cared for, is used as a* shoin *room in the social contact of* daimyô, *and gourmets and drunkards organize feasts in the* sôan *hermitage and, since they are unable to act according to their spirit and their ideas, the* wabi *tea then becomes repugnant to them."* [B]

Not social pleasure, but spiritual concentration and depth should characterize a tea gathering in the spirit of the *wabi* philosophy. While Rikyû was still philosophically and artistically motivated to turn to design elements of the houses of the poorer classes and attempt to discover humanistic and artistic values in them gradually turned into a pure formalism. Although the outer form of the *wabi* style was still preserved, only the best craftsmen were employed, the most exquisite materials selected, the most artistic techniques used, the most precious teas prepared and served in precious bowls, which finally made the tea ceremony as a whole and the teahouses in particular an extremely expensive affair. This was a paradox of an esthetics that pretended to appreciate the values of poverty. Rikyû's grandson Sen Sôtan commented on this: "It is a great mistake, indeed, to make an ostentious show of *wabi* while inwardly nothing is consonant with. Such people construct a tea-room as far as appearances go with all that is needed for *wabi*; ... they think a life of *wabi* is here. But far from it."[C] With the tea style of the ruling princes and high samurai (*daimyô-cha*) there were drastic changes within the tea ceremony. With Rikyû the tea room was open to all classes without exception; the samurai now claimed the tea ceremony as a leisure activity appropriate to their position for themselves. More and more it became a pleasure reserved for the upper class, and the democratic spirit of the *chanoyu* was lost. The Tokugawa rulers supported this tendency, and the shogunate even began to set certain standards and regulations for the tea ceremony.

155 Portrait of Furuta Oribe;
18th century

A   Quoted from Horst Hennemann
B   Sen no Rikyû in the *Nampôroku*,
quoted from Horst Hennemann,
p. 212
C   Sen Sôshitsu XV, p. 134

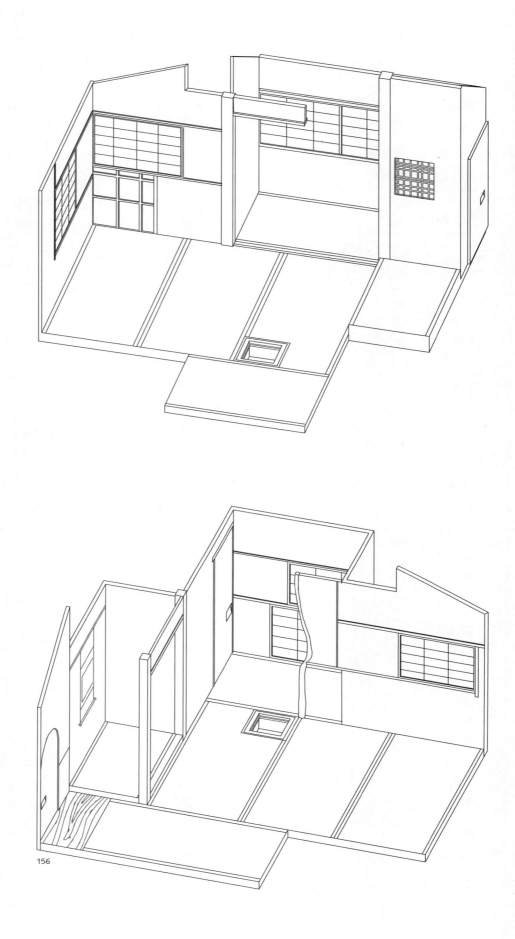

Furuta Oribe (1544–1615) was the first to take a leading role in the tea world after Rikyû's death. He was a powerful *daimyô* from Mino Province who shared Nobunaga's and Hideyoshi's passion for the tea ceremony. Certain sources suggest that he had learned the art of making tea from Rikyû, in any case becoming one of his closest friends in later years.[D] Oribe is considered the founder of the *daimyô-cha*. His fame and closeness to the new rulers opened the gates to the new capital Edo for him. He succeeded in building a bridge between the *wabi* esthetics and the social requirements of the samurai class, and it is thanks to him that a tea cult was able to spread among the elite of the Edo shoguns. In 1605 he launched his career as a tea teacher of Ieyasus' son Tokugawa Hidetada. According to an entry in the *Annals of Suruga* in 1612, Oribe was "[...] the master of tea [*suki*] of these times. Everyone in the shogunate reveres him. All the samurai aspire to learn *chanoyu*, and there are tea functions morning and night."[E] The *daimyô-cha* was the perfect embodiment of the ruling social hierarchy. It was entirely in the spirit of the new rulers and was able to establish itself in connection with the concepts of neo-Confucianism.[F] This ideology seemed perfect for legitimating the Tokugawa state, which assigned each citizen a precisely defined position within society. Despite his success Oribe met the same fate as his teacher Rikyû: 1615 he had to commit suicide (*seppuku*) as an alleged spy. Perhaps it was his free artistic will that was ultimately incompatible with the norms and the orderliness of the ruling sword nobility that sealed Oribe's fate, like that of his mentor.

After his death, Oda Uraku (1547–1621), the younger brother of Oda Nobunaga, assumed the role of leading tea master for a short time – a reputation he owed above all to his creativity in designing teahouses and his extensive collection of famous tea utensils. The third great tea master from the class of the samurai nobility to succeed Rikyû was Hosokawa Sansai (1563–1645). He began to practice tea under Hideyoshi's influence and became one of Sen no Rikyû's favorite disciples. Although Sansai, like Oribe and Uraku, came from a *daimyô* family, he remained much more committed to his teacher's *wabi* spirit and memory than the other two. He only attempted minor changes, and did not break with the style of his teacher neither in the way of making tea (*temae*) nor in the design of his tea rooms. The *Matsuya Hikki* ("The Matsuya family records") notes, that "For this reason, Furuta Oribe prospered, while Hosokawa Sansai, being so close [to Rikyû's practice], could not make a name for himself."[G] In the art of *chanoyu* following Rikyû, Furuta Oribe and Hosokawa Sansai represent the two opposite poles, which also determined the further history of *chanoyu*.

THE EN-AN TEAHOUSE

The En-an teahouse, the most famous building designed by Furuta Oribe, was built on the Yabunouchi family property in Kyoto. It was situated in a corner of the estate, far away from the main buildings, and thus corresponded to the classic type of a free-standing teahouse, which apart from the tea room only contained a service room (*mizuya*) and a small adjoining room. The tea room was a 3¾-mat room (*sanjô-daime*), equipped with the elements characteristic of this tea room type: ¾-mat (*daime*), center post (*naka-bashira*) and sleeve wall (*sode-kabe*). For Oribe, a tea room with 3¾ mats was the ideal size, and teahouses of this format are still called *En-an-keshiki* ("En-an-style teahouses") after the teahouse he designed. This tea room type offered sufficient space for the comfort of the samurai nobility, which is why it quickly received the approval of a large number of tea lovers and was often copied. The host entered the tea room from the *mizuya* through a host entrance (*sadô-guchi*) closed with a "drum" sliding door (*taiko-busuma*), while the guests entered

156 To Oribe, a tea room with 3¾ mats was the ideal size. Teahouses of this format are still called *En-an-keshiki* ("En-an-style teahouses") after the teahouse he designed. Axonometric projection of the interior of the En-an

D   Cf. Shosei Nakamura, "Furuta Oribe and En-an", in: *Chanoyu Quarterly*, p. 10
E   Sen Sôshitsu XV, p. 24 f.
F   The Tokugawa regime promoted neo-Confucianism, for contrary to the Buddhist concept of transience of all being, Confucianism propagated a perfect and stable order in the universe. A strict hierarchical social structure reflected this order.
G   Sen Sôshitsu XV, p. 24

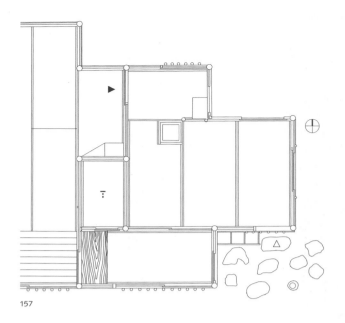

157

158

through the crawl-in entrance (*nijiriguchi*). Opposite the *daime* mat, a double sliding door (*fusuma*) separated the area of a lower seat (*shôbanseki*) from the tea room. This seat in the size of a single *tatami* mat was intended for the companions of the highest guest. With this innovation, Oribe was able to give architectural expression to the social differences in rank and at the same time create a new etiquette in the tea room. The possibility of opening and closing the *fusuma* also gave the tea room the flexibility that characterized the Japanese residential building and which had not yet been realized in tea rooms. Several room constellations could be created in this way, so that, depending on the occasion, more or fewer visitors could be accommodated. Below the *tatami* the floor of the *shôbanseki* was made of cedar wood; if a particularly high guest was invited, the entire *tatami* was removed and the companions had to sit on the wooden floor. A similar measure was also implemented for the waiting bench in the tea garden: Whereas the guests had previously sat on a common, uniformly designed bench, the seating area of the guest of honor was now covered with a *tatami*, while the seat of the companions was made of wood and lay somewhat lower.

The strict social hierarchy of the Tokugawa regime made it necessary for Oribe to clarify and determine the social position of each individual guest during the tea ceremony. He created a separate entrance for the highest guest, so that he no longer had to crawl through the *nijiriguchi*, but could enter the tea room in an upright position. Compared to Rikyû's frugal meals, he served more refined and elaborate meals, and the guests were again allowed to carry their short swords in the tea room, a practice that would have been impossible with Rikyû. Oribe also deviated from the design principle of reducing the floor space to an absolute minimum and criticized the 2-mat rooms and the spatial concept behind them, in which the distance between host and guest was almost abolished: "When a man of high rank is invited to a tea house, there should exist some space distinction between him and the host."[H] A room too small would bring the guest unseemly close to the host, making it impossible to maintain the ruling class barriers. He even mocked his teacher's Taian when he said that the only purpose of such small tea rooms was to torture the guests.[I] Oribe therefore expanded the tea room and provided the host with an additional *daime* mat. The structure of a ¾-mat was already made possible in *wabi* tea style by the disappearance of the shelf (*daisu*), as the host needed less space to prepare tea. Rikyû already used this type of mat in his teahouse designs, but it was only with his successors that this spatial structure matured to such an extent that it eventually became a defining element of teahouse design.

While Rikyû preferred as few openings as possible in his teahouses to emphasize the introverted character of the tea ceremony, Oribe brightened up the dark and austere atmosphere of the *sôan* teahouse. He inserted a larger number of windows, and some of his teahouses like the Hasso-an or the Hasso-no-seki were even named after the number of windows.[J] The En-an had a window arrangement (*shikishi-mado*) on the side of the *tatami* on which the tea was prepared (*temae-tatami*), in which two windows were offset slightly off-center one above the other. Oribe used this type of window repeatedly in his tea room designs, as they were a highly efficient means of enhancing the "stage effect" of the host side. He inserted a calligraphy window (*bokuseki-mado*) into the side wall of the *tokonoma*, which was originally intended to accentuate the picture scroll suspended in the *tokonoma* by means of side light. Oribe reversed the window structure and placed a hanging *shoji* on the outside of the wall, so that the bamboo wickerwork remained visible from the inside. He hung a flower vase on a nail in the wickerwork of the window, creating a

157 En-an, floor plan
158 Due to the strict social hierarchy of the Tokugawa regime, Oribe had to determine the social position of each individual guest. Among other things, he created a separate entrance for the highest guest so that he no longer had to crawl through the *nijiriguchi*.

H   Shosei Namakura, "Furuta Oribe and En-an", in: *Chanoyu Quarterly*, p. 11
I   Teiji Itoh, "Sen Rikyû and Taian", in: *Chanoyu Quarterly*, p. 14
J   *Hasso-an* respectively *Hasso-no-seki* means "eight window hut".

159

160

completely new scenic effect within the room. Until now, the flower vases had stood at the bottom of the *tokonoma* or had been hung on the *tokonoma* post.

If you look at Rikyû, the individual elements, in accordance with their function, served to generate a spatial unity; individual spatial areas were never emphasized. Oribe, on the other hand, planned a spatial composition through the combination of coordinated individual elements. The result was a relaxed spatial tension in which individual parts of the ensemble were given more space to unfold their visual effects.

THE JOAN TEAHOUSE

Oda Uraku cultivated a creative approach to Rikyû's and Oribe's heritage; his tea room designs captivated with a surprising reinterpretation of elements of the *sôan* teahouse, which he also combined with new design elements: A type of window in which vertical bamboo bars standing close to one another are set in the openings was named *Uraku-mado* after its inventor. Joan, his most famous teahouse, – originally built in the Shoden-in sub-temple of Ken-nin-ji, today situated on the grounds of the Shiroyama Villa of the Mitsui family in Kanagawa Prefecture – already attracted a lot of attention at his time due to its many innovations and special style. With a size of only about four by five meters, the teahouse contained nothing more than the tea room, a *mizuya*, and a small anteroom. It was designed as a free-standing structure very close to the house so that it could be easily reached by the host via a short covered veranda. The guests approached the entrance area of the building, which was distinguished by a reorganization of the spatial connections, through the tea garden (*roji*). The gabled hip roof, covered with thin wooden shingles, covered an open anteroom into which the stepping stones of the tea garden led. This area cut out of the building was still part of the *roji*, although it was protected by the roof. The *nijiriguchi* was not located at the front of the building, but was arranged on a side wall; opposite it, a clay wall, into which a circular window was cut by omitting the clay covering (*shitaji-mado*), shielded the area. The tendency towards a re-evaluation of the transition area between teahouse and tea garden was already evident in Oribe's En-an teahouse, where the entrance area was designed similarly to the Joan. But Uraku used this element much more pointedly – a development that culminated in Hosokawa Sansai's buildings.

The interior of the Joan was also exceptional: Although the room was no larger than 3½ mats, a new and unconventional room division led to an unprecedented flowing room quality. A curved trunk sat as *naka-bashira* in the middle of the room and separated a corner area the size of half a mat with a *sode-kabe*. Even the arrangement of this sleeve wall was remarkable: Its narrow side pointed into the room, thus avoiding the usual visual separation of the host mat. Moreover, it was not made of clay, as usual, but of a wooden board from which a semicircle had been cut – a shape that reflected the opening of the guest entrance. From the *tokonoma* a sloping wall led to this entrance, a triangular wooden board covered the floor, creating a gentle transition to the guests' sitting area. With this extremely unusual division, the small room was given the spatial width of a 4½-mat room and an open atmosphere, which was underlined by large window areas and a skylight in the sloping roof. Although Uraku has certainly achieved some of the most interesting spatial structures in the history of the teahouse, its architectural language has not been as influential as that of Furuta Oribe. Despite all innovations he tried to satisfy the spirit of his teacher Sen no Rikyû. The walls, wallpapered with old calendar sheets in the lower part, achieved a very beautiful *wabi* effect, and the ceiling was also kept entirely in the *sôan* style: At the height of the *naka-bashira*, divided into

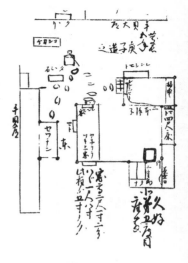

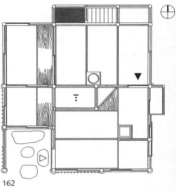

162

159 En-an, interior
160 The tea masters of the *daimyô* class preferred tea rooms with more and larger windows; tea room in the Daitoku-ji, Kyoto
161 Teahouse and tea garden in Oribe style in the house of Matsuya Hisayoshi; *Cha-no-yu Hisho* ("Secrets of the Tea Ceremony"), 1738
162 Joan, floor plan

163

164

163 The gabled roof of the Joan teahouse, covered with thin wooden
shingles, covered an open anteroom
into which the stepping stones of
the tea garden led; this area was
thus protected by the roof and yet
still part of the *roji*.

164 Joan, perspective of the interior

165 Although the tea room in the Joan
was no larger than 3½ mats, a new
and unconventional room division
led to a never-before-seen flowing
room quality.

165

166

two areas, it was horizontal and extremely simple above the host mat and in front of the *tokonoma*, while above the *nijiriguchi* the slope of the roof decorated with bamboo poles remained visible.

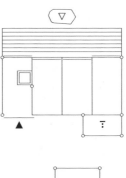

TEAHOUSES OF HOSOKAWA SANSAI

While Oribe and Uraku made modifications to the interior, Hosokawa Sansai's teahouses offered attractive redesigns of the entrance area. Repeatedly, he inserted intermediate elements that softened the hard line between teahouse and garden. Today there is only one building left according to his plans, but the designs of other teahouses that still exist reveal the peculiarities of his style. The drawing of a tea room in a part of the Tôdai-ji temple in Nara, for example, shows a buffer room mediating between the interior and exterior, which was entered through a narrow and low door opening. One arrived in an anteroom, which contained stepping stones and the sword shelf (*katakake*). In this way, Sansai created a kind of "inner roji", a "gray" space similar to the veranda (*engawa*) of the Japanese house, which eluded a clear classification as an interior or exterior space. Only from this room did one climb through a two-part sliding door, also only 120 centimeters high, to the level of the tea room.

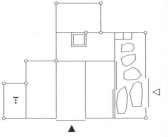

Sansai was able to realize a similar concept in a teahouse in the Shinjoin sub-temple of the Tenryu-ji temple in southern Kyoto: The 4¾-mat room (*yojô-daime*) had an L-shaped floor plan, rather unusual for teahouses, which left an earth-covered corner area the size of two *tatami* mats under a roof overhang. A narrow veranda in this entrance area was also used here as a waiting bench (*koshikake-machiai*), an element that was usually found at a certain point in the tea garden before reaching the teahouse. The roofed ground area intervened as *roji* into the interior of the house. The entrance was equipped with four sliding doors, two of which were made of wood and the other two were translucent *shoji*. By rearranging the sliding elements during the ceremony, different lighting effects could be created. In this way, Sansai also followed the new trend of a freer and more creative lighting in the tea room.

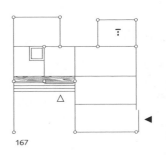

167

Located in the Kôtô-in, a sub-temple of Daitoku-ji, Shôkô-ken is the only surviving tea room of Hosokawa Sansai and one of the few remaining teahouses from the early Edo period. It was built in 1628 in the style of the teahouse that Sansai had built for the Grand Kitano Tea Gathering, and this is also the origin of the name: Shôkô-ken – "opposite the pine" – because the building was located near a famous pine tree. Probably due to the location of the Shôkô-ken in an important Zen temple, Sansai – contrary to his habits – varied the spatial structure of the building much less than his other teahouses. Embedded in the structure of the temple building, the 2¾-mat room (*nijô-daime*) was an example of a classic *sôan* in the sense of Rikyû: Sansai merged three different ceiling levels, one with clay plastered *tokonoma* (*murodoko*), *nijiriguchi*, *katakake* and *shitaji-mado* with the elements *daime* together with *naka-bashira* and *sode-kabe* into a new unit. Small windows and dark walls created an atmosphere of high spatial density without creating the feeling of confinement.

166 The Shonan-tei teahouse in the Saiho-ji, Kyoto, shows the new relationship between interior and exterior space.

167 Teahouses of Hosokawa Sansai: tea room with veranda, teahouse in the Tôdai-ji, teahouse in the Shinjoin

168

169

166

After Oribe's death in 1615, his disciple Kobori Enshu (1579–1647), a high representative of the *daimyô* class, succeeded him as the leading man of the tea world. Enshu was a man of extraordinary talent: Known as a master builder and garden designer and also skilled in other arts, trained in the Daitoku-ji in Zen, he became particularly famous for his design of teahouses and utensils in Enshu style. His ability to inspect tea utensils was also highly regarded, and he lent many precious pieces poetic names borrowed from Japan's classical literature. His definition of the tea ceremony referred to the values of neo-Confucianism typical of the samurai class of the Tokugawa period: "The way of tea ... contains nothing very new, consisting simply of loyalty and filial piety, the diligent execution of the business of each household, and above all the need to insure that old friendships do not die."[K] Enshu's esthetic criteria of *chanoyu* were deeply rooted in the esthetics of the imperial house that had developed during the Heian period. It was exactly the kind of taste that appealed to the representatives of the Tokugawa regime and the military elite, which became more powerful: an atmosphere of alleged poverty, which, however, left enough room for splendor and was sophisticated enough for the demands of the rich *daimyô*. This combination of decorative beauty and restrained simplicity (*kirei-sabi*), which led to a seamless fusion of Rikyû's spiritual austerity with Oribe's imaginative innovations, remains one of the foundations of Japanese esthetics today. The reduced space for decorations in the *sôan*-style teahouses to the *tokonoma* contradicted the *daimyô's* need to present their wealth and their possessions of valuable utensils. Enshu responded by modifying the tea ceremony: Before or after the *chanoyu*, people met for a banquet in a separate room, which, like the former tea preparation room in the reception buildings (*kaisho*), was known as the chain room (*kusari-no-ma*), but which was now furnished and richly decorated in the style of *shoin* architecture in keeping with its role as a reception room.

The formal expressions of Enshu's teahouse designs show his esthetic preference for the *shoin* style. Circumferential horizontal hinges, walls covered with printed paper, sliding doors with black lacquered frames, decorated shelves, writing niches (*tsuke-shoin*) and blinds (*ranma*) with carvings above the doors were combined with *daime*, *naka-bashira* and *sode-kabe*. Enshu thus created a connection between the elements of the *sôan* teahouse and the decorative side of the *shoin* architecture, which, next to the recognition of the *daimyô*, brought him contempt of Rikyû's followers. Suzuki Masamichi, publisher of *Chajin Keifu* ("Genealogy of the Tea Men") made mockery of his style: "Collecting old utensils, he loads the shelves with them" and "It looks as though he had set up a shop for selling Chinese goods."[L] Using a variety of windows, he followed Oribe and Uraku, but allowed himself a more vivid distribution than his predecessors. A characteristic feature of his tea rooms was a window constellation in which a *shitaji-mado* was arranged above the *nijiriguchi* above a window with a vertical bamboo grid (*renji-mado*). Although the *nijiriguchi* continued to serve as entrance, some of his tea rooms could be entered by aristocrats through sliding doors on a veranda, which saved them not only the bowed posture, but also the path in the sandals through the garden. In his quest to transform the *chanoyu* into a "show" – both in terms of the presentation of the utensils and the stage-like performance – the ideal of the *daimyô-cha* can be seen. His most famous tea rooms Mittan and Bosen were built in sub-temples of the Daitoku-ji Zen temple in Kyoto. The Mittan tea room is embedded in the structures of the temple buildings of the Ryoko-in and named after Mittan Kanketsu[M], a Chinese Zen priest of the Sung Dynasty. Allegedly the tea room was built to house a particularly beautiful calligraphy of this monk, which was brought to Japan and mounted by Sen no Rikyû on a picture scroll. The room is built in the style of the early Edo period

168 The Shôkô-ken in the Koto-in, Kyoto, is the only preserved teahouse of Hosokawa Sansai.
169 Portrait of Kobori Enshu; attributed to Kano Tan'yu; 17th century

K   Tatsusaburo Hayashiya/ Masao Nakamura/Seizo Hayashiya, p. 91
L   Tatsusaburo Hayashiya/ Masao Nakamura/Seizo Hayashiya, p. 112
M   The Chinese name of the priest was An Hsien Chieh.

and is an example of Enshu's design philosophy of furnishing tea rooms with elements of the *shoin* style. The 4½-plus-*daime* room featured a *tokonoma* in the north, a shelf at right angles to it (*chigaidana*) and the crossbeam (*nageshi*), all the typical design elements of *shoin* architecture. Originally, the room might also have had a *tsuke-shoin* next to the host mat. In the course of a reconstruction, however, the window cut into the rear wall was closed, so that today the niche has the function of a second *tokonoma*. Also the paintings of the famous artist Kano Tanyu on *fusuma* and walls represented a clear departure from Rikyû's strict *wabi* esthetics. But despite the clear orientation towards *shoin* architecture, Enshu incorporated many elements of the *sôan* style. The ceiling, for example, was quite simply made of plain boards, and the bark was left at the corners of some posts, features that are usually associated with teahouses in grass hut style. It was particularly noticeable in the area of tea preparation: The *daime* mat with lowered top, a simple shelf suspended from the ceiling by a bamboo pole, a *naka-bashira* with bark left on the trunk and a *sode-kabe* made of a wooden board with a strong grain still reflected Rikyû's philosophy and ensured that the simultaneous use of *sôan* and *shoin*-style elements could develop a completely new sense of space. The fusion of the two styles was so perfect that it was hardly possible to tell where one style ended and the other began.

The Bosen-seki, a large 12-mat room built in 1608 in the Koho-an, was also equipped with architectural features of the *shoin* style. The *nageshi* ran across all wall surfaces, the posts were square and sharp-edged in cross section, the walls were covered with paper and painted, and only the simple surface of the sanded ceiling of Cryptomeria wood was a break from the austerity of a typical *shoin* room. The Bosen tea room, destroyed by fire in the middle of the Edo period and rebuilt by Matsudaira Fumai$_N$, became famous in particular for its reinterpretation of the entrance area: a veranda extended between the narrow *roji* and the tea room, which was separated from the tea garden by *shoji* elements suspended from the roof overhang. The *shoji* did not reach to the floor of the veranda, but formed a crevice about one meter high, through which one could slip from the last stepping stone to the veranda. Formally solved completely differently, this arrangement fulfilled the same task as a *nijiriguchi*: Every visitor was forced to adopt a humble attitude before taking part in a tea ceremony. Next to the veranda stood a stone washbasin set far down, and this could also only be used in a low bowed posture. From the veranda one could enter the tea room through the *shoji* in an upright position. When these doors were open, the tea garden was perceived from the tea room as a picture framed by the hanging *shoji*.

Although the Bosen tea room had discarded most of the *sôan* elements, including the *daime* mat, Enshu continued to use grass hut design concepts: Stepping stones, water basins, and *nijiriguchi* were ingeniously incorporated into the *shoin* style and reinterpreted. It was not least Enshu himself who admitted that he owed most of his success to Sen no Rikyû.

170

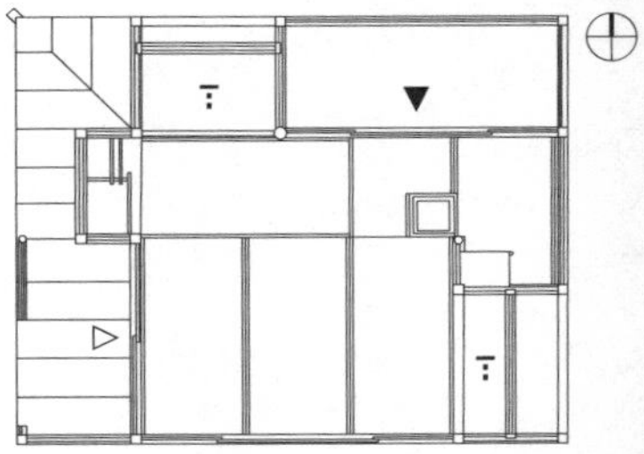

171

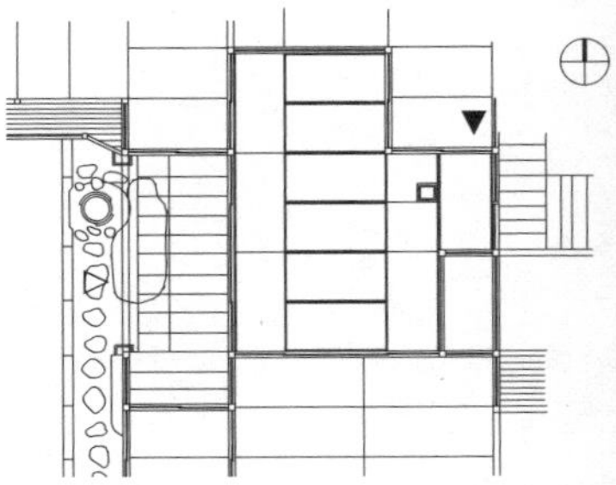

172

170 Mittan, interior
171 Mittan, floor plan
172 Bosen, floor plan

N   For the person of Fumai see chapter "The influence of the bourgeoisie and the Meiji Restoration", p. 193.

174

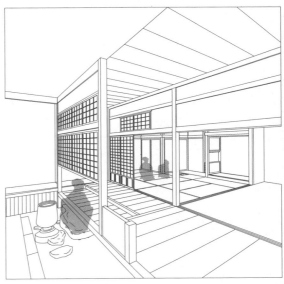

175

173 Bosen was particularly known for its
reinterpretation of the access area:
Between the narrow *roji* and the tea
room there was a veranda that was
separated from the tea garden by
shoji elements suspended from the
roof overhang. These formed a crevice
about one meter high, through which
one could slip from the last stepping
stone to the veranda.

174 Bosen, interior

175 Bosen, perspective of the veranda

176

177

SUKIYA ARCHITECTURE
AND THE RETURN OF THE WABI

"Chanoyu to wa   "Tea is to teach the ears,
mimi ni tsutaete   eyes and the heart
me ni tsutae
kokoro ni tsutau   without even writing
hitofude mo nashi."   a word."
SEN NO SÔTAN~A~

178

THE SUKIYA STYLE

The Japanese feudal society under Tokugawa rule was subject to strict regulations. Even in the Heian period, special architectural elements had been reserved for certain social classes, but the regulations of the Tokugawa shogunate
eventually went so far as to dictate every detail of architecture, and ultimately
led to a complete ossification in construction. Especially in the official residences
of the samurai and *daimyô* there were no possibilities to use new techniques
and stylistic means, since everything was the object of strict architectural conventions.

However, at the same time there was great interest in the tea ceremony,
and the individual touch of the teahouse buildings was highly appreciated.
Teahouse architecture was thus given the freedom to evade these regulations
and to place esthetic considerations above social status and ideology. Based on
the architecture of the teahouse, a new architectural style could develop, which
was the direct expression of these freedoms and was named after the teahouse:
Since from the second half of the Muromachi period *suki* ("exquisite taste")
was used as a synonym for the tea ceremony, the term "room for *suki*" (*sukiya*)
became customary for the teahouses and rooms in the residences of the *daimyô*.
The *sukiya* style, inspired by this, refers to buildings erected with the architectural elements of the teahouse: Naturalness, asymmetry, a free spatial arrangement and an airy and elegant atmosphere characterized this architectural style.
However, the *sukiya* style could only gain a foothold where status symbols did
not play a role for the time being. In addition to private villas, these were mainly
semi-public facilities used for entertainment: Tea shops, elegant restaurants or
houses where geishas entertained their customers were places where men of
wealth and high social rank could escape the burden of daily life and the formalities of their official residences. In this way, these semi-public buildings became
the model for the houses of ordinary city dwellers.

THE TEA OF COURTLY SOCIETY

The court aristocracy was skeptical about the *chanoyu* for a long time, as
it was inseparably connected with the rise of the samurai class and the middle
classes. In contrast to other arts such as poetry or calligraphy, the representatives of the nobility were not involved in the development of the tea ceremony.
Until Toyotomi Hideyoshi organized a tea ceremony for the emperor and his
family in the emperor's palace, for which he prepared the tea himself,~B~ led to
gradual interest. Individual members of the imperial family became interested
in the tea ceremony, and in the first half of the 17th century *chanoyu* already
enjoyed great popularity at court. The aristocratic tea style was less oriented on
the *daimyô-cha* than to courtly norms of behavior and was strongly influenced
by the *shoin* tea of the Higashiyama tradition.~C~ The buildings of the imperial
palaces Shûgakuin and Katsura Rikyû, which both had rooms for the tea ceremony and were influenced in their entire appearance by the style of the
teahouse architecture, were an immediate expression of this renaissance of

176 The natural nature and elegance of
sukiya architecture: Villa Katsura in
southern Kyoto is not only regarded
as the culmination of *sukiya* style,
but also as the epitome of Japanese
architecture in general.
177 Villa Katsura, views of the Shôkintei
pavilion
178 Villa Katsura, detail of the Old
shoin Palace

A   Quoted from Horst Hennemann, p. 198
B   This was Hideyoshi's proof
of gratitude to the emperor for
the award of the shogunate title.
C   See chapter "The development
of the *soân* teahouse", p. 131

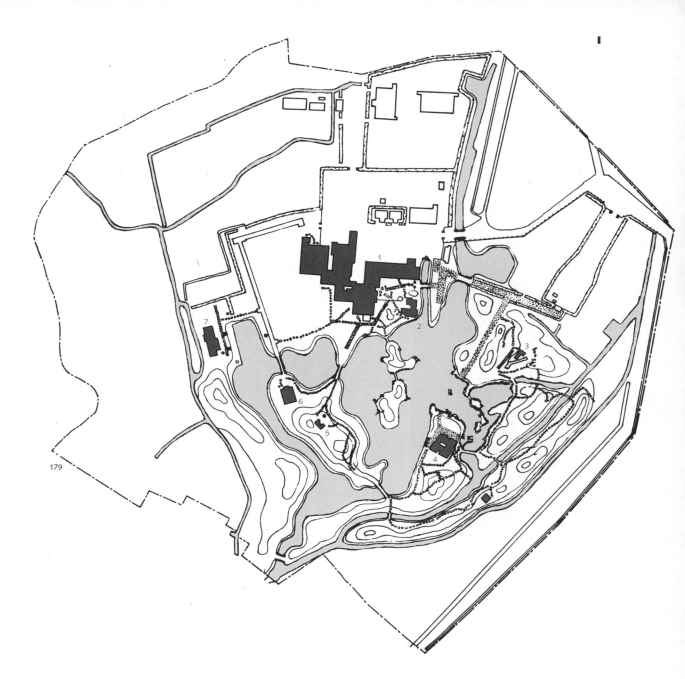

179

180

a courtly tea culture. The nobility were attracted to the grass-covered *sôan* houses, but at the same time let the refinement of their lifestyle flow into the design of the buildings. The filigree elaboration of details, the artistic design of the paper covering on walls and sliding doors (*fusuma*), the use of decorative shelves even in small rooms with ¾-mat arrangements (*daime*) and the laying out of verandas with *tatami* mats gave the buildings a touch of noblesse and restrained elegance despite the appearance of a rustic hut.

VILLA KATSURA

The imperial Villa Katsura is not only the culmination of the *sukiya* style but also the epitome of Japanese architecture. The integration of the buildings into nature, the modular order of the buildings, the orthogonal design of the structural elements, and the strong limitation of any decoration are evidence of perfect mastery of materials and forms. The palace complex is located in the southwest of Kyoto, close to the banks of the Katsura River, which gave the complex its name. The construction of the palace began in 1620 on the orders of Prince Hachijônomiya Toshihito (1579–1629), and in the year of his death the basic structure of the garden and the building had already been determined. From 1642 his son Prince Noritada (1619–1662) dedicated himself to the completion of the project. Whether the high-quality designs of the garden and the buildings came exclusively from Toshihito and Noritada, or whether they can be ascribed to Kobori Enshu[D], as is often assumed, remains unclear to this day. What is certain is that the design of Katsura Rikyû was strongly influenced by Enshu's work. The total area of the villa is not particularly large: The heart of the complex is a pond around which the residential buildings and the various tea and amusement pavilions are grouped in a loose arrangement. The garden, equipped with stone lanterns (*ishi-dôrô*), stone washbasins (*tsukubai*), and a waiting bench (*koshikake-machiai*), is designed like a tea garden (*roji*), and despite its small size, one gets many different impressions when walking through the skilful and varied design. The architectural structures do not follow a uniform style or pattern, but what they have in common is the fusion of every single element of the architecture with the surrounding landscape. In the flexible, often diagonally staggered arrangement of the individual rooms – the "flight formation of the wild geese" –, the use of natural materials and the elaboration of details, the buildings of Katsura Rikyû feature all aspects of the *sukiya* style. In addition to the main buildings of the "old, middle and new *shoin* palace", several pavilions are distributed in the garden: Gepparô ("tower of moonlit waves"), Shôiken ("hut of smiling thoughts"), Shôkatei ("pavilion of admired flowers"), Erindô ("hall of garden groves") and Shôkintei ("pavilion of sounds in the pines") are all made of simple materials. Posts and beams are often used in their natural form together with the bark and, similar to the thatched roofs and unrendered clay walls, they express the philosophy of the tea ceremony. The largest and most lavishly designed pavilion, Shôkintei, was specially designed for a summer stay: Oriented towards the north, located near the pond, shaded by nearby trees and with a wide roof overhang, it was designed to make the heat and sultriness of the summers in Kyoto bearable. The different rooms are grouped around a small inner courtyard, and there was also a classic tea room in the building. From the main room (*ichi-no-ma*) one has a wonderful view of the pond and the garden, which is why the Shôkintei was used as a pavilion for aristocratic pleasures like moon observations or poetry competitions. Built in the style of a thatched farmhouse (*minka*), the interior is surprisingly exquisitely designed. The strict *shoin* design is given a completely new face in combination with the natural materials. In the *ichi-no-ma*, for example, hemp stalks are set in blinds above a door next to a paper-covered niche (*tokonoma*) printed with a blue and white checkered pattern, and in the

179 Villa Katsura, general plan
  1 *Shoin* palace
  2 Gepparô
  3 Waiting bench
    (*koshikake-machiai*)
  4 Shôkintei
  5 Shôkatei
  6 Enrindô
  7 Shôiken
180 The staggered arrangement of the *shoin* buildings in Villa Katsura was also known as the "flight formation of wild geese".

D   See chapter "The *daimyô* tea after Rikyû", p. 167

181

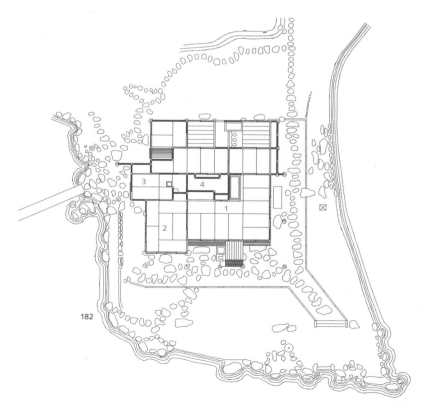

182

second room (*ni-no-ma*) rough *shitaji-mado* windows form a strong contrast to the rest of the formal design. The *ni-no-ma* is connected to the tea room, which is named after the number of its windows "eight window tea room" (*yatsumado-kakoi*). Measuring 3¾ mats (*sanjô-daime*) it is designed entirely according to the principles of the *sôan* teahouses: A canopy over an area of crushed clay protects the entrance to the tea room, which consisted of a crawl-in entrance (*nijiriguchi*) before which the swords were laid down. *Shitaji-mado*, different ceiling levels and a center post (*naka-bashira*) are used in classical *sôan* style. A window (*bokuseki-mado*) is cut into the side wall of the *tokonoma*, which is covered with a *shoji* on the inside. A skylight is arranged in the sloping roof above the already well-lit *daime* of the host mat, a circumstance which, like many other details – such as the placement of two windows above the *nijiriguchi* –, suggests Kobori Enshu's authorship, or at least reveals his strong influence.

The unification of two life philosophies of the nobility within one building – the preference for lively entertainment and the search for spiritual enlightenment – led to a dual spatial concept in the Shôkintei: The large room with a veranda in front and an unobstructed view of the garden accommodated the elegant lifestyle of the nobility, at the other end the quiet, inwardly facing tea room was used for contemplation during the tea ceremony.

181 Shôkintei was the largest and most lavishly designed pavilion and specially designed for use on sultry summer days.
182 Shôkintei, floor plan
  1 Main room *(ichi-no-ma)*
  2 Second room *(ni-no-ma)*
  3 Tea room
  4 Courtyard

183 Yatsumado-kakoi tea room in the Shôkintei, view of the *daime* mat

183

184

185

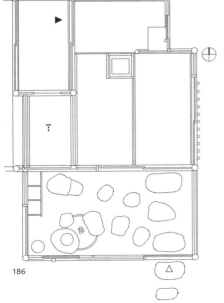

186

184 Main gate of Daitoku-ji, Kyoto:
In Sôwas time Daitoku-ji was the
spiritual center of the tea world.
The tombs of Sen no Rikyû and
Murata Shûko are located in its
sub-temples.

185 The way to the Teigyokuken
teahouse in the Shinjuan, Kyoto

186 Teigyokuken, floor plan

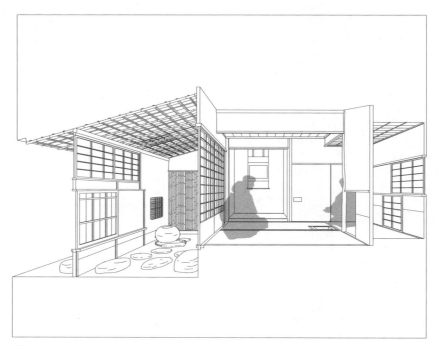

187

188

While Kobori Enshu was the tea master of the shoguns and samurai, his contemporary Kanamori Sôwa (1584–1656) played the same role in courtly society. His grandfather had been a tea disciple of Rikyû, and his father learned the tea ceremony from Rikyû's son Dôan. Sôwa was first instructed by both in the art of tea, before he got to know the *daimyô-cha* in the style of Enshu, from whom he adopted the esthetic ideal of the *kirei-sabi*ₑ. He maintained close contact with members of the imperial house and became the leading tea master at the court, where he created his own tea style – the "tea of the palaces" (*dôjôcha*). *Dôjôcha* was characterized by a special esthetic sensitivity and refinement, which suited the lifestyle of his students and earned him the nickname "princess" (*hime*). His most famous tea room is the Teigyokuken ("jewel of the garden") in the Shinjuan sub-temple of the Daitoku-ji in Kyoto. At that time Daitoku-ji was undoubtedly the spiritual center of the tea world. The tomb of Sen no Rikyû is located in one of its sub-temples as well as that of Murata Shûko. In the Shinjuan temple the memory of the great monk Ikkyû was upheld.ₑ One can imagine the challenge a building site like this posed for a tea master of the level of Sôwa; moreover, the wood for the building came from the imperial palace in Kyoto: It was donated to the temple by the emperor in the course of a reconstruction. The tea room was directly attached to the temple and could be entered by the host directly from the main building. Due to the limited space available on the temple site, the *roji* was no more than a narrow garden strip running alongside the temple building. Nevertheless, even in this minimalist tea garden, all the characteristic elements were present. The teahouse had a rather cramped and tense atmosphere, contrary to Sôwa's custom, a fact that can certainly be explained by its location on the grounds of a Zen temple. The tea room itself is a small 2¾-mat room (*nijô-daime*), whose spatial narrowness was underlined by diffuse lighting through low north windows. Sôwa, however, extended the interior by adding an earth-covered vestibule before the tea room. He thus made use of a spatial concept that Hosokawa Sansai had already implemented in his tea room in Tôdai-ji.ₑ In contrast to Sansai's tea room, however, the buffer zone of the outer area in the Teigyokuken was entered by a *nijiriguchi*, a sign that the transition area was already to be understood as part of the interior. The fact that this area nevertheless included elements of the *roji* such as stepping stones, sword shelf and the *tsukubai* can possibly be explained by Sôwa's longer stay in the north of Japan. The placement of the *tsukubai* inside the building certainly offered advantages during the harsh winters there.

Even within this narrow framework, Sôwa tried to implement a concept in which the anteroom and the actual tea room formed a continuum, because in his opinion no tea room should have a restrictive effect. His efforts to create a certain level of comfort also explain the high esteem in which he was held among members of the nobility.

THE RESTORATION OF THE SEN FAMILY

After Rikyû's suicide, the Sen family's entire family fortune was confiscated, and his two sons Shôan and Dôan were forced to leave Kyoto. It was not until a few years later that the shogun gave the Sen family permission to return so that Shôan and his son Sen Sôtan could settle again in Kyoto. Despite the pre-dominance of *daimyô* tea, they sought to revive Rikyû's style of tea ceremony, which had been displaced by Enshu's tea style. Rikyû's second son, Sen Shôan, laid the foundation stone for the Sen family's new rise with the construction of a tea room on a plot of land in front of the Hompo-ji temple in Kyoto. He immediately followed his father's legacy by erecting the Zangetsutei ("pavilion

187 Sôwa expanded the interior of the Teigyokuken by placing an earth-covered anteroom in front of the 2¾-mat tea room. Perspective of anterior area and interior

188 The anteroom of the Teigyokuken tea room was entered through a *nijiriguchi*.

E   Combination of decorative beauty and restrained simplicity, see chapter "The *daimyô* tea after Rikyû", p. 167
F   See chapter "The development of the *sôan* teahouse", p.135
G   See chapter "The *daimyô* tea after Rikyû", p. 165

189

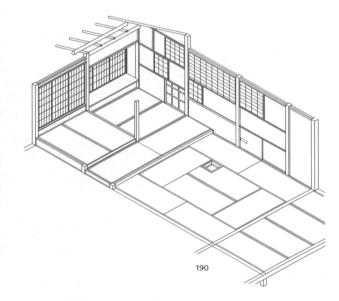

190

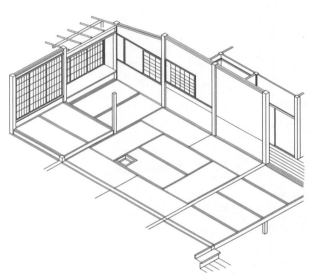

of the decreasing moon") as a reproduction of the "Colored Shoin", a tea room from Rikyû's Juraku-dai residence.ₕ While Rikyû's room was still 18 mats in size and his floor space was staggered on three different levels, Shôan reduced the Zangetsutei to twelve *tatami*, which he arranged on one level. Only a raised corner area in the size of two *tatami* remained, which, however, did not serve as a seat for the highest guest, but marked the place of the *tokonoma*. Otherwise the large, bright room with its extensive windows and a niche (*tsuke-shoin*) completely follows its model. In front of the *tsuke-shoin* the ceiling was inclined and revealed the bamboo trunks of the roof construction. The entrance was formed by two pairs of *fusuma*, which, like the paper of the wall surfaces, were printed with a Paulownia₁ pattern, a reference to shogun Hideyoshi, who was probably a frequent guest of Rikyû in the "Colored Shoin" and whose coat of arms was the leaf of the Pauwlownia. Although the room had all the attributes of a *shoin* structure, it still differed greatly from the classic style of samurai houses: The thresholds of the raised area (*iodan-no-ma*) were made of polished Japanese cedar in its natural form, freed from the bark but not sawn, the corner posts were square, but the corners were only rough trimmed to obtain an octagonal shape, while the ceiling, unlike in *shoin* rooms, was not coffered, but designed with wide boards like a simple home. The Zangetsutei was destroyed in a fire, but a 19th-century reconstruction still exists on the grounds of the Omotesenke tea school in Kyoto.

SEN NO SÔTAN

Sen no Sôtan (1578–1658) studied Zen in the Daitoku-ji on his return to Kyoto and tried to bring the tea ritual back into line with the principles of his grandfather Rikyû's Zen and *wabi* philosophy. Although the tea ceremony prospered in his time as a leisure activity for the feudal lords and a large number of tea masters found employment this way, Sôtan's life was marked by poverty and simplicity, which earned him the nickname "beggar" (*kojiki*). Despite the many offers he received for his excellent reputation, he never worked for the feudal aristocracy, perhaps to escape the entanglements of power his grandfather had fallen victim to. In the *Chawa Shigetsu Shû*, a contemporary chronicle, his tea style is described as follows:

"There is a man called Sotan whose grandfather is Rikyu. He never searches for fame and wealth, and lives a simple life. Now he is in his seventies. Sometimes on a snowy morning or a moonlit night when he is in the mood, he spends his days meditating. If someone comes to beg him to teach his way, he answers there is no way to teach because his life depends on Zen." ⱼ

191

189 Rikyû's second son, Sen Shôan, reproduced with the construction of the Zangetsutei in the Hompo-ji, Kyoto, the "Colored Shoin" which Rikyû had built in the Juraku-dai residence. Reconstruction of the Zangetsutei, Omotesenke tea school, Kyoto
190 Axonometries of the "Colored Shoin" (left) and of the Zangetsutei (right)
191 Portrait of Sen no Sôtan

H   The name "Colored Shoin" is due to the fact that all wooden parts inside were painted with a mixture of *sumi* ink and iron oxide.
I   Ornamental tree
J   Kaisen Iguchi, "Sen Sôtan and Yûin", in: *Chanoyu Quarterly*, p. 10

192

Like his tea style, Sôtan's architectural concept was dominated by Sen no Rikyû, and his tea rooms breathed the spirit of renewal of the *wabi* philosophy. He continued the intentions of his grandfather when he resumed Rikyû's concept of a 1½-mat tea room in 1615 with the construction of Fushin-an ("uncomplicated hut") on today's site of the Omotesenke school. Although it was mockingly said about this room that it would be doubtful whether there would be room for someone other than Rikyû himself, Sôtan took the *wabi* approach of simplification even further: In addition to the minimum room size, he used a *tokonoma* plastered on all sides with clay (*murodoko*) similar to the one in Taian, but additionally he even made the *tokonoma* floor, usually covered with *tatami*, from clay. Sôtan's son Kôshin later changed the room with his father's consent and expanded it into a *sanjô-daime* room, in which form the room still exists today.

With his retirement from active tea life, Sen Sôtan designed his three most important tea rooms: Kon'nichian, Kanuntei and Yûin. The Kon'nichian ("hut of this day") is the ultimate embodiment of the *wabi* spirit of Sôtan, the end of a long process in which he reduced his tea rooms to the essential until he even eliminated the *tokonoma*. Today the teahouse is located on the premises of the Urasenke tea school in Kyoto, on the south side of the complex. The construction of the building is very simple: Four round supports in the corners of the tea room support a simple pent roof projecting over the entrance area. The underside of the roof construction is visible inside and the ceiling has a uniform design over the entire surface. The Kon'nichian is a 2-mat tea room, in which, however, only an area the size of 1-plus-*daime* mats is laid out with *tatami*, the remaining area, which is separated from the rest of the room by a sleeve wall reaching to the floor (*sode-kabe*), is covered by a wooden board. Next to this the *nijiriguchi* is arranged. The room has no *tokonoma*, so that the scrolls are simply hung on the wall next to the host's entrance and the flower vase is placed directly on the wooden board without the usual base board (*usuita*). Instead of a service room (*mizuya*), the room has a utensil cupboard on the host side, an element that was already found in the early teahouses of Rikyû. *Renji-* and *shitaji-mado* are cut into three wall surfaces, so that the spatial narrowness is somewhat loosened despite the small size.

After the completion of the Kon'nichian, Sôtan continued to work for the family business before finally withdrawing from all secular concerns. At this point he built another teahouse and called it Yûin – "second retreat". The defining feature of the exterior was its imposing rush-covered roof, which gave the building a tremendous plasticity. The interior followed exactly the model of a 4½-mat room in Rikyû's Juraku-dai residence and showed a classic tea room with a *tokonoma* in the north and the *nijiriguchi* in the south. Above the *nijiriguchi* the ceiling was inclined and a skylight cut in, the rest of the room had a horizontal ceiling only 1.80 meters high. Apart from the skylight, there were only two other windows, a *shitaji-mado* each arranged above the *nijiriguchi* and on the wall of the guest side.

192 Fushin-an, Omotesenke tea school, Kyoto; view towards *daime* mat

κ   1 *shaku* = 1.81813 meters

After Kon'nichian and Yûin as teahouses in the *wabi* style were not suitable to fulfill the new demands of the aristocracy, Sôtan additionally built the Kanuntei tea room ("pergola of the cool cloud") in order to be able to receive members of the nobility. The 8-mat *shoin*-style room had a *tsuke-shoin* and a six *shaku*κ wide *tokonoma*. The famous painter Kano Tan'yu decorated the six *fusuma* of the main room with depictions of Chinese sorcerers. Although it was basically a *shoin* room, Sôtan also used techniques here that corresponded to

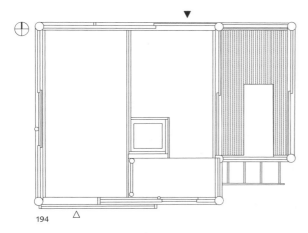

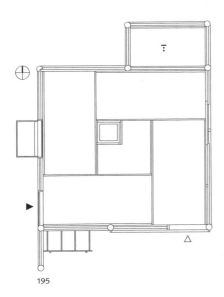

193 In the absence of a *tokonoma*, the scroll is hung on the wall of the entrance of the host. Kon'nichian, Urasenke tea school, Kyoto

194 Kon'nichian, floor plan

195 Yûin, Urasenke tea school, Kyoto, floor plan

196 The defining exterior feature of the Yûin was an imposing rush-covered roof, which gave the building a tremendous plasticity.

196

197

198

his *wabi* mentality. The ceiling was divided into several areas according to the model of small tea rooms, and the arrangement of the sunken stove (*rô*) corresponded to the use in smaller rooms.

UKIYA ARCHITECTURE
AND THE RETURN OF THE WABI

The fascination of the dense spatial tension that characterized Rikyû's tea rooms was also found in Sôtan. With the minimalist spaces of Fushin-an and Kon'nichian, he finally underlined his role as an advocate of his grandfather's tradition. The Yûin tea room was also intended as a model for a myriad of tea rooms from the Edo period, as it best represented the classic Sen no Rikyû-style 4½-mat room.

Sôtan divided the family property – the front (*omote*) and rear (*ura*) half of the property on Ogawa Street and a narrow plot of land on Mushanokôji Street – among his sons, who became the founders of the three most important tea schools to this day: Mushanokôjisenke, Omotesenke and Urasenke, named after the location of the possessions. Over the centuries, the three plots of land have undergone various extensions by the respective tea masters (*iemoto*), so that today a whole complex of nested teahouses, rooms and gardens exists mainly on the plots of land of Urasenke and Omotesenke. The sons of Sôtan saw themselves as custodians of Rikyû's heritage because of their ancestry, a role that was contested by various sides, including the four famous students of Sôtan (*shitenno*): Fujimura Yoken, Sugiki Fusai, Yamada Sohen and Miyake Boyo not only continued the style of their teacher, but also achieved remarkable successes themselves in the design of their teahouses and gardens, in their literary works and other creative activities. Like Sôtan's sons, they actively sought to spread the *wabi* esthetics in influential circles, as the country lived in an era of relative peace, and *daimyô* and rich merchants showed renewed interest in the tea ceremony, Nô theater, and other traditional arts.

197 Yûin was a classic 4½-mat tea room with *tokonoma* in the north and *nijiriguchi* in the south.
198 Sôtan built the Kanuntei tea room in order to welcome members of the nobility. The 8-mat *shoin*-style room had a *tsuke-shoin* and a six *shaku* wide *tokonoma*. Kanuntei, Urasenke tea school, Kyoto

91

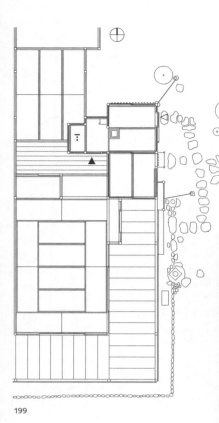

199

200

THE INFLUENCE OF THE BOURGEOISIE
AND THE MEIJI RESTORATION

"[...] and a few of the other usual movements [during a tea ceremony] are certainly grotesquely formal enough; but I question whether the etiquette of a ceremonious dinner-party at home, with the decorum observed in the proper use of each utensil, does not strike a Japanese as equally odd and incomprehensible when experienced by him for the first time."[A]

201

KATAGIRI SEKISHU AND HON'AMI KOETSU

The names of Katagiri Sekishu and Hon'ami Koetsu, two tea masters with high prestige in the tea world, stand for the spread of *chanoyu* in the bourgeois class. Sekishu (1605–1673) studied tea under Rikyû's son Dôan, and like many tea masters before him he practiced Zen at the Daitoku-ji. Although he followed Enshu and the *daimyô-cha*, his style was influenced by Rikyû's *wabi* philosophy as well as by the elegance of courtly culture. Although his tea style had neither Rikyû's religious austerity nor Enshu's artistic significance, it was precisely this synthesis of different contemporary tendencies that laid the foundation for a *chanoyu* that was not reserved solely for the upper classes, but could also be perceived and practiced by the merchant class. In his most important building, the Jikoin temple in Koizumi near Nara, which he founded in 1663 as a memorial temple for his parents, he was able to implement his esthetic ideas of a *wabi* esthetics that was as natural and restrained as possible. Situated on a hill at the edge of the Yamato plain, the *shoin*-style main room offered an overwhelming view of the landscape around Nara, which today is severely impaired by urban sprawl and industrial buildings. From the *shoin* reception room a corridor led to the Korin-an tea room, in between there was a 2-mat room, which was separated from the main room by two sliding doors (*fusuma*). If these are removed, the small 2¾-tea room (*nijô-daime*) can be enlarged to 4-plus-*daime* mats. Two *shoji* window bands along the guest mats create a bright area that strongly contrasts with the dark host side, which is separated by the center post (*naka-bashira*) and the sleeve wall (*sode-kabe*). While the representatives of the *daimyô-cha* were keen to move the place of the host as far as possible into the center of the tea room, Sekishu remembered the roots of Rikyû, who placed the host mat in a subordinate position. The niche (*tokonoma*) was arranged next to the host mat and radiated a calm simplicity with its plastered inner corners, the post (*toko-bashira*) and the lower *tokonoma* frame (*toko-gamachi*) made of cedar wood, as well as the *naka-bashira*, a cedar trunk where the bark was left on the trunk. The view revealed a dual design concept that revealed Sekishu's various influences: While the *shoin* wing on one side was regularly and generously structured, the small, asymmetrical yet balanced order of the teahouse style was attached to it.

Hon'ami Koetsu (1556–1637) also contributed significantly to the spread of tea in the merchant class. A descendant of the tea specialist (*dôbôshû*) Hon'ami, he learned the art of tea from Oribe and Uraku. He studied painting, calligraphy, garden design, was a lacquer and ceramic artist, a universal genius who influenced the tea world of his time in many ways. He spent his life in seclusion and contemporaries described him as someone who rejected the restrictions of the ruling feudal system and did not submit to its authority. By that time, the Edo shogunate had almost completely taken power over the provincial princes, the feudal order had become more and more entrenched, and the free and creative spirit characteristic of the Momoyama period had been increasingly suppressed. Since drastic regulations of the Tokugawa shogunate regulated all areas of life of the citizens, the *chanoyu* also lacked the space

199 Korin-an tea room in the Jikoin,
Koizumi, floor plan

200 With its plastered inner corners, the
post (*toko-bashira*) and the lower
tokonoma frame (*toko-gamachi*)
made of cedar wood as well as the
naka-bashira, a cedar trunk where
the bark was left on the trunk, the
tokonoma radiated a calm simplicity
in the Korin-an.

201 View of Korin-an

A   Edward S. Morse, *Japanese
Homes and their Surroundings*,
p. 151

for free development. There were hardly any more interesting new creations, rather they were limited to refining individual areas of tea art. Ossification in formalism and tradition was thus inevitable, and in this sense Koetsu's death in 1637 can be seen as the symbolic decline of an entire era.

With the peak of the Edo culture in the Genroku era (1688–1704), the rise of the merchant class reached its zenith. While merchants used to be regarded as inferior to warriors, farmers and craftsmen, their role became more and more important due to their economic possibilities. They turned the Confucian value system upside down and over time became the bearers of a new urban culture: Suddenly they were the ones who determined fashion, style and literary taste, instead of court or warrior nobles. Bourgeois theater forms such as the *kabuki* or the *bunraku* puppet theater flourished and woodcuts (*ukiyo-e*)ₙ were the focus of the fine arts. Elegant leisure activities such as ikebana or *chanoyu* were widespread, and if at the time of Rikyû it was still the top of the merchant class (*machi-shû*) alone that practiced it, now the entire urban class of merchants (*chônin*) was involved in the development of the tea ceremony. The increasing need to learn and practice the necessary manual skills and rituals led to the establishment of a large number of tea schools, each with extensive hierarchies under a grandmaster (*iemoto*), who had the right to national certification and authorization of teachers. From the second half of the 17th century onwards, the *iemoto* system was responsible for the rapid spread of tea within the merchant class. A huge new market was opened up, which the former personal relationship between master and pupil could never have accommodated. The *iemoto* system eventually led to a democratization of the *chanoyu* and made it possible to preserve the tea ceremony to this day.

202 Bourgeois tea culture: the Iseya teahouse, woodcut by Isoda Koryusai, 18th century

B The "images of the flowing world" featured the entertainment districts of the capital.

203

204

NEW TEAHOUSE CONCEPTS

Despite the favorable conditions, the Senke schools entered a long phase of stagnation. When it became apparent that Rikyû's legacy could not survive in the sole context of *wabi*, the grandmasters of these tea schools tried to introduce new elements that would be more compatible with the prevailing zeitgeist. The tea style and the architecture of the teahouse were modified so that the tea schools could gradually consolidate again. The fact that the *iemoto* of these schools were direct descendants of Rikyû was a decisive decision factor for many pupils. Kakukakusai (1678–1730), sixth *iemoto* of the Omotesenke school, set new trends in tea room design in addition to many innovations in teaching: He preferred a tea room type with a separate host area (*uraku-gakoi*) and created two new forms of *tokonoma*: a niche the size of a *daime-tatami* (*genso-doko*) and a square *tokonoma* that was only half a mat wide (*masu-doko*).

Kakukakusai's successor, Joshinsai Tennen (1705–1751), continued on the path he had chosen, and under his leadership Omotesenke took the leading role among the three Senke schools. His friend Konoike Ryoei built a memorial chapel in the Gyokurin sub-temple of Daitoku-ji around 1740 and called it Namyo-an. The Saan tea room and a *shoin* room, which was also used as a tea room, were connected to the chapel. If necessary, Buddhist ceremonies could be held in the form of a tea ritual. The *shoin* room was 4½ mats and had a *tokonoma* with a full width shelf (*chigaidana*) of staggered boards in it, a highly unusual combination of elements that were usually arranged side by side. Behind the *chigaidana* there was a picture scroll with a depiction of Mount Fuji, the form of the *chigaidana* was to evoke in a poetic way the memory of rising wafts of mist, which lent the name to both the *tokonoma* and the space itself: Kasumi-doko-no-Seki ("room of the *tokonoma* of the rising mist"). Although the room had many of the classic *shoin* elements – the *tokonoma* with six *shaku* as wide as a *tatami* mat, the walls covered in paper and the ceiling designed as a coffered ceiling – the details revealed new design ideas: The use of untreated bamboo for the normally wooden crossbeams (*nageshi*), smoked bamboo for the *tokonoma* threshold and the insertion of a *chigaidana* across the entire width of the *tokonoma* was a bold concept that brought elements of the *sôan* style into a *shoin* space and aimed at a novel fusion of both styles. The dark interior of the Saan tea room, on the other hand, breathed at first sight the austerity of the Rikyû tea rooms. A closer look, however, also revealed a changed spatial feeling: The 3-mat room was extended by the insertion of a wooden board in the middle of the room (*nakaita*), and the stove was moved out of the middle in relation to the host's seat. At the same time, the position of the *naka-bashira*, a fragile-looking trunk with a strong curvature, which was no longer at the intersection of the ceilings of the guest side with those of the host, was shifted. These visual variations caused a relaxation of the spatial tension, a trend that could also be observed in the Kannin-no-seki tea room designed by Joshinsai Tennen in the Juko-in sub-temple of Daitoku-ji. For traditional tea masters, these approaches were initially incomprehensible, but not for the society of the Genroku merchant class, which took such unusual concepts for granted, and even expected them. However, these innovations only appeared sporadically; the tea room design of the 18th century was primarily characterized by stereotypical reproductions of well-known teahouses.

Only Matsudaira Fumai (1751–1818), a member of the Isa section of the Sekishû school, succeeded in bringing new impulses into tea room architecture. At the age of 20, he published his work *Mudagoto* ("words of idleness"), a highly regarded critique of the contemporary tea world, in which he denounced the extravagances of tea ceremonies and the lack of sensitivity and spirituality of

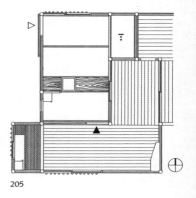

205

203 From the end of the 17th century onwards, the grandmasters of the Senke tea schools tried to introduce new elements that would be more compatible with the spirit of the times. *Kabutomon*, the "helmet" gate of the Urasenke tea school, Kyoto

204 Gate of the Omotesenke tea school, Kyoto

205 The 3-mat room was extended by the insertion of a wooden board in the middle of the room (*nakaita*); Saan tea room in the Gyokurin, Kyoto, floor plan

206

207

冨貴臺

清水谷茶室

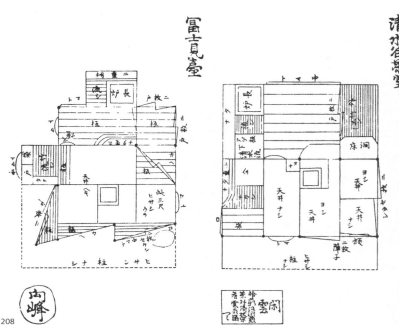

208

tea esthetics. In addition, he designed a large number of teahouses and broke through the stagnation that teahouse architecture was stuck in with the liberty of his style. Fumai's credo, not to be a slave to conventions of any kind, was implemented in a series of teahouses. By no means did he arbitrarily disregard the conventions of his time; the basis of his freedom of expression lay rather in the works of classical teahouse architecture. Several teahouses were situated on the property of his Osaki-en residence in Edo. Although none of these buildings has survived, the drawings reveal his unconventional interpretation of well-known tea rooms. The Koho-no-on teahouse was a tea room the size of 2½ mats with an adjoining service room (*mizuya*). It had triangular niches lined with wooden floors, which certainly created an interesting spatial effect and altered previously common spatial patterns. The drawings of the Yugetsu-ken clearly show the influence of the Kon'nichian, and the Kann'un teahouse contained many elements of Rikyû's Taian. In choosing his models, Fumai did not limit himself to any particular school, and in his notes on the tea ceremony he clearly stated that one should take advantage of the works of the predecessors without paying attention to their affiliation to a particular school. His extensive studies of the architecture of classical teahouses had a strong influence on other tea masters, and the respect for classicism and the fashion for copying that characterized the teahouse architecture of the entire Meiji period can be traced back to no small extent to Fumai's efforts.

CHANGES IN THE MEIJI RESTORATION

In 1868 the Meiji Restoration took place, when the united military power of the families Satsuma, Chosu, Tosa and Hizen conquered Kyoto and forced the shogunate to give up political rule. The emperor was reinstated as the supreme ruler and Shintoism was proclaimed as the state religion. With this historical turning point, tea art along with the Nô theater and many other artistic genres that depended on and were associated with the donations of the shogunate were threatened with extinction. All of Japan's traditional arts were confronted with the fact that, after more than 200 years of isolation, the country was completely untouched by the industrial age and wanted to catch up with the West in a national feat of strength. With the opening of the country, a wave of Western influence spread across the nation, and many traditions were seen as hindering progress. With the slogans "civilization and enlightenment" or "Let's flee Asia, let's enter Europe" typical Japanese traditions were often dismissed as anachronism. The takeover of Western values also brought European architectural styles to Japan. Many public buildings were built in historicizing styles, and for the architecture of residential buildings a mixture of Japanese and European traditions was preferred: Non-Japanese structures were provided with Japanese details and described as a "quasi-European style" (*giyôfû*). Outside the conurbations, however, the traditional Japanese way of building and living remained largely unchanged initially, and even in the large cities, large sections of the population remained unaffected by the changes at first. The lost support of the princes increasingly undermined the *iemoto* system. The *iemoto* of the Urasenke and Mushanokôjisenke schools were forced to vacate their residences in Kyoto, and the grandmaster of the Urasenke tea school even left Kyoto, the heart of the tea tradition, for Tokyo.[c] The impoverished *iemoto* and other tea masters were looking for a way out of their financial difficulties by selling their tea utensils, but this brought in little income, as the market for such goods was scarce in those days. Gengensai Sôshitsu (1810–1877), eleventh *iemoto* of the Urasenke school, fought against this current: As head of the largest tea school and thus representative of the tea world, he addressed his protest note *Chado Gen'i* ("The true meaning of tea") to the Meiji government, which had discredited the tea ceremony as a leisure activity of the old ruling classes. Due to his

206 Kasumi-doko-no-Seki ("room of the *tokonoma* of the rising mist") in the Gyokurin, Kyoto: The shape of the shelf was poetically reminiscent of rising wafts of mist, which gave both the *tokonoma* and the space itself its name.

207 New concepts in teahouse design: wooden floor in a tea room in the Sesshu-ji, Kyoto.

208 With *Mudagoto*, Matsudaira Fumai published a much acclaimed critique of the contemporary tea world and, with his liberal style, disrupted the stagnation in which teahouse architecture was stuck: Koho and Kann'un teahouse, floor plans

c   Paul Varley/Isao Kumakura (eds.), *Tea in Japan – Essays on the History of Chanoyu*, p. 189

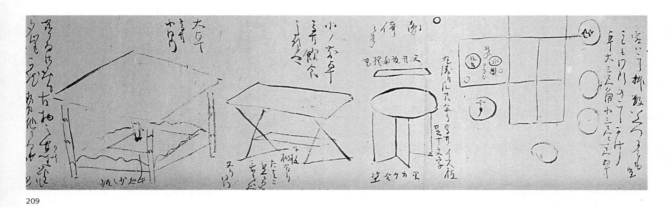

209

210

persistent efforts, the tea ceremony finally regained official recognition as a true art form. This success earned him the nickname "father of the restoration of the *Chado*". Nevertheless, Gengensai was aware that the art of tea had to be adapted to the new times. At an exhibition in Tokyo in 1873 he therefore presented a tea ceremony in which tables and chairs were used for the first time (*ryurei*). Thus he reacted on the one hand to the changing customs, such as the Westernization of clothing, which was not suitable for dignified sitting on a *tatami*, but also took into account the increased interest of Western visitors in *chanoyu*. Traditionalists rejected this type of tea ceremony and regarded it as a makeshift. As late as the 1930s, the *ryurei* ceremony was described in this sense: "This style was devised about sixty years ago by a tea-master of the Ura Senke School in Kyoto, but has scarcely been improved since it was originally devised as a makeshift only. It is natural that some tea-masters and devotees of the orthodox type should attach little importance to the practice of using tables and chairs, for they do not quite harmonize with a Japanese room."ᴅ From today's point of view, the introduction of chairs as part of the tea ceremony refers to the roots of tea practice in the Heian period, when tea was drunk sitting on chairs according to Chinese custom. At Gengensai's time, however, the use of chairs became an absolute novelty, necessitating new structural measures. For example, the raising of the *tokonoma*, which was usually aimed at a much lower view point. Gengensai also foresaw the increased travel activity, which would take more and more people away from their homes for ever longer periods of time, and invented the *chabako*, a mobile tea set, which enabled the traveler to hold a tea ceremony anywhere and at any time.

The Westernization of the Japanese architectural style naturally also had an impact on the architecture of the teahouses. The adoption of Western building techniques led to *sukiya* buildings and teahouses being increasingly constructed with Western methods, and wherever possible timber was replaced by bricks. The results were larger rooms and wide, unstructured wall surfaces, which painfully lacked the high spatial density of the former teahouses. Tea rooms with the flair of earlier buildings were the exception, and only rarely were they erected in residential buildings and sometimes in restaurants.

209 Gengensai recognized that the art of tea had to be adapted to the new times and therefore presented a tea ceremony in Tokyo in 1873, in which tables and chairs were used for the first time (*ryurei*). Sketch for the equipment of the *ryurei* ceremony
210 A mobile tea set for the traveler

ᴅ Yasunoke Fukukita, *Tea Cult of Japan*, p. 38

OKAKURA AND "THE BOOK OF TEA"

In the first decades after the Meiji Restoration, the traditional Japanese art forms were hardly noticed. Western means of expression were taught and eagerly received by Japanese artists. A renewed interest in the local arts developed only gradually, not least due to the work of the American philosopher Ernest Fenellosa (1853–1908) and his Japanese student Kakuzo Okakura (1862–1913). They recognized the fundamental importance of traditional Japanese culture and tea ceremony, and their efforts preserved much of the national cultural heritage. Convinced of the international importance of Japanese art, Okakura published *The Awakening of Japan* in 1904 and *The Book of Tea* in 1906, both in English. In it he presented the Japanese tea ceremony to the West as an artistic tradition and philosophy that for him was one of the greatest achievements of Japanese culture. In the first chapter he described the central position of the tea ceremony in Japan:

"The long isolation of Japan from the rest of the world, so conducive to introspection, has been highly favourable to the development of Teaism. Our home and habits, costume and cuisine, porcelain, lacquer, painting – our very literature – all have been subject to its influence. No student of Japanese culture could ever ignore its presence." [E]

When the book was first published in Japanese in 1927, this led to a new understanding of the tea ceremony in its country of origin as well. After the first wave of enthusiasm for Japanese culture gradually subsided abroad, the Japanese realized, in view of the impending loss, the importance of traditions for their cultural self-identification. In particular, the tea ceremony played an important role in finding a definition of what was typically Japanese as opposed to what was Western, with its unification of different artistic genres. With the steady growth of the capitalist system in Japan and its return to the status of a typical Japanese art form, the tea ceremony received the support of new powerful families: The industrial clans Mitsubishi, Mitsui, Konoike and Sumitomo continued the tradition of the princes of collecting tea utensils and undoubtedly profited from the fact that at the beginning of the Meiji period large quantities of antiques had come onto the market. Some collectors even established museums to present their treasures and contributed much to a higher understanding of Japanese culture among the general public with exhibitions of old art objects. The industrial families can be credited for the renewed popularization of the tea ceremony, although there was a new danger that the ceremony would be too focused on the possession of utensils.

211 Geishas making tea

E   Kakuzo Okakura, p. 11

212 At the beginning of the 20th century, the 14th head of
     the Urasenke school recognized the *ryurei* ceremony.
     The Yûshinken tea room in the complex of the Urasenke
     tea school in Kyoto is the first tea room of an Urasenke
     master since Gengensai, which was designed especially
     for this ceremony.

212

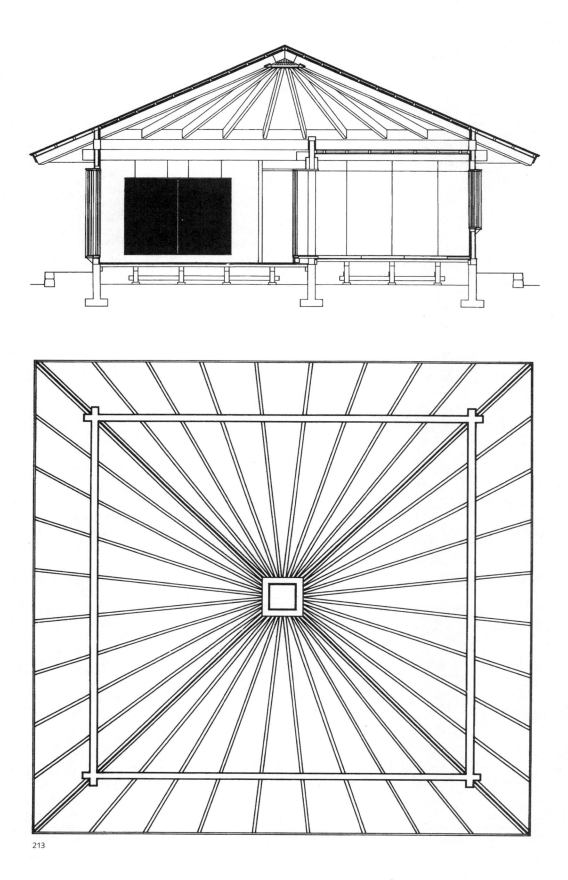

213

TEAHOUSE TODAY

"But since the teahouse is not painting, and neither is architecture, one could call it built poetry."

BRUNO TAUT[A]

214

The sufferings of the Second World War and the burdens of the post-war years meant that teahouses were initially neglected as building projects. But soon the premises for the tea ceremony again became a challenge for Japanese architects. They directly continued a building tradition that saw its roots in the *sukiya* style. To this day, there is an ongoing engagement with the teahouse style and the basic principles of Japanese architecture, ranging from Kazuo Shinohara and Kisho Kurokawa to Tadao Ando. In 1950 an architect designed two *ryurei* tea rooms[B] for the exhibition *The Japanese Way of Tea* in the Matsuzakaya department store in Tokyo, but these met with only limited approval in the tea world. Only with Tantansai (1893–1964), the 14th tea master (*iemoto*) of the Urasenke school, this type of ceremony received the final recognition of the grandmasters. In 1953 his wife Kayoko designed the Yûshinken tea room with tables and low benches in the complex of the Urasenke tea school on the occasion of his 60th birthday. This was the first tea room of a Urasenke master since Gengensai that was specially designed for the *ryurei* ceremony. In 1956, the Chadô Kaikan, a center for tea studies at the Urasenke school, was built in Kyoto, where two tea rooms were also set up for this type of ceremony. Tantansai founded an international department of the Urasenke school and sent his son Sen Sôshitsu XV, the father of today's *iemoto* Sen Sôshitsu XVI (born 1956), to Europe and America after the Second World War to introduce and spread the Japanese Way of Tea. The philosophy of the Way of Tea, valid beyond the borders of nations and cultures, was so convincing that today it is practiced by a multitude of people all over the world. The *iemoto* of the Urasenke school of the 20th century have thus not only managed to preserve the basic features of their *chanoyu*, but embarked on a path towards modernization and universality.

Even today, teahouses are still built in the traditional *sôan* style. However, these rarely express the spirit of earlier buildings. In the choice of materials and in the general layout they remind us of their role models. However, the complicated old techniques necessary for the construction, which only a few highly specialized craftsmen can master, require an enormous financial expenditure. The costs for a new, traditionally manufactured teahouse amount to up to ten million yen (86,000 euros) per square meter, which is far above the price of a single-family house and makes the teahouse one of the most expensive architectural square meters in the world. An alternative to the expensive buildings in the original style are teahouses that are built with modern construction methods. Thus, of course, the outer shape is subject to certain changes: Whereas the structural elements in *sôan* were extremely slender, thicker posts are used today, and instead of simply placing them on buried stones, they are placed on concrete strip or slab foundations. Today there are also prefabricated teahouses on the market at relatively low prices, which are advertised on the Internet and sold worldwide. According to the homepage of a Japanese construction company, the Chosei-an teahouse ("hermitage of long life") costs about 60,000 dollars. The materials for the building are delivered about two months after the order and can be assembled by the customer. Although it allows everyone to own their own teahouse, this standardization contradicts the principle that each teahouse should be designed according to the specific circumstances of its environment.

213 The roof of Shinohara's Umbrella House is reminiscent of the Karakasatei teahouse.

214 Sen Sôshitsu XV preparing tea in a Shinto shrine.

A   Bruno Taut, p. 162
B   At the *ryurei* ceremony, chairs and tables are used, see chapter "The influence of the bourgeoisie and the Meiji Restoration", p. 193

215

For architects, the teahouse has lost none of its charm. In the last two decades there have been a number of well-known Japanese architects who have tackled this construction task and designed new interpretations of the classic teahouse. The different ways in which they dealt with tradition will be demonstrated using selected examples.

KISHO KUROKAWA

Already since the 17th century it was common practice to build more or less exact copies of famous teahouses. The well-known architect Kisho Kurokawa (1934–2007) took up this tradition when he decided to rebuild a teahouse by Kobori Enshu. In an essay he explained his motives for the undertaking:

"My purpose in designing Yuishikian was to recreate a particular tea room that one existed but has disappeared, and in doing so to recreate a symbol that represents a formative, crucial, and yet forgotten model of Japanese aesthetics. This forgotten model is profoundly linked to what have long been considered the basic principles of the Japanese aesthetic, wabi *and* sabi.*"* [C]

Since the building no longer existed, Kurokawa had to adhere to sketches and contemporary reports. These meticulously recorded all elements, materials and dimensions, described even the slightest deviations from the perfect form, for example in the *tokonoma* post (*toko-bashira*), or the surface treatment of the woods, but during the practical reconstruction he found himself confronted with the problem that decisive information was missing or not clear enough. One text, for example, mentions that the *toko-bashira* is made of "kunogi", an old term that could only be identified as a local dialect for "kunigi" – a species of oak – after painstaking research. According to Kurokawa, he searched for ten years before he found the appropriate old calendar pages to stick on the *tokonoma* in antiquarian bookshops, and it took even longer before his carpenter was able to present him with a post with that particular natural curvature that seemed suitable for the *tokonoma*. [D] This description throws a significant light on the doggedness and determination that make this hunt for a maximum of authenticity necessary. They probably have only little in common with the original intention of the early tea masters.

HIROSHI HARA

Hiroshi Hara (born 1936) became famous in the last millennium for his major projects such as the railway station in Kyoto or the Umeda Sky Building in Osaka. He knows how to combine large buildings with a peculiar, post-modern formal language. In the late 1980s he built a teahouse in Mizusawa, a location in northwestern Tokyo, which attracted attention due to its spatial concept. Two teahouses are placed as "house in the house" in a building, one measuring 4½ *tatami*, and the second eight *tatami*. These are placed as open structures in the five-meter-high room and allow views into the other tea room through the glazed wall surfaces. The outer shell is closed except for a few window slits, so that most of the light penetrates into the room through two skylights. As clear and simple as the principle is, the built space appears a little overloaded due to the variety of materials – wood, concrete, marble, plaster, granite, glass and metal – and the decorative effects typical of Hara. Playful elements such as cloud forms drawn into the plaster, sunlight refracted in color by prisms, or different patterns on etched glass obscure the spatial concept rather than providing decorative added value.

215 *Tokonoma* of a contemporary tea room

C   Kisho Kurokawa, *Rediscovering Japanese Space*, p. 81
D   Ibid.

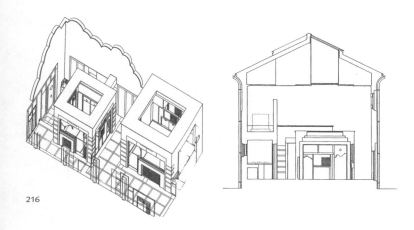

216

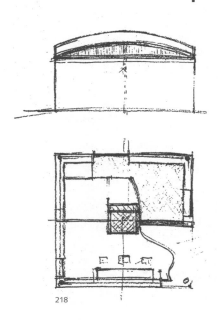

218

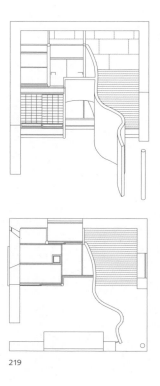

219

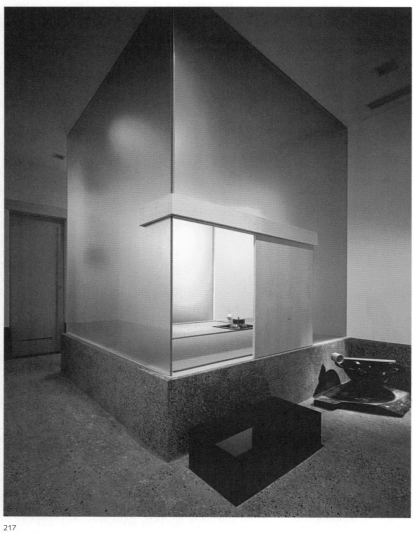

217

In 1983, the Leo Castelli Gallery in New York organized an exhibition entitled *Folly*. The invited architects were asked to exhibit drawings of structures whose sole function is to act as an esthetic eye-catchers when placed in a garden, i.e. buildings with a strong sculptural effect. For the exhibition, Arata Isozaki chose the design of a Japanese teahouse that, in his opinion, perfectly represented the title and meaning of the exhibition: A pavilion building in a garden that served nothing but the "useless" purpose of the tea ceremony. The design attracted the attention of Toshio Hara, who had the design implemented on his property in Tokyo and named the teahouse "Uji" after a philosophical concept of the founder of Soto Zen Buddhism, Dogen. The result is a sandstone building under a mighty curved lead roof, the undersides of which are clad with stainless steel plates. One enters the interior through a crawl-in entrance (*nijiriguchi*), also made of stainless steel, or through a sliding door (*shoji*) made of aluminum, which leads into an inner waiting area (*uchi-machiai*), which is also suitable for *ryurei* ceremonies. Directly next to it and separated only by a *shoji*, the actual tea room is the size of a 2¾-mat (*nijô-daime*). Great importance was attached to the selection of materials: The *tokonoma* is covered with lead slabs like the roof surface, and an old wooden beam from the Yakushi-ji temple was chosen as the *toko-bashira*. A curved wall of titanium steel separates the entrance area and service room (*mizuya*) from the main rooms. Isozaki explains the variety of materials used – taking up the concept of "here and now" (*ichigo-ichie*)ᴇ – as follows:

*"The spatial composition of tea-ceremony is organized by the aesthetics of combination, following a method of combining …The set of tea-things and the hanging-scroll assembled for a tea ceremony will be rearranged for every tea ceremony meeting. This is a unique, one-time-only assemblage, including the guest of the day, and this particular combination will never be replaced again. The building composition of the tea-house is also organized according to this principle of assemblage. Materials including even some which are inappropriate for ordinary buildings are incorporated, while preserving the individuality of each material, as part of the expression of the microscopic space of the tea ceremony room."*ꜰ

SHIGERU UCHIDA

Shigeru Uchida (1943–2016) is one of Japan's most famous interior designers. In his works, he often deals with the question of the extent to which traditional Japanese culture and modernity can be linked, which is why teahouses are always part of his work: In 1998, in collaboration with Aldo Rossi, he designed the Hotel Mojiko in Moji City, Kyushu. As the person responsible for the interior design, he planned a room for the tea ceremony, which is designed as a room-in-room principle. He placed the actual tea room, a cube made of frosted glass, in a room covered with soft, cream-colored *washi* paper. One enters the interior of the 2-mat room, which is slightly elevated from the floor, through a classic *nijiriguchi*. For an exhibition in 1993 Uchida designed three simple teahouses, Ji-an, Gyo-an and So-an. There were three cubes of the same size, which differed only in the design of the walls and ceilings. By using different materials, he created completely different spatial experiences despite having the same cubature. With this means he tried to express the different degrees of formalization – *shin, gyô, sô* ɢ.

216 Two tea rooms by Hiroshi Hara in Mizusawa: axonometry and section

217 Shigeru Uchida designed a room for the tea ceremony for Hotel Mojiko, which is designed as a room-in-room principle. One enters the interior of the 2-mat room, which is covered with soft, cream-colored *washi* paper and slightly elevated from the floor, through a classic *nijiriguchi*.

218 Uji teahouse, Tokyo: sketch by Arata Isozaki

219 Uji teahouse, Tokyo: axonometric projection and floor plan

E   See chapter "The development of the *soân* teahouse", p. 123

F   *Japan Architect*, 1993, p. 274

G   The terms are derived from *kai-gyô-sô*, a terminology for three different types of calligraphy, where *kai* corresponds to block letters, *gyô* uses rounded characters and *sô* represents the italic, free writing style. Usually translated as "formal – semiformal – informal", *shin* is used in relation to things that are strongly controlled or designed by humans, such as the esthetics of the standardized decoration of a *shoin* room. Rikyû-style teahouses, on the other hand, can be considered informal – *sô* – and the esthetics of Shukô corresponds to *gyô* in this system, the semiformal style.

220

Kan Izue (born 1931) dealt with another aspect of the teahouse tradition in his teahouse Bou-Bou-an in Nagoya, which was awarded a prize by the International Academy of Architecture in 1996. He used cheap industrial materials – zinc sheet, old newspapers, simple steel I-beams – and thus offered a reinterpretation of traditional teahouse esthetics, as the old teahouses were often made of recyclable old materials and building materials found in the surrounding area. It is not only the cozy atmosphere of the traditional wooden structure that is at the center of his teahouse esthetics, but also the fundamental question of materials, from where they could be obtained, and how they change over time. In an interview with David N. Buck he remarked on his design philosophy: "Because of the expense involved, traditional Japanese things have started to die out. But originally Sen-no-Rikyu made the tea ceremony for the common people, not for the privileged, the aesthetic of the poor people was the tea room. […] the materials for the tea room were those that poor people had access to. The origin of aesthetics in Japan was the tea room for the poor people. Great architecture all over the world is the architecture of kings and the upper classes. Japan was the only country to make *sukiya* architecture, to make aesthetics for the poor people, and the original creator was Sen-no-Rikyu."[H]

221

The 10.6-square-meter building would have cost 50 to 100 million yen (430,000 to 860,000 euros) according to the standard of traditional teahouses, but Izue managed to make do with just five million yen, less than a tenth, by using industrial materials. The exterior, with its barrel roof and zinc plate cladding, is more reminiscent of industrial architecture or a garden shed than of a teahouse. The interior is covered with galvanized metal plates with a pattern on the surface resembling the straws in the mud walls of former teahouses. The space of the *tokonoma* is a slightly curved apse, which, like a *tokonoma* plastered with clay (*murodoko*), gives it an indefinite depth. The *toko-bashira* consists of an I-beam, which has been covered with soy sauce in order to initiate and accelerate the process of rust formation. On the wall of the host side, in the tradition of former teahouses, where old letters or calendar sheets were used to cover the walls, cutouts of old newspapers are glued on. In the same interview he commented on the teahouse: "I wanted […] a renaissance of the tea ceremony. I wanted to destroy, to hammer a big nail into the traditional Japanese way. Usually the tea room is very expensive using costly materials and craftsmen, but I used only very cheap materials. The H-beam I used cost only 1,000 yen for the whole thing. I wanted to shock the traditional way of Japanese architecture. […] I wanted to return the tea ceremony to the ordinary people, to say to people that you don't need high-class stones or high-class columns to make a tea house but that you can do it with zinc plate. You can do it with old newspapers. […] I wanted to show that there is nothing cheaper to use to make a tea house."[I]

In another teahouse, the Pipia-an in Takarazuka, he did the same. The teahouse is situated on the roof of a skyscraper and serves the local population as an easily accessible tea ceremony room. It is a public building and can be rented by anyone interested. This teahouse with a 2-mat tea room is designed as a steel structure made of inexpensive materials, paying great attention to the proportions, connections and different textures of the individual elements. Here, too, Izue used old roof tiles in the garden design and metal plates to clad the interior, thus following the intentions of Bou-Bou-an.

220 Ji-an, Gyo-an, So-an, night view: By using different materials, Shigeru Uchida created completely different spatial experiences despite having the same cubature and gave expression to the principles *shin*, *gyô*, *sô* ("formal, semiformal, informal").
221 Interior of the Gyo-an

H David N. Buck, *Responding to Chaos – Tradition, Technology, Society and Order in Japanese Design*, p. 29
I David N. Buck, p. 29

222

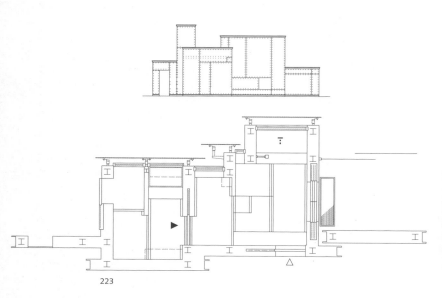

223

224

TADAO ANDO

Teahouses are also a recurring theme in the work of Tadao Ando (born 1941). Many of them are realized as exposed concrete buildings, and despite this modern material, these rooms are permeated by the poetry of the tea ceremony. With the design of a tea room made of concrete blocks with a floor area of only 1.4 x 2.8 meters, Ando continues the *sôan* tradition of minimal spatial structures. Through a story-high frosted glass pane, into which the outline of a ginkgo leaf is etched, the light penetrates as if filtered through paper *shoji* into the room, where it is reflected by the polished concrete walls. Another teahouse is built on the roof of an old wooden merchant house in Osaka. The lack of space led to a completely new arrangement of the tea garden, which is now conceived as a vertical structure: One climbs a steep ladder to the waiting room, from which a narrow bridge over the roof of the house leads to the tea room. This marks the highest point of the building. All surfaces of the room are covered with a veneer of Japanese lime; the cubic structure of the room is proportioned by an inscribed sphere, which is taken up by a vaulted ceiling in the form of a sixth of a cylinder.

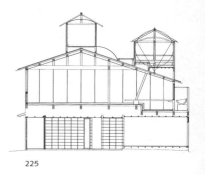

225

SABIE-ZEN

The Sabie Cultural Institute has set itself the goal of further spreading the Way of Tea, starting from the impending loss of the spiritual values of the tea ceremony. Open to experimental trends, it supported an event called *SABIE-Zen* in 1992 that was initiated by some well-known Japanese creative artists and aimed at a reinterpretation of the tea ceremony. Of the over 60 domestic and foreign designers and architects invited to participate, 52 contributed to the exhibition, including such well-known names as Ettore Sottsass and Issey Miyake. Masayuki Kurokawa designed the Quest Hall in Harajuku, Tokyo. He provides information on the furnishings of the room in the exhibition catalog: "I want the hall to represent a microcosm, just as a tearoom does. Very commonplace materials that are well suited to the hall will be integrated into the existing space to create a design consisting solely of a floor – the key concept in Japanese architecture. Lighting will be focused around the perimeter of the floor to highlight the gap between floor and the four surrounding walls and to create an impression of a gigantic stage suspended in mid-air, into which six tearooms have been inlaid.",

The tea rooms were designed by Shigeru Uchida, Toshiyuki Kita, Takashi Sugimoto, Jae-Eun Choi and Teruhiku Negishi. The formal variety ranged from more classic tea rooms to innovations that even went so far as to change the shape of the *tatami*. Of particular interest was the contribution of designer Toshiyuki Kita, who constantly explores the tension between tradition and modernity in his works. For him, the experience that has accumulated over centuries in traditional craft techniques is of central importance. For the exhibition he created a tea room whose simplicity can hardly be surpassed: The space of a cube with a side length of 1.8 meters is defined by a frame of lacquered wooden strips, the floor is formed by two *tatami*. For Kita this space represents – in the sense of the *I-Ching* – an entire universe.

222 The Pipia-an teahouse in Takarazuka is situated on the roof of a skyscraper and serves the local population as an easily accessible tea ceremony room.

223 Pipia-an, view and floor plan

224 Interior of the Pipia-an

225 Section of the teahouse with lime veneer, Oyodo, 1985

Teahouses are being built all over the world to also convey an authentic feeling of the tea ceremony to those who have not had the opportunity to visit Japan. However, the global distribution of the tea ceremony has not yet been completed, as the Austrian daily *Der Standard* reported under the title "Tea Ceremony in Space": "Tokyo – Japanese scientists want to set up a place for tea ceremonies in the International Space Station ISS to relax the astronauts. 'Space travel can be psychologically stressful, hence the idea of a space for relaxation',

J *SABIE-Zen, The Way of Tea; a fresh perspective*, exhibition catalog

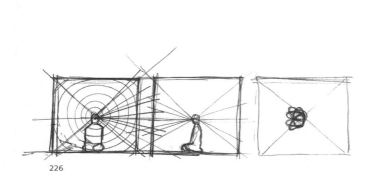

226

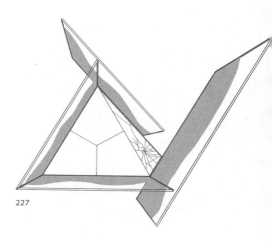

227

228

said a spokesman for the Japanese space agency Nasda on Tuesday evening. The authority is working with art professors and students on a proposal for a four-square-meter room equipped with reed mats." K

To a certain extent, the Way of Tea has become a pleasure again today, reserved for the wealthy. The tea utensils, not to speak of a classical teahouse, are immensely more expensive, and so tea is practiced by many Japanese not only because it is a genuine Japanese art form that relates them to their own history, but also because the ceremony connects them to the upper class. With this attitude, tea culture has lost much of the egalitarian, spiritual principles that shaped it in Rikyû's day. Many Japanese are painfully aware of this problem and hope that the spirit of Rikyû is still alive in Japan. Masakazu Izumi, the second son of Sen Sôshitsu XV and director of the Sabie Cultural Institute, outlines the ideological background: "It is very disappointing to note that, if this is the case, the existence of today's Way of Tea, is considered merely as one of the traditional entertainments or a training for a bride to be. Is is no exaggeration to say that this disappointing fact is my driving force in the development of Sabie, which is to establish new ways of expressing movements and actions of the Way of Tea. [...] The main purpose of establishing Sabie is not to redesign the tea gathering and pretend it anew by destructing the tradition of the *Chanoyu*, but to customarily examine the diverse factors the culture of *Chanoyu* possesses and to convey its essence to the public, the majority of people who live under the contemporary life style without any contact with the tea gathering." L

The fact that a large number of architects and designers are still involved with the tea ceremony today, and some even see it at the center of their design philosophy, is proof of the unbroken attraction and significance of the Japanese Way of Tea. Attempts to break away from the entrenched traditions – but without losing sight of them – may be regarded with suspicion by purists, but may indicate a way for *chanoyu* to continue as a living part of Japanese cultural life.

226 Sketch by Toshiyuki Kita for his contribution to the *SABIE-Zen* exhibition, 1992
227 Tea room with triangular *tatami* shape, *SABIE-Zen* exhibition, 1992
228 Students drinking tea in the Jikoin

229 Following page: bamboo wall and ceiling in a teahouse by the architect Issiki

K   *Der Standard*, 7 February 2002
L   *SABIE-Zen*

IMPORTANT TERMS
OF THE TEA CEREMONY

IMPORTANT TERMS
OF TEAHOUSE ARCHITECTURE

CHRONOLOGICAL TABLE

BIBLIOGRAPHY

PICTURE CREDITS

ACKNOWLEDGEMENTS

akatsuki-no chaji Twilight ceremony, held in the coldest time of the year. The guests arrive between three and four in the morning, even before the sun rises

asa-cha Early morning ceremony, held before the sun gets too hot in the summer months

bokuseki Scroll with the calligraphy of a Zen priest

cha Tea

chabako Literally "tea box"; contains all utensils except the wastewater tank, > furo and kettle

chabana Flowers exhibited in the > tokonoma unlike ikebana, only one or two flowers are arranged in a simple vase

chadô Way of Tea

cha-e Former name for the tea ceremony in Buddhist temples

cha-ire Tea tin, a small container for powdered tea; one of the most important utensils in the tea ceremony. The container for the thick tea is called > cha-ire, the one for the thin tea > cha-ki

chaji A tea ceremony in full extent, includes the ritual of adding charcoal to the fire, a > kaiseki meal and both > koicha and > usucha

chajin "Tea man", a follower of the culture of tea ceremony

cha-ki > cha-ire

chakin Narrow, rectangular white linen cloth used to wipe the tea bowl before and after the tea ceremony; moistened with water beforehand and folded in a predetermined manner

chanoyu Tea ceremony

chasen Bamboo broom used for mixing powder tea and hot water (> koicha) or beating it into a foamy liquid (> usucha)

chashaku Long curved spoon used to put the powder tea into the tea bowl; formerly made of ivory or iron, today made almost exclusively of bamboo. Most tea masters carve their own teaspoons

chawan Tea bowl, always without handle and made of ceramic without exception

dôbôshû Monks, who were employed by the Ashikaga shoguns as specialists for Chinese art objects and who had a great influence on the development of the tea ceremony

fukusa Almost square silk cloth with which the host cleans the utensils in front of the guests

furo Mobile charcoal container used in the summer season instead of the sunken stove (> rô); can be made of iron, bronze, silver or ceramic and is named according to size and shape

futa-oki Piece of bamboo, ceramic or metal on which the water ladle or the lid of the kettle is placed

haboki Feather-broom in two sizes: the larger one is used for cleaning the > tatami; the smaller one, consisting of three feather layers, for cleaning the stove frame or the > furo

hai Literally "ash", usually refers to the ash in the > furo or > rô; ash is shaped into elegant shapes that are admired by the guests as part of the ceremony

haiki Flat bowl filled with a special ash spread over the ashes in the stove

haisaji Large spoon with which the special ash is removed from the > haiki

hakama A kind of skirt, worn by men

hana-ire Flower vase, mostly made of ceramic, metal or bamboo. Either placed on the > tokonoma floor, hung on the pillar next to the *tokonoma* or suspended from the ceiling

hantô Host assistant

hatsugama First ceremony of the new year, usually held on the fifth or sixth day of the new year

hibashi Pair of long metal sticks with which the charcoal is arranged

hishaku Bamboo or wooden ladle; one bamboo ladle is used in the tea room for water from the kettle, one made of wood is placed at the stone sink in the garden

ichigo ichie Literally "a time, a meeting"; formulates the non-repeatability of each individual tea gathering in its specific form

kaiseki Literally "warm stone"; simple, but with highest refinement made meal, served at a tea ceremony before the thick tea (> koicha)

kaishi Soft paper that the guests bring with them to eat sweets on

kakemono Hanging scroll with a painting or a calligraphy

kama A kettle for boiling water, usually made of iron, but sometimes also of gold or silver

kasa A broad-brimmed, flat straw hat that guests wear when it rains

kensui Wastewater container

Kitano-dai-chakai "Grand Kitano Tea Gathering" in Kyoto in October 1587

kobako/kogo A holder for incense made of porcelain or lacquer, a very small but valuable object of art; one of the most important utensils used in the tea ceremony

kôboku Particles of an aromatic wood species, such as sandalwood, added to the fire during the ceremony

kobukusa Square piece of fabric made of expensive material (brocade); during the ceremony, valuable tea bowls are placed on top of it

koicha Thick tea, named after its viscous consistency

kokoroire Literally "the laying down of the heart"; the host should devote all his/her strength and attention to the well-being of the guest

kuchikiri Special tea ceremony in which the seal of the container containing fresh tea is broken

kuromoji Chopsticks with which sweets are eaten

kyaku Guest; during a ceremony the first (shôkyaku) and the last (otsume) guest are particularly challenged; the first leads the conversation, the last helps the host to clear the room

meibutsu Famous tea containers and tea bowls; collectibles each with its own name, history and description

mizusashi Water container for fresh water in the tea room, often made of Chinese porcelain

nagori Tea ceremony at the end of October, when the tea supply of the year comes to an end and the days become colder; melancholy of farewell

nakadachi A break of ten to fifteen minutes between each part of the tea ceremony. Guests leave the tea room to smoke or chat on a specially designed bench

natsume Tea container made of lacquer for > usucha

raku Best known tea ceramics; potted without wheel and fired at low temperature

sadô Tea master

sakazuki Cup for drinking sake

sencha Green tea, in which the tea leaves are left to brew and then drained

sensu Fan; if > fukusa is the sign of the host, then sensu is the sign of the guest

shifuku Silk or damask bag in which the ceramic tea containers are packed

shoburo First date in the year (May) on which the > furo is put into operation

shôgo-no-chaji Lunchtime tea ceremony; the most common type of tea ceremony

shozumi Procedure in which the charcoal is added to the fire in front of the guests

sumi Charcoal in different lengths and thicknesses

tabako-bon Tobacco stand, a deep tray containing a small fire pot; used during the break

tabi Japanese socks with detached big toe

temae General term for the ritual preparation of tea

tenmoku Special tea bowl, which is used in very formal tea ceremonies and stands on a stand made of lacquer or wood (tenmoku-dai)

usucha Thin tea, not so pasty, but stronger

yobanashi Tea ceremony in the cold season; from early evening to late night

yûzari Tea ceremony in the warm season; from early evening to late night

zori Straw sandals

amado Wooden sliding doors, storm doors, which protect the > shoji situated behind from the weather; are installed at night to secure the house

arakabe Rough clay wall without fine plastering

bashira Column, post

bokuseki-mado Window in the side wall of the > tokonoma

bu Traditional unit of length, 1 *bu* = 3.03 mm

buke-zukuri Architectural style of the samurai residential building

chanoyu-ma Tea preparation room in the > kaisho

chanoyu-dana Shelf on which the tea was prepared in the > chanoyu-ma

chaseki/chashitsu Tea room or teahouse, specially designed for holding tea ceremonies

chigaidana Shelf with staggered shelves, which was installed in the > shoin rooms next to the > tokonoma

chiri-ana Small garbage pit placed in the tea garden near the teahouse and filled with leaves of the tea garden.

chôzubashi Stone washbasin

chûmon Middle gate between inner and outer garden

daime ¾-*tatami* mat used exclusively in tea rooms; indicates the host's location and is separated from the rest of the tea room by means of > naka-bashira and > sode-kabe

daisu Tea utensil stand used in the most formal type of tea ceremony

dojon Fortified castle complex

doma Earth-covered floor area inside the house

engawa Veranda

fumi-ishi High stone in front of > nijiriguchi

furosaki-mado Small window on the side of the host, in front of the > furo

fusuma Sliding doors with paper covering. In contrast to > shoji, *fusuma* are not translucent and are usually used as dividing elements between rooms; they are often painted decoratively

gorota-ishi Area of differently shaped pebbles laid in front of the > chôzubashi

hasamishikii Rails of the > nijiriguchi

hiroma Literally "big room", a tea room that is bigger than 4½ mats; sometimes 4½-mat rooms themselves are called this; for more details on the different room names see the chapter "Tea room structure".

ishi-dôrô Stone lantern

itanoma Wooden floor

jodan-no-ma Elevated area of a room

kaisho Meeting room

karakami Paper with regular woodprint pattern in Chinese style

katô-guchi Door with round lintel

ken Japanese unit of length: 1 *ken* = 6 > shaku = 1.81813 m

keshoyaneura-tenjo Sloping ceiling

kinin-guchi Entrance for guests which they use in an upright posture, as opposed to the > nijiriguchi

kirei-sabi Esthetics that combine decorative beauty with restrained simplicity

kissa-no-tei Simple tea pavilions from the early days of Japanese tea culture

kiwari jutsu Dimensional reference system for timber construction: *ki* = wood, *wari* = division, *jutsu* = system

koma Literally "small room"; a tea room that is smaller than 4½ mats; for more details on the different room names see the chapter "Tea room structure".

koshikake-machiai Waiting hut where guests wait before the tea ceremony and during the break

kusari-no-ma "Chain room"; named after the iron chain on which the kettle is suspended from the ceiling

mae-ishi Stone that is placed in front of the > tsukubai

me Woven lines on the surface of the > tatami

miegakure Special technique of garden design, in which only part of the garden is shown at any one time; frequently used in tea gardens

minka Japanese farmhouse

mizuya "Water room"; a service room in the immediate vicinity of the tea room, where utensils are washed and arranged

muro-doko Clay *tokonoma*, in which the inner corners are plastered with clay and rounded off

nageshi Crossbeams attached to the side of the column

naka-bashira Center post; often used with the > daime arrangement in combination with a > sode-kabe

narashi-ishi Flat foundation stones

nijiriguchi "Crawl-in entrance"; miniature entrance to the teahouse for the guests

nobedan Paved path in the tea garden

nuki Crossbeams running through the column

okoshiezu Literally "fold-out drawing"; model of a tea room where all surfaces can be folded into one level

oshiita Precursor of the > tokonoma

otoshi-gake Upper > tokonoma frame

ranma Blind in the area above the sliding door; often decorated with elaborate carvings

renji-mado Window with vertical bamboo bars grille

rô Sunken stove

rôbuchi Stove frame

rôdan Part of the > rô, designates the stove pit

roji Tea garden; essential part of the tea ceremony, as a way to the teahouse

sadô-guchi Entrance of the host

sekimori-ishi Single stone wrapped with a black hemp rope, which blocks the wrong way at forks; also called *tome-ishi*

shaku Traditional unit of length, 1 *shaku* = 303.02 mm

shikishi-mado Window arrangement with a > renji-mado sitting over a > shitaji-mado

shitaji-mado Window created by omitting the clay covering of the wall. The bamboo substructure is exposed

shôbanseki Area of a lower seat in the teahouse

shoin style Building style mainly used in samurai houses; derived from > tsuke-shoin

shoji Sliding doors that are covered with only one layer of white paper and are therefore translucent

sôan Teahouse made of natural materials, which imitates a remote hermit's hut; as an architectural style "grass hut style"

sode-kabe Literally "sleeve wall"; separates the host's niche from the rest of the tea room in the > daime arrangement.

sotomon Outer gate

sukiya Originally a free-standing teahouse, later used to describe an architectural style derived from the principles of teahouse architecture

sun Traditional unit of length, 1 *sun* = 30.302 mm

taiko-busuma "drum" *fusuma*; > fusuma on which the paper is stretched over the frame so that it forms a single white surface

tana-ishi Round foundation stones

tatami Japanese floor mat made of rice straw with a rush pad; standard size for the tea room: 90 x 180 cm

tenjo Blanket

tobi-ishi Stepping stones in the garden

toko-bashira > tokonoma post

toko-gamachi Lower > tokonoma frame

tokonoma A niche that is a few centimeters higher than the rest of the room; it refers to the most important part of the tea room, decorated with a hanging scroll or flowers; for more detailed classifications of the different *tokonoma* types see the chapter "Tea room structure"

tome-ishi > sekimori-ishi

tsuboniwa Inner garden of the house, inner courtyard; design influenced by the tea gardens

tsugi-no-ma Room for the extension of the tea room

tsuke-shoin Writing area in front of a window in a priest's residence

tsukiage-mado Skylight windows

tsukubai Arrangement around the stone washbasin, where the guests clean their hands and mouth before entering the tea room

uwa-nuri Last, fine layer of the wall; in teahouses in the *sôan* style it is usually omitted

yaku-ishi Stepping stones with special function

yoritsuki Room where guests can meet before the tea ceremony and take off their outer wear

Political and cultural events	Historical period (AD)	History of the chanoyu and the teahouse
– Yamato and Izumo are the regional centers, government by the clan system – Relations with the Asian mainland via Korea	Late Yayoi and Kofun periods	
– Introduction of Buddhism (558) and increased cultural exchange with the Kingdom of Korea – First Japanese legation to the court of the Chinese T'ang dynasty	Asuka period 592–710	
– 710: Foundation of Nara – State is organized under the emperor Shomu (reign 724–749) based on the Chinese model of the T'ang dynasty – Dispute at court; Kuni, Naniwa and Shigaraki become capitals – Nara becomes capital again (745–794)	Nara period 710–794	– Around 730 first testimonies of tea drinking in Japan, which, like many other cultural techniques, is taken over from China – 772: Lu Yu writes the *Cha Ching* in China, the first book about tea – Tea is mainly enjoyed at the imperial court and is part of the leisure activities of the nobility
– Kyoto (Heiankyo) becomes imperial capital – Closer ties to China – Flourishing of aristocratic culture, but soon the central power must increasingly relinquish the power regional princes – War between the Taira and Minamoto families	Heian period 794–1185	– 815: Emperor Saga is served tea by the monk Eichû – 1191: Monk Eisai returns to Japan after several years in China and imports tea seeds and the Chinese etiquette of the tea ceremony
– Minamoto no Yoritomo becomes 1192 first shogun, military regency in Kamakura – Growing influence of Zen Buddhism – 1274: Mongol invasion of Kyushu, 1281 Mongol defeat	Kamakura period 1185–1333	– 1211: Eisai writes *Kissa Yôjôki*, in which the medical advantages of drinking tea are emphasized – Tea ceremony becomes more and more common in the monasteries – Samurai also discover tea that is often enjoyed in garden pavilions and embedded in lavish *tocha* games that enjoy high popularity
– 1333: Downfall of the Kamakura shogunate, beginning of the civil war of the northern and southern dynasties – 1338: Ashikaga Takauji founds the Muromachi shogunate – With the end of the civil war in 1392, the Higashiyama and Kitayama court cultures flourish – 1467–1477: Onin revolt in which Daitoku-ji is burned down along with other temples – 1543: Arrival of the Portuguese – 1549: Jesuit Father Francisco de Javier begins the missionary work of Japan	Muromachi period 1333–1573 Period of the northern and southern dynasties (1336–1392) Kitayama era (late 14th and early 15th century) Higashiyama era (2nd half of the 15th century) Period of civil wars (1478–1568) . . .	– Rapid spread of the drink, tea is also accessible to the lower classes – Tea gatherings take place in the reception rooms (*kaisho*) of the palaces, the furnishing of the rooms corresponds to the magnificent *shoin* architecture – Tea specialists (*dôbôshû*) are responsible for the ceremonial use of the tea, they also establish the rules according to which the tea utensils are presented

Political and cultural events	Historical period (AD)	History of the chanoyu and the teahouse
	. . .	– 1476: *Dôbôshû* Nôami writes the *Kundaikan Sôchô-ki*, which describes the arrangement of tea utensils – 1486: Construction of the Dojinsai room with sunken stove (*rô*), which is today regarded as the first tea room – Murata Shukô (1422–1502), founder of the Japanese tea ceremony. Beginning of the construction of small tea rooms based on the model of the hermitages – Takeno Jôô (1502–1555), development of the *wabi* philosophy, the 4½-mat teahouse becomes standard
– Process of national unification under Oda Nobunaga and Toyotomi Hideyoshi – 1590: Pacification and unification of the empire by Toyotomi Hideyoshi – 1592: Korea campaign	Azuchi-Momoyama period 1568–1600	– Sen no Rikyû (1522–1591), most famous and influential tea master. Perfection of the *wabi* idea and development of the *sôan* teahouse: dark atmosphere, minimization of room size. Construction of the Taian teahouse – 1587: Grand Kitano Tea Gathering, more than 800 tea huts are built – Furuta Oribe (1544–1615) is considered the founder of the *daimyô* tea style: larger rooms, brighter atmosphere, high respect for etiquette. Most famous tea room En-an – Rikyû's son, Sen Shôan (1546–1614), erects the Zangetsutei – Oda Uraku (1547–1621) erects the Joan tea room: many innovations, interesting interior structure
– 1600: Battle of Sekigahara; Tokugawa Ieyasu subdues the last opponents and forces the unification of the country – 1603: Tokugawa Ieyasu establishes shogunate in Edo, consolidation of political authority – 1635–1639: Increased control of the state and complete isolation of the country (*sakoku*) – 1690–1774: Peak of bourgeois culture – 1820–1835: Revolts, decline of the currency, decline of the Tokugawa rule – Growing pressure from abroad contributes to destabilization of the regime – 1853: US commander Perry arrives in Japan – 1854: Forced signing of trading contracts	Edo period 1600–1868 Kann'ei era (ca. 1600–1670) Genroku era (ca. 1625–1725) . . .	– Hosokawa Sansai (1563–1645) varies the transition between interior and exterior space in his tea rooms – Kobori Enshu (1579–1647), peak of *daimyô* tea style: large rooms with a fusion of *sôan* and *shoin* stylistic elements. The best-known tea rooms are Mittan and Bosen – Kanamori Sôwa (1584–1656) arouses the court nobility's interest in tea, builds the Teigyokuken tea room – 1620: Construction of Villa Katsura begins and a new esthetics, the *sukiya* style, is born, influenced by the teahouse style – Rikyû's grandson, Sen Sôtan (1578–1658), strives to revive the *wabi* philosophy. Builds important teahouses Fushin-an, Kon'nichian, Yûin and Kanuntei. Founds the most important tea schools: Urasenke, Omotesenke, Mushanôkjisenke

Political and cultural events	Historical period (AD)	History of the chanoyu and the teahouse
	. . .	– Hon'ami Koetsu (1556–1637) and Katagiri Sekishu (1605–1673) popularize the tea ceremony among the wealthy trading classes – Around 1740: Establishment of Kasumi-doko-no-seki and Saan create new trends in tea room design; at the same time frequent copying of meanwhile classical models – Matsudaira Fumai (1751–1818) with refreshing innovations in teahouse design
– 1868: End of the Tokugawa rule, restoration of the empire – Establishment of Shintoism as state religion – Rapid process of modernization and industrialization – 1889: Meiji constitution and parliamentary government – Colonial expansions – 1894–1895: First Sino-Japanese War – 1904–1905: Russo-Japanese War	Meiji period 1868–1912	– Tea culture collapses due to socio-political change, impoverishment of princes and tea masters – Gengensai Sôshitsu (1810–1877) fights for official recognition of the tea ceremony as an art form. Responds to new trends with *ryurei* tea ceremony held on tables and chairs – 1906: Kakuzo Okakura (1862–1913) publishes *The Book of Tea* and initiates a revaluation of tea culture in Japan
– 1914: Japan enters the First World War as Germany's opponent – 1923: Great earthquake of Kanto (Tokyo)	Taisho period 1912–1926	– Stagnation of tea culture until after the Second World War
– 1937–1945: War against China – 1941: Attack on Pearl Harbor – 1941–1945: Pacific War – 1945: Atomic bombing on Hiroshima and Nagasaki – 1945–1952: Occupation by the Allies – 1964: Olympic Games take place in Tokyo	Showa period 1926–1989	– After the surrender slow emergence of a new consciousness for tea
– Until 1991 so-called "bubble economy", whose bursting leads to unstable coalition governments – 1995: Hanshin earthquake (Kobe)	Heisei period since 1989	– Especially the Urasenke tea school makes a contribution to the dissemination and internationalization of *chanoyu*

– **Peter Ackermann,** "The four seasons", in: Pamela J. Asquith/Arne Kalland (eds.), *Japanese Images of Nature – Cultural Perspectives,* (Nordic Institute of Asian Studies – Man and Nature in Asia), no.1, Richmond: Curzon Press, 1997

– **Stephen Addiss,** *The Art of Zen,* New York: Harry N. Abrams, Incorporated, 1989

– **Yoshinobu Ashihara,** *The Hidden Order – Tokyo through the Twentieth Century,* New York/London/Tokyo: Kodansha International, 1989

– **Pamela J. Asquith/Arne Kalland (eds.),** *Japanese Images of Nature – Cultural Perspectives,* (Nordic Institute of Asian Studies – Man and Nature in Asia), no.1, Richmond: Curzon Press, 1997

– **Pamela J. Asquith/Arne Kalland (eds.),** "Japanese Perception of nature – Ideals and Illusions", in: Pamela J. Asquith/Arne Kalland (eds.), *Japanese Images of Nature – Cultural Perspectives,* (Nordic Institute of Asian Studies – Man and Nature in Asia), no.1, Richmond: Curzon Press, 1997

– **Roland Barthes,** *Das Reich der Zeichen,* Frankfurt am Main: Suhrkamp, 1981

– **Heinrich Bechert/Richard Gombrich,** *Der Buddhismus,* Munich: C.H. Beck, 1984

– **Ruth Benedict,** *The Chrysanthemum and the Sword – Patterns of Japanese Culture,* Boston: Houghton Mifflin Co., 1989

– **Vito Bertin,** "Ein Teeraum", in: *deutsche bauzeitung,* 12/1991

– **Werner Blaser,** *Tempel und Teehaus in Japan,* Basel/Boston/Berlin: Birkhäuser, 1988

– **Werner Blaser (ed.),** *Tadao Ando. Sketches – Zeichnungen,* Basel/Boston/Berlin: Birkhäuser, 1990

– **Werner Blaser,** *Tadao Ando – Nähe des Fernen/The Nearness of the Distant,* Sulgen/Zurich: Verlag Niggli AG, 2005

– **Werner Blaser,** *Japan – Wohnen + Bauen/Dwelling Houses,* Sulgen/Zurich: Verlag Niggli AG, 2005

– **Botond Bognar,** *Contemporary Japanese Architecture,* New York: Van Nostrand Reinhold Company Inc., 1985

– **Klaus Bosslet/Sabine Schneider,** *Ästhetische Gestaltung in der japanischen Architektur,* Düsseldorf: Werner-Verlag, 1990

– **Heinz Brasch,** *Kyoto – Die Seele Japans,* Olten/Lausanne/Freiburg i. Br.: Urs Graf-Verlag, 1974

– **Martin Brauen,** *Bambus im alten Japan,* Stuttgart/Zurich: Arnoldsche Art Publishers – Völkerkundemuseum Zurich, 2003

– **David N. Buck,** *Responding to Chaos – Tradition, Technology, Society and Order in Japanese Design,* London/New York: Spon Press, 2000

– **Noel Burch,** *To the Distant Observer – Form and Meaning in the Japanese Cinema,* London: Scolar Press, 1979

– **Norman F. Carver,** *Form and Space in Japanese Architecture,* Kalamazoo: Documan Press Ltd., 1993

– **Amos Ich Tiao Chang,** *The Tao of Architecture,* Princeton University Press, 1956

– **Ching-Yu Chang,** "Japanese Spatial Conception", in: *Japan Architect,* 1–12/ 1984

– **William H. Coaldrake,** *Architecture and Authority in Japan,* London/New York: Routledge, 1996

– **Edward Conze,** *Eine kurze Geschichte des Buddhismus,* Frankfurt am Main: Suhrkamp, 1986

– **Michael Cooper,** "The Early Europeans and Tea", in: Paul Varley/Isao Kumakura (eds.), *Tea in Japan – Essays on the History of Chanoyu,* Honolulu: University of Hawaii Press, 1994

– **Louise Allison Cort,** "The Grand Kitano Tea Gathering", in: *Chanoyu Quarterly,* vol. 31, Kyoto: Urasenke Foundation

– **Florian Coulmas,** *Die Kultur Japans. Tradition und Moderne,* Munich: C. H. Beck, 2003

– **J. C. Covell,** "Kanamori Sowa and Teigyokuken", in: *Chanoyu Quarterly,* vol. 17, Kyoto: Urasenke Foundation

– **Design Exchange Company (ed.),** *Japanese Design – Modern Approaches to Traditional Elements,* Hamburg/Corte/ Madera/Tokyo: Gingko-Press, 2001

– **Tetsuo Doi,** *Amae – Freiheit in Geborgenheit,* Frankfurt am Main: Suhrkamp, 1982

– **Arthur Drexler,** *The Architecture of Japan,* New York: The Museum of Modern Art, 1956

– **Franziska Ehmcke,** *Der japanische Tee-Weg,* Cologne: DuMont, 1991

– **Franziska Ehmcke/Heinz Dieter Reese (eds.),** *Von Helden, Mönchen und schönen Frauen – Die Welt des japanischen Heike-Epos,* Cologne/Weimar/ Vienna: Böhlau Verlag, 2000

– **Mircea Eliade,** *Das Heilige und das Profane – Vom Wesen des Religiösen,* Frankfurt am Main: Insel Verlag, 1998

– **Heino Engel,** *Measure and Construction of the Japanese House,* Rutland/Tokyo: Charles E. Tuttle, 1985

– **Gabriele Fahr-Becker,** *Ryokan – Zu Gast im traditionellen Japan,* Cologne: Könemann, 2000

– **Jorge M. Ferreras,** "Frontal Perception in Architectural Space", in: Koji Yagi (ed.), *Process Architecture 25: Japan: Climate. Space and Concept,* Tokyo: Process Architecture Publishing Co., Ltd, 1981

– **Gisela Fleig-Harbauer,** *Der japanische Garten – Wege zur modernen Gestaltung,* Herrsching: Pawlak-Verlag, 1992

– **Willi Flindt/Manfred Speidel,** "Zur Struktur des japanischen Raumes", in: Manfred Speidel (ed.), *Japanische Architektur – Geschichte und Gegenwart,* Stuttgart: Verlag Gerd Hatje, 1978

– **Kenneth Frampton/Kisho Kudo,** *Japanese Building Practice From Ancient Times to the Meiji Period,* New York: Van Nostrand Reinhold Company Inc., 1997

– **Margarete Fujii-Zelenak,** *Strukturen in den modernen Architekturen. Pier-Luigi Nervi – Kenzo Tange,* Frankfurt am Main: Verlag für interkulturelle Kommunikation, 1992

– **Yasunoke Fukukita,** *Tea Cult of Japan,* Tokyo: Board of Tourist Industry, 1937

– **Masao Furuyama,** *Tadao Ando,* Zurich: Artemis, 1993

– **Wolfram Graubner,** *Holzverbindungen – Gegenüberstellung japanischer und europäischer Lösungen,* Stuttgart: DVA, 1990

– **Kôshirô Haga,** "The Wabi Aesthetic through the Ages", in: Paul Varley / Isao Kumakura (eds.), *Tea in Japan – Essays on the History of Chanoyu,* Honolulu: University of Hawaii Press, 1994

– **Seiji Hagiwara / Yasunobu Tachikawa,** *Creators File for Living,* vol. 2, Tokyo: GAP Publication Co., Ltd., 2000

– **John W. Hall / Takeshi Toyoda (eds.),** *Japan in the Muromachi Age,* Berkeley / Los Angeles: University of California Press, 1977

– **Horst Hammitzsch,** *Zen in der Kunst des Teeweges,* Bern / Munich / Vienna: O. W. Barth Verlag, 2000

– **Masao Hayakawa,** "The Microcosmic Space Created by Sen Rikyû", in: *Chanoyu Quarterly,* vol. 80, Kyoto: Urasenke Foundation

– **Shino Hayashiya,** "Teabowls – Part I–IV", in: *Chanoyu Quarterly,* vol. 55, 56, 58, 59, Kyoto: Urasenke Foundation

– **Tatsusaburo Hayashiya / Masao Nakamura / Seizo Hayashiya,** "Japanese Arts and the Tea Ceremony", in: *The Heibonsha Survey of Japanese Art,* vol. 15, New York / Tokyo: Weatherhill / Heibonsha, 1980

– **Christoph Heinrichsen,** *Historische Holzarchitektur in Japan – Statische Ertüchtigung und Reparatur,* Stuttgart: Konrad Theiss Verlag, 2003

– **Joy Hendry,** "Nature Tamed – Gardens as a Microcosm of Japan's View of the World", in: Pamela J. Asquith / Arne Kalland (eds.), *Japanese Images of Nature – Cultural Perspectives,* (Nordic Institute of Asian Studies – Man and Nature in Asia), no. 1, Richmond: Curzon Press, 1997

– **Horst Hennemann,** *Chasho – Geist und Geschichte der Theorien japanischer Teekunst,* Wiesbaden: Harrasowitz, 1994

– **Wolfgang Hesselberger,** "Eine japanische Spielart von Bautradition", in: *Baumeister,* 11 / 1984

– **Shin'ichi Hisamatsu,** *Zen and the Fine Arts,* Tokyo / New York: Kodansha, 1971

– **Shin'ichi Hisamatsu,** "The Way of Tea and Buddhism", in: *Chanoyu Quarterly,* vol. 74, Kyoto: Urasenke Foundation

– **Kaisen Iguchi,** "Sen Sôtan and Yuin", in: *Chanoyu Quarterly,* vol. 13, Kyoto: Urasenke Foundation

– **Mitsue Inoue,** *Space in Japanese Architecture,* New York / Tokyo: Weatherhill, 1985

– **Sojin Ishikawa,** "An Invitation to Tea", in: *Chanoyu Quarterly,* vol. 11–13, Kyoto: Urasenke Foundation

– **Arata Isozaki,** "Ma: Japanese Time-Space", in: *Japan Architect,* 2 / 1979

– **Yoshiaki Ito / Masaaki Arakawa / Masashiro Karasawa / Toshiko Tsubonaka,** *Momoyama togei no katen (The flower exhibition of momoyama ceramic art),* Nagoya: NHK Nagoya hoso kyoku, NHK chubu purenzu, NHK promoshyon, 2000

– **Teiji Itoh,** "Sen Rikyû and Taian", in: *Chanoyu Quarterly,* vol. 15, Kyoto: Urasenke Foundation

– **Teiji Itoh,** "The Development of Shoin-Style Architecture", in: John. W. Hall / Takeshi Toyoda (eds.), *Japan in the Muromachi Age,* Berkeley / Los Angeles: University of California Press, 1977

– **Teiji Itoh,** *Die Gärten Japans,* Cologne: DuMont, 1999

– **Tetsuo Izutsu,** *Die Theorie des Schönen in Japan – Beiträge zur klassischen japanischen Ästhetik,* Cologne: DuMont, 1994

– **Kamo no Chômei:** *Aufzeichnungen aus meiner Hütte,* Frankfurt am Main / Leipzig: Insel Verlag, 1997

– **Daniel R. Kane,** "The Epic of Tea. Tea Ceremony as the Mythological Journey of the Hero", in: *Kyoto Journal,* winter 1987

– **Shuichi Kato,** *Form. Style. Tradition. Reflections of Japanese Art and Society,* Tokyo / New York / San Francisco: Kodansha, 1971

– **Masao Katsushiko,** *Zen Gardens,* Kyoto: Suiko, 1996

– **Mitsugu Kawakami / Masao Nakamura / Tetsuo Aiga,** *Katsurarikyu to chashitsu (katsurarikyu and tea house),* Tokyo: Shogakkan Co., Ltd., 1967

– **Marc P. Keane,** *Japanese Garden Design,* Rutland / Tokyo: Charles E. Tuttle Company, 1996

– **Donald Keene (ed.),** *Anthology of Japanese Literature from the Earliest Era to the Mid-nineteenth Century,* Rutland / Tokyo: Charles E. Tuttle Company, 1968

– **Yoshida Kenkô,** *Betrachtungen aus der Stille – Tsurezuregusa,* Frankfurt am Main: Insel Verlag, 1963

– **Karin Kirsch,** *Die neue Wohnung und das alte Japan,* Stuttgart: DVA, 1996

– **Brigitte Kita,** *Tee und Zen – der gleiche Weg,* Munich: Verlag Peter Erd, 1993

– **Harumichi Kitao,** *Interior Elevation of Tea Room,* Tokyo: Mitsumura Suiko Shoin Co., Ltd., 1978

– **Leonard Koren,** *Wabi-sabi, für Künstler, Architekten und Designer,* Tübingen: Wasmuth, 2000

– **Wybe Kuitert,** *Themes, Scenes and Taste in the History of the Japanese Garden Art,* Amsterdam: J. C. Gieben Publisher, 1998

– **Isao Kumakura,** "Kan'ei Culture and Chanoyu", in: Paul Varley / Isao Kumakura (eds.), *Tea in Japan – Essays on the History of Chanoyu,* Honolulu: University of Hawaii Press, 1994

– **Isao Kumakura,** "Sen no Rikyu. Inquiries into his Life and Tea", in: Paul Varley / Isao Kumakura (eds.), *Tea in Japan – Essays on the History of Chanoyu,* Honolulu: University of Hawaii Press, 1994

– **Kisho Kurokawa,** "Architecture of Grays", in: *Japan Architect,* 266 / 1979

– **Kisho Kurokawa,** *Rediscovering Japanese Space,* New York: Weatherhill, 1988

– **Masayuki Kurokawa,** "Disymmetrical Architecture", in: *Japan Architect,* 280 / 1980

– **Joseph A. Kyburz,** "Magical thought at the interface of nature and culture", in: Pamela J. Asquith / Arne Kalland (eds.), *Japanese Images of Nature – Cultural Perspectives,* (Nordic Institute of Asian Studies – Man and Nature in Asia), no. 1, Richmond: Curzon Press, 1997

– **Lao Tze,** *Tao Te King – Das Buch vom rechten Wege und von der rechten Gesinnung,* Frankfurt am Main / Berlin: Ullstein Verlag, 1996

– **Theodore M. Ludwig,** "Chanoyu and Momoyama: Conflict and Transformation in Rikyu's Art", in: Paul Varley / Isao Kumakura (eds.), *Tea in Japan – Essays on the History of Chanoyu,* Honolulu: University of Hawaii Press, 1994

– Fumihiko Maki, "Japanese City Spaces and the Concept of oku", in: *Japan Architect*, 5/1979

– Ekkehard May, *Shômon. Das Tor der Klause zur Bananenstaude*, Mainz: Dietrich'sche Verlagsbuchhandlung, 2000

– Hisao Maye, "Theorizing about the Origins of the Tokonoma", in: *Chanoyu Quarterly*, vol. 86, Kyoto: Urasenke Foundation

– Michiko Meid, "Der Prozess der Einführung der europäischen Architektur in Japan", in: Manfred Speidel (ed.), *Japanische Architektur – Geschichte und Gegenwart*, Stuttgart: Verlag Gerd Hatje, 1978

– Kogen Mizuno, *Basic Buddhist Concepts*, Tokyo: Kôsei Publishing, 2000

– Edward S. Morse, *Japanese Homes and their Surroundings*, New York: Dover Publications, 1961

– Governor Mosher, *Kyoto – A Contemplative Guide*, Rutland/Tokyo: Charles E. Tuttle Company, 1964

– Yasuhiko Murai, "The Development of Chanoyu: before Rikyû", in: Paul Varley/Isao Kumakura (eds.), *Tea in Japan – Essays on the History of Chanoyu*, Honolulu: University of Hawaii Press, 1994

– Adolf Muschg, *Im Sommer des Hasen*, Frankfurt am Main: Suhrkamp, 1975

– Masao Nakamura, *Kokyo Chashitsu (The public tea house)*, Tokyo: Kenchiku shiryo kenkyu-sha, 1994

– Shosei Nakamura, "Kobori Enshu and Mittan", in: *Chanoyu Quarterly*, vol. 14, Kyoto: Urasenke Foundation

– Shosei Nakamura, "Furuta Oribe and Ennan", in: *Chanoyu Quarterly*, vol. 17, Kyoto: Urasenke Foundation

– Shosei Nakamura, "Katagiri Sekishu and Korin-an", in: *Chanoyu Quarterly*, vol. 18, Kyoto: Urasenke Foundation

– Shosei Nakamura, "The Tearooms of Hosokawa Sansai", in: *Chanoyu Quarterly*, vol. 18, Kyoto: Urasenke Foundation

– Shosei Nakamura, "Oda Uraku and Joan", in: *Chanoyu Quarterly*, vol. 19, Kyoto: Urasenke Foundation

– Toshinori Nakamura, "Reconstructing the Taian Tearoom", in: *Chanoyu Quarterly*, vol. 81, Kyoto: Urasenke Foundation

– Kano Nakane, *Die Struktur der japanischen Gesellschaft*, Frankfurt am Main: Suhrkamp, 1970

– Kazuo Nishi/Kazuo Hozumi, *What is Japanese Architecture?*, Tokyo/New York/London: Kodansha, 1983

– Günter Nitschke, *From Shinto to Ando*, London: Academy Editions/Ernst und Sohn, 1993

– Günter Nitschke, *Japanische Gärten – Rechter Winkel und natürliche Form*, Cologne: Taschen, 1999

– Cees Nooteboom, *Im Frühling der Tau*, Frankfurt am Main: Suhrkamp, 1995

– Klaus-Josef Notz, *Lexikon des Buddhismus*, Wiesbaden: Fourier Verlag, 2002

– Ryôsuke Ôhashi, *Kire – Das Schöne in Japan. Philosophisch-ästhetische Reflexionen zu Geschichte und Moderne*, Cologne: DuMont, 1994

– Kakuzo Okakura, *Das Buch vom Tee*, Frankfurt am Main: Insel Verlag, 1981

– Naomi Okawa, "Edo Architecture: Katsura and Nikko", in: *The Heibonsha Survey of Japanese Art*, vol. 20, New York/Tokyo/Weatherhill/Heibonsha, 1975

– Satô Osamu, "A History of Tatami", in: *Chanoyu Quarterly*, vol. 77, Kyoto: Urasenke Foundation

– Hirotarô Ota, *Japanese Architecture and Gardens*, Tokyo: Kokusai Bunka Shinkôkai, 1966

– Robert Treat Paine/Alexander Soper, *Art and Architecture of Japan*, Middlesex/New York: Penguin Books, 1981

– Henri Plummer, *Light in Japanese Architecture*, Tokyo: a+u Publishing, 1995

– Herbert E. Plutschow, *Historical Chanoyu*, Tokyo: The Japan Times Ltd., 1986

– Herbert E. Plutschow, *Rediscovering Rikyû and the Beginnings of the Japanese Tea Ceremony*, Folkestone: Global Oriental, 2003

– Manfred Pohl, *Japan*, Munich: C.H. Beck, 1991

– Peter Pörtner, "Japan und einige Aspekte der Weltgeschichte des Nichts", in: Peter Pörtner (ed.), *Japan – Ein Lesebuch*, (konkursbuch 16/17), Tübingen: Verlag Claudia Gehrke, 1986

– Bernard Rudofsky, *The Kimono Mind. An Informal Guide to Japan and the Japanese*, Rutland/Tokyo: Charles E. Tuttle Company, 1983

– A. L. Sadler, *Cha-no-yu, The Japanese Tea Ceremony*, Rutland/Tokyo: Charles E. Tuttle Company, 1962

– A. L. Sadler: (ed.), *The Ten Foot Square Hut and Tales of the Heike*, Rutland/Tokyo: Charles E. Tuttle Company, 1972

– Kiyosi Seike, *The Art of Japanese Joinery*, New York/Tokyo: Weatherhill, 1977

– Kazuo Shinohara, *Kazuo Shinohara*, Berlin: Ernst und Sohn, 1994

– Sen Sôshitsu XV, *Chanoyu – The Urasenke Tradition of Tea*, New York/Tokyo: Weatherhill, 1988

– Sen Sôshitsu XV, *Tea Life. Tea Mind*, New York/Tokyo: Weatherhill, 1997

– Sen Sôshitsu XV, *Chanoyu – Handbook one*, Kyoto: Urasenke Foundation

– Manfred Speidel (ed.), *Japanische Architektur – Geschichte und Gegenwart*, Stuttgart: Verlag Gerd Hatje, 1978

– Manfred Speidel, "Das japanische Wohnhaus und die Natur", in: Manfred Speidel (ed.), *Japanische Architektur – Geschichte und Gegenwart*, Stuttgart: Verlag Gerd Hatje, 1978

– David B. Stewart, *The Making of a Modern Japanese Architecture*, Tokyo/New York: Kodansha International, 1987

– Daisetz T. Suzuki, *Zen and Japanese Culture*, Rutland/Tokyo: Charles E. Tuttle Company, 1997

– Sen'ô Tanaka/Sendô Tanaka, *The Tea-Ceremony*, Tokyo/New York/London: Kodansha International, 2000

– Jun'ichiro Tanizaki, *Lob des Schattens – Entwurf einer japanischen Ästhetik*, Zurich: Manesse Verlag, 2002

– Bruno Taut, *Das japanische Haus und sein Leben – Houses and People of Japan*, Berlin: Gebr. Mann Verlag, 1997

– Sen Tomiko, *Ima ni ikiru cha no kokoro, Cha no bi (Beauty of tea)*, Kyoto: Tanko-sya Co., Ltd., 1999

– Victor Turner, *Dramas, Fields and Metaphors: Symbolic Action in Human Society*, Ithaca: Cornell University Press, 1974

–   Atsushi Ueda, *The Inner Harmony of the Japanese House*, Tokyo/New York/London: Kodansha, 1998

–   Paul Varley, *Japanese Culture*, Honolulu: University of Hawaii Press, 1973
–   Paul Varley/Isao Kumakura (eds.), *Tea in Japan, Essays on the History of Chanoyu*, Honolulu: University of Hawaii Press, 1994
–   Paul Varley, "Chanoyu: from the Genroku Epoch to Modern Times", in: Paul Varley/Isao Kumakura (eds.), *Tea in Japan – Essays on the History of Chanoyu*, Honolulu: University of Hawaii Press, 1994
–   **Vitra Design Museum/Foundation Zeri/C.i.r.e.c.a (eds.)**, *Grow Your Own House – Simón Vélez und die Bambus-architektur*, Weil am Rhein: self-publication of the Vitra Design Museum, 2000

–   **Robin Noel Walker**, *Shoko-ken. A Late Medievial daime sukiya Style Japanese Tea-house*, New York/London: Routledge, 2002

–   **Koji Yagi (ed.)**, *Process Architecture 25: Japan: Climate, Space and Concept*, Tokyo: Process Architecture Publishing Co., Ltd., 1981
–   **Masao Yanagi**, *Proportion in der Architektur – dargestellt in der Gegenüberstellung der Villa Barbaro (Palladio) und des Chashitsu Taian (Rikyû)*, dissertation, Stuttgart University, 1986
–   **Soetsu Yanagi**, *The Unknown Craftsman – A Japanese Insight into Beauty*, Tokyo/New York/London: Kodansha International, 1972
–   **Asano Yasuhiro (ed.)**, *The Tea Garden – Kyotos Culture Enclosed*, Kyoto: Mitsumura Suiko Shoin Co., Ltd., 1992
–   **Tatsuhiko Yoshida**, *kyabuki chashitsu (Thatched tea house)*, Kyoto: Gakugei shuppan-sha Co., Ltd., 1995
–   **Hiroko Yoshino**, "The I-Ching and Chanoyu", in: *Chanoyu Quarterly*, vol. 65, Kyoto: Urasenke Foundation
–   **Lu Yu**, *Cha Ching – Das klassische Buch vom Tee*, Graz: edition aktuell im Verlag Styria, 2002

–   **Klaus Zwerger**, "Verstecken und zur Neugier zwingen – japanische Verbindungen als Rätselspiel", in: *Detail*, Juli 1994

–   **Klaus Zwerger**, *Das Holz und seine Verbindungen – Bautechniken in Europa und Japan*, Basel/Berlin/Boston: Birkhäuser, 1997

CATALOGS AND BROCHURES
–   *Ginkaku-ji*, brochure
–   *The History and Aesthetics of Tea in Japan*, exhibition catalog, Kyoto National Museum, 2002
–   *Katsura Rikyû Imperial Villa*, brochure
–   *Nijo Castle*, brochure
–   *SABIE – Zen, The Way of Tea; a fresh perspective*, exhibition catalog, Tokyo: no date
–   *Shugakuin Imperial Villa*, brochure

PICTURE CREDITS

I

PHOTOGRAPHS

- **Wolfgang Fehrer** Illus. 8, 11, 13, 14, 15, 18, 20, 25, 27, 32, 33, 39, 43, 47, 51, 54, 62, 64, 78, 79, 88, 90, 92 (top left and bottom right), 93, 96, 98, 106, 108, 109, 116, 123, 124, 129, 133, 158, 160, 168, 184, 203, 204, 207, 210, 215, 222, 224, 229
- **Kerstin Gödeke** Illus. 1, 3, 4, 61, 63, 107, 113, 115, 211
- **Jens Hvass** Illus. 5, 7, 30, 31, 35, 46, 48, 49, 50, 57, 72, 87, 92 (top right and bottom left), 95, 99, 101, 110, 111, 147, 150, 166, 173, 176, 178, 180, 181, 183, 185, 200, 228
- **Martina Rössl** Illus. 163, 165, 192
- **Shigeru Uchida** 217, 220, 221

GRAPHICS CREATED BY THE AUTHOR

- Illus. 12, 19 – after **Günter Nitschke**, *From Shinto to Ando*, London 1993
- Illus. 26, 37, 38, 40, 41, 56, 59, 65, 67, 68, 70, 73, 74, 81, 97, 102, 118, 127, 128, 146, 151, 153, 156, 157, 162, 164, 167, 171, 172, 175, 177, 182, 186, 187, 190, 194, 195, 199, 201, 205, 219, 223
- Illus. 53 – after **Design Exchange Company (ed.)**, *Japanese Design – Modern Approaches to Traditional Elements*, Hamburg/Corte/Madera/Tokyo 2001

REPRODUCED PHOTOGRAPHS AND GRAPHICS

- Illus. 2, 89: **Cha-no-yu-Postcards**, Genre Pictures by Toshikata, Tokyo: Fukui Asahido Co., Ltd.
- Illus. 6: **Sen Tomiko**, *Ima ni ikiru cha no kokoro, Cha no bi (Beauty of tea)*, Kyoto 1999
- Illus. 9, 105: **Heinz Brasch:** *Kyoto – Die Seele Japans*, Olten/Lausanne/Freiburg i. Br. 1974
- Illus. 10, 16: **Arthur Drexler**, *The Architecture of Japan*, New York 1956
- Illus. 17, 60, 112: **Sen'ô Tanaka/Sendô Tanaka**, *The Tea-Ceremony*, Tokyo/NewYork/London 2000
- Illus. 21, 52: **Edward S. Morse**, *Japanese Homes and their Surroundings*, New York 1961
- Illus. 22, 149: *Miyako rinsen meisho zue*
- Illus. 23, 24: **Manfred Speidel (ed.)**, *Japanische Architektur – Geschichte und Gegenwart*, Stuttgart 1978
- Illus. 28, 134, 140, 193, 196, 197, 198, 212, 214: **Urasenke Foundation (ed.)**, *The Urasenke Tradition of Tea*, Kyoto 2001
- Illus. 29, 76, 91, 121: **Stephen Addiss**, *The Art of Zen*, New York 1989
- Illus. 34: **Botond Bognar**, *Contemporary Japanese Architecture*, New York 1985
- Illus. 36, 100: **Günter Nitschke**, *Japanische Gärten – Rechter Winkel und natürliche Form*, Cologne 1999
- Illus. 42: **Chado**, *Cha no yu meiwan (The tea bowl name of Cha no yu)*, Kyoto 1999
- Illus. 44, 45: **Vito Bertin**, "Ein Teeraum", in: *deutsche bauzeitung*, 12/1991
- Illus. 55, 75: **Christoph Heinrichsen**, *Historische Holzarchitektur in Japan – Statische Ertüchtigung und Reparatur*, Stuttgart 2003
- Illus. 58, 191: **Fushin'an Foundation (ed.)**, *Japanese Tea Culture – The Omotesenke Tradition*, Kyoto 2002
- Illus. 69: **Sen Soshitsu XV**, *Chanoyu – Handbook one*, Kyoto, no date
- Illus. 71, 152, 159, 174, 188, 189, 206: **Mitsugu Kawakami/Masao Nakamura/Tetsuo Aiga**, *Katsurarikyu to chashitsu (katsurarikyu and tea house)*, Tokyo 1967
- Illus. 77: **Vitra Design Museum/Foundation Zeri/C.i.r.e.c.a (eds.)**, *Grow Your Own House – Simón Vélez und die Bambusarchitektur*, Weil am Rhein 2002
- Illus. 80: **Klaus Zwerger**, "Verstecken und zur Neugier zwingen – japanische Verbindungen als Rätselspiel", in: *Detail*, Juli 1994
- Illus. 82, 83: **Tatsuhiko Yoshida**, *kyabuki chashitsu (Thatched tea house)*, Kyoto 1995
- Illus. 84: **Harumichi Kitao**, *Interior Elevation of Tea Room*, Tokyo 1978
- Illus. 85, 86 : **Teiji Itoh**, "Sen Rikyû and Taian", in: *Chanoyu Quarterly*, vol. 15, Kyoto, no date
- Illus. 94: **Masao Nakamura**, *Kokyo Chashitsu (The public tea house)*, Tokyo 1994
- Illus. 103, 131, 136, 139, 141, 161, 170, 208: **Tatsusaburo Hayashiya/Masao Nakamura/Seizo Hayashiya**, *Japanese Arts and the Tea Ceremony*; the graphics are from the Japanese version: Tatsusaburo Hayashiya, *cha no bijutsu*, Tokyo 1965

- Illus. 120: **Yoshiaki Ito / Masaaki Arakawa / Masashiro Karasawa / Toshiko Tsubonaka,**
  Momoyama togei no katen (The flower exhibition of momoyama ceramic art), Nagoya 2000
- Illus. 122, 126, 130, 135, 144, 155, 169, 202: *The History and Aesthetics of Tea in Japan,*
  exhibition catalog, Kyoto 2002
- Illus. 132: *Ginkakuji,* brochure of the temple, no date
- Illus. 137, 154, 209: *Hajimete no cha no yu (The first time cha no yu),* no place and date
- Illus. 142, 145: postcard – Osaka Castle Museum
- Illus. 148: brochure of the Kodai-ji temple, no place and date
- Illus. 213: **Kazuo Shinohara,** *Kazuo Shinohara,* Berlin 1994
- Illus. 216, 218: *Japan Architect,* unknown vol.
- Illus. 225: **Masao Furuyama,** *Tadao Ando,* Zurich 1993
- Illus. 226, 227 **Masakazu Izumi / Junji Ito / Ikko Tanaka,** *SABIE – Zen,*
  The Way of Tea; a fresh perspective, exhibition catalog, Kyoto 1993

The publisher and author have made every effort to obtain the necessary reproduction rights for
all illustrations. In spite of intensive research, it was not possible to find the authors of some of
the illustrations. We kindly ask you to inform us accordingly. Upon notification, legal claims will
be settled within the usual scope.

ACKNOWLEDGEMENTS

I would like to express my sincere thanks to the following persons and institutions who supported
me in writing this work with suggestions, information and pictures. Without them, the book had not
been realized:

Gary Cadwallader, Marion Elmer, Rolf Gerber, Kerstin Gödeke, Ulrich Haas, Kunihiko Horinouchi,
Jens Hvass, Yuki and Tetsuo Kawai, Nazuki Konishi, Bettina Langner-Teramoto, Niggli Verlag,
Günter Nitschke, Tamaki Ohori, Omotesenke Foundation, Osaka Castle Museum, Martina Rössl,
Naomi Saito, Shigeru Uchida, Urasenke Foundation, Junko Yamada